4-12-79

Time After Time...It's Magic...Three Coins in the Fountain...People...Just in Time...Everything's Comin' Up Roses...Let It Snow...I'll Walk Alone... Let Me Entertain You...Don't Rain on My Parade... Diamonds Are a Girl's Best Friend...The Party's Over...Make Someone Happy...

Jule Styne's been writing memorable songs for almost half a century. Over 1400 songs in fact. His hits read like a top-40 in *Billboard* magazine. His Broadway successes include *Gypsy, Funny Girl, Gentlemen Prefer Blondes, Bells Are Ringing.* And here, for the first time, is his rambunctious and revealing story, from mob-ruled Chicago in the twenties to Hollywood and Broadway.

When he was four, Julius Stein leaped on the stage of the Hippodrome in London to do an impromptu act with Harry Lauder. Soon after, his family moved to the United States, where Jule began taking piano lessons; it wasn't long before he was playing with symphony orchestras in Chicago, Detroit and Cincinnati. And then he was told he could never be great, his hands were too small.

So Jule began playing in local Chicago bands—alongside the likes of Benny Goodman, Glenn Miller and Jack Teagarden. Once when he had his own band, Al Capone insisted on directing an evening of George Gershwin. Jule complied.

When the gang wars got too hot, Jule came to New York and became a voice coach for girlfriends of the underworld. He actually improved their performances so much that Hollywood called him out West, where he coached stars at Twentieth Century-Fox, including Shirley Temple and Alice Faye. At Republic Studios he began writing songs for Gene Autry and Roy Rogers, and teaming up with Frank Loesser and Sammy Cahn, wrote more movie song hits than any other songwriter in history.

But New York beckoned. When he returned back East, he composed the score of *High Button Shoes,* drawing on his memory of his own New York City

Adolph Green, and many, many more.

In *Jule,* Theodore Taylor captures the essence of the man Margaret Styne has called "...impossible, infuriating, inconsistent, irresponsible and illogical. Exhilarating, exciting, irrepressible, irreplaceable and never ever boring.

"He calls himself Peter Pan—he must be right because he's never grown up enough to forget where dreams are born. I'm glad."

HIGH BUTTON SHOES
PHIL SILVERS
NANETTE FABRAY
JULE STYNE & SAMMY CAHN
STEPHEN LONGSTREET
OLIVER SMITH
MILES WHITE
JEROME ROBBINS · GEORGE ABBOTT
"A SONG AND DANDY Gayer Than a Mardi Gras" — WALTER WINCHELL
SHUBERT THEATRE
44th ST W. of B'WAY
MATS WED & SAT.

HERMAN LEVIN & OLIVER SMITH present
GENTLEMEN PREFER BLONDES
A NEW MUSICAL COMEDY
JOSEPH FIELDS & ANITA LOOS · JULE STYNE · LEO ROBIN
AGNES deMILLE
CAROL CHANNING · YVONNE ADAIR
JACK McCAULEY · ERIC BROTHERSON
ALICE PEARCE · REX EVANS · ANITA ALVAREZ
OLIVER SMITH
MILES WHITE
MILTON ROSENSTOCK
DON WALKER
HUGH MARTIN
PEGGY CLARK
ENTIRE PRODUCTION STAGED BY JOHN C. WILSON
ZIEGFELD THEATRE
54th STREET and 6th AVENUE
MATINEES WEDNESDAY and SATURDAY

"BEST DAMN MUSICAL I'VE SEEN IN YEARS!"
DAVID MERRICK LELAND HAYWARD
ETHEL MERMAN
GYPSY
a new musical
ARTHUR LAURENTS
JULE STYNE
STEPHEN SONDHEIM
GYPSY ROSE LEE
JACK KLUGMAN SANDRA CHURCH
JO MIELZINER RAOUL PÈNE DU BOIS
ENTIRE PRODUCTION DIRECTED AND CHOREOGRAPHED BY
JEROME ROBBINS
BROADWAY THEATRE

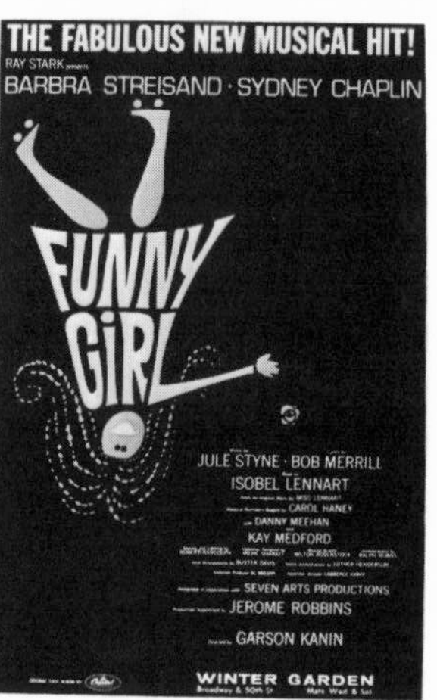
THE FABULOUS NEW MUSICAL HIT!
RAY STARK
BARBRA STREISAND · SYDNEY CHAPLIN
FUNNY GIRL
JULE STYNE · BOB MERRILL
ISOBEL LENNART
CAROL HANEY
DANNY MEEHAN
KAY MEDFORD
SEVEN ARTS PRODUCTIONS
JEROME ROBBINS
GARSON KANIN
WINTER GARDEN

JULE

THE STORY OF COMPOSER JULE STYNE

THEODORE TAYLOR

Random House New York

Grateful acknowledgment is made to the following for permission to reprint previously published material:

Barton Music Corp. Excerpt from "Time After Time." Lyrics by Sammy Cahn. Music by Jule Styne. © 1947 Sands Music Corp. © 1975 Sands Music Corp. Excerpt from "The Christmas Waltz." Lyrics by Sammy Cahn. Music by Jule Styne. © 1954 Sands Music Corp. Permission granted.

Chappell Music Company. Excerpt from "Small World." Copyright © 1959 and 1960 by Norbeth Productions, Inc. and Stephen Sondheim. Excerpt from "Rose's Turn." Copyright © 1960 by Norbeth Productions, Inc. and Stephen Sondheim. Stratford Music Corporation and Williamson Music, Inc., owners of publication and allied rights. Chappell and Co. Inc., sole selling agent. International Copyright Secured. ALL RIGHTS RESERVED including public performance for profit. Used by permission of Chappell and Co., Inc.

Paramount Music Corporation. Excerpt from "I Don't Want to Walk Without You," by Frank Loesser and Jule Styne. Copyright © 1941 by Paramount Music Corporation. Copyright © renewed 1968. Used by permission.

All photographs are courtesy of Jule Styne Productions except as noted.

Library of Congress Cataloging in Publication Data
Taylor, Theodore, 1922–
Jule: The story of composer Jule Styne.
1. Styne, Jule, 1905– 2. Composers—
United States—Biography. I. Title.
ML410.S9426T4 784'.092'4 [B] 77-90294
ISBN 0-394-41296-6

Manufactured in the United States of America

2 4 6 8 9 7 5 3

First Edition

For the late
BENNETT CERF,
who was first to suggest that the life of "Jule" be put into print.

In Appreciation

I DO SO MUCH APPRECIATE the following, who graciously sat for *Jule* taping sessions at odd hours of the day and night in New York and California: Jon Baines, Barry Brown, Claire Bregman, Irving Brown, Sammy Cahn, Betty Comden, Robert Conzleman, Lillian Conzleman, Harry Crane, Buster Davis, Dorothy Dicker, Ruth Dubonnet, Cy Feuer, Herb Gardner, Adolph Green, Sylvia Herscher, Joseph Kipness, Arthur Laurents, Herman Levin, Goddard Leiberson, Josh Logan, Anita Loos, Ethel Merman, Bob Merrill, Buddy Robbins, Jerome Robbins, Leo Robin, David Rose, Walter Scharf, Morris Stoloff, Maurice Stein, wife Margaret Styne, sons Stanley and Norton Styne. Stephen Sondheim corresponded freely about *Gypsy,* adding immeasurably to those scenes. And of course, I'm forever grateful to Jule Styne, the main source of this material.

THEODORE TAYLOR
LAGUNA BEACH, CALIF.
NOVEMBER 1978

Contents

Book I

THE LONDON STORY

1

People often ask Jule which comes first, words or music. Song to song, either one. For Barbra Streisand's classic "People," Jule wrote the music first, then Bob Merrill wrote the lyrics. The idea for the words or the melody is what is important, not the numerical order.

—DOROTHY DICKER, 1977

Snow was falling over New York City that afternoon in December 1955 when Comden and Green made their way to Jule Styne's little office in the Mark Hellinger Theatre building on West Fifty-first Street, just off Broadway. The pair had a notion for a new musical comedy, and Green held in one hand the bulky, improbable seed for that idea: a Manhattan telephone directory.

Betty Comden and Adolph Green had worked with Styne (formerly Julius Stein) before, writing sketches and lyrics to his music for *Two on the Aisle,* starring Bert Lahr and Dolores Gray, staged in 1951 and justly lamented as the last "big-time" Broadway revue. They'd also collaborated with Jule in some hasty repair work on Mary Martin's *Peter Pan,* which reached *the street* (and for him, none other really existed) in 1954. From these two very successful teamings, Comden–Green had learned that Jule, pronounced "Joolie," quite possibly more than any other Broadway composer, was apt to express instant, electric enthusiasm for even a wisp of an idea. Of course, he might well discard it the next morning with a phone call unhindered by the grace of a hello, as if everyone on earth knew, or should know, his distinctive voice.

"Listen, it won't work!"

"What won't work, darling?"

"The thing yesterday, the thing . . ."

Then again, Jule could be wildly writing music by sundown, shouting to everyone around that it would be his gre-aaatest score ever, and during the period of its creation firmly believing himself. His optimism was often of flood-tide force; seldom did he stand on safe ground. This wintry day, Comden and Green were counting on Jule's instant response to the back cover of the telephone directory.

Any idea by way of Comden–Green likely had some merit. For more than ten years in the musical theater they'd combined in writing witty and sophisticated librettos and lyrics. They'd also written for films. The initial blending of their talents took place in the late 1930's, when, as "The Revuers," a trio doing satirical numbers in Greenwich Village clubs, they were joined by another youthful star, Judy Holliday. Offstage, away from her writing chores, the attractive, chic Betty Comden was Mrs. Steven Kyle, mother of two children, involved in the P.T.A. and cookie bakes. Adolph Green was unmarried, an urbane, socially sought-after man about town. The pair moved, professionally speaking, throughout Manhattan, within a select circle of theatrically very "in" people.

For several reasons, the 1944 Comden–Green Broadway debut—with *On the Town*—was auspicious. A young composer, Leonard Bernstein, also made his musical-comedy entry that night at the Adelphi Theatre. The show was an adaptation of Bernstein's ballet *Fancy Free,* from a foolproof idea by choreographer Jerome Robbins—three sailors on shore leave, chasing girls. The libretto was crisp and funny; the lyrics, rollicking when needed, haunting for the ballads, had an undeniable freshness. Comden and Green also performed in the wartime hit, coming away established as major new contributors to Broadway. They were then in their mid-twenties.

Now, eleven years and five shows later, they were approaching a fellow craftsman who was still finding it difficult to shake off a reputation as one of the busiest lords of Tin Pan Alley. More than fifty of his melodies, out of some nine hundred, had been blessed with the chart status of *hit.* Few radio stations in America ever passed a day without spinning one or another of them.

Jule Styne's melodies, often pounded out in a matter of minutes, almost disrespectfully, played to near perfection under the words of such songs as "I Don't Want to Walk Without You, Baby," "I'll Walk Alone," "Five Minutes More," "Let It Snow," "It's Magic," "I've Heard That Song Before," "The Things We Did Last Summer" and the Academy Award winner, "Three Coins in the Fountain." The words to many of them were written by Sammy Cahn, and for a period, the Sammy–Jule combination was Hollywood's most prolific; perhaps even its best. Hit song followed hit song, almost to the point of embarrassment—certainly to the point of riches. During the period of the "Great Swoon," their work was pretty much the private property of Frank Sinatra.

But on *the street,* tricky and fickle Broadway, the Tin Pan Alley fame sat on Jule's shoulder like an albatross. Even Comden and Green had winced on being notified that their collaborator for *Two on the Aisle* would be none other than jukebox champion Jule Styne. To them he was still a pop songwriter, a peacockish, movie-jaded tunesmith, not necessarily a composer and certainly not one of Broadway quality. Snobbery got them nowhere, except another hit show, music by J. Styne.

Comden and Green did not set out to write popular songs. If a show tune happened to reach smash proportion, such as their "New York, New York . . . (is a wonderful town)," they were delighted, of course. They welcomed money, but they didn't make any special effort to fashion words for the disc jockeys and Wurlitzers. Jule, on the other hand, did, attempting to provide at least one hit song for each show, a singable whistler for the way home. Though he sometimes denied it indignantly, he was very commercial, whether he wanted to be or not.

A hard ache inside Mr. Styne ever since Comden and Green started doing their biting satires in Village clubs was a desire to compose fine, complete musical scores for Broadway shows. And while Comden–Green were taking deserved bows for *On the Town,* Jule was stuck with a thoroughly mauled ego because his first entry in the musical theater, *Glad to See You,* hadn't made it past Boston and tryout time. The show was nothing less than awful, and Jule had returned to the "music tables" at one studio or another, there to suffer sly digs from such film music men as Johnny Mercer and Harry Warren and Jimmy McHugh.

However, a few good things had happened to Jule, too, since 1944: He'd written the scores for *High Button Shoes* and *Gentlemen Prefer Blondes,* as well as producing the award-winning revival of Rodgers and Hart's *Pal Joey.*

• • •

No discriminating Broadway composer-producer would ever have an office at 237 West Fifty-first Street, almost under the marquee of the Mark Hellinger. Empty bottles were often kicked aside as one walked up two dank flights of unpainted concrete steps to reach two small, cluttered rooms with more nicotine than paint on the walls. Yet this is where Jule had been comfortably operating since the early 1950's. He had inherited the converted dressing-room space from the late owner of the theater, Anthony Farrell. But the walk-up and the rooms in the Hellinger building had the theater's faint odor of stale sweat and disinfectant and urine; during matinees, the sound of music and applause crept up the dim steps, a reminder of live drama. Perhaps that was reason enough to work well away from the luxury of Madison or Park Avenues.

Try as he might, Jule couldn't keep away from the musty halls, seemingly extracting joy from the chill dampness during rehearsals. He didn't seem to mind banging his knees on the hard iron of the theater seats, drinking stale coffee and eating junk food. It was noticed by his associates that he actually thrived on the wearing, argumentative production meetings that were usually held in the foyers, near the toilets, the group often sitting on dirty, moth-eaten carpets. The only conceivable answer was that he was childishly, sometimes irresponsibly in love with harridan Broadway.

While the somewhat austere Richard Rodgers recognized Jule's talent, entrusting the production of *Pal Joey* to him, the composer remained an enigma to the partner of Oscar Hammerstein. Jule was nothing like Leonard Bernstein or Cole Porter or Harold Arlen. He was a mad bee, buzzing all over the place. Yet from his head and hands came beautiful music: sometimes sad and sweet, sometimes rowdy, full of flesh and brass.

When Milton Rosenstock, conductor of most of Styne's Broadway hits, first heard Jule play piano he was puzzled. There was a different sound to the hammers, like in boogie or cow-cow. He phoned a fellow conductor and described the touch to him: short, percussive phrases improvised by the right hand against the steady rolling bass set up by the left hand. "Sure, that's Chicago piano," said the friend. "Whorehouse piano. Barrelhouse. Brought up from New Orleans by the blacks, with some Texas mixed in." It didn't take long for Rosenstock to discover that Jule also had a wide classical background. Yet at their first meeting Rosenstock had elevated his nose, too. God help us, he thought. Another of those half-assed people from Tin Pan Alley and Hollywood.

Comden and Green wound up the steps, said hello to Jule's calm, reserved associate, Sylvia Herscher—who did everything from managing productions to buying pastrami at the nearby deli—and to a new secretary, Dorothy Dicker, a small, sharp-minded blonde who was preparing to devote her life to Jule, though not in matrimony. Comden–Green went on into the inner office, which barely accommodated a desk and a small upright piano. Heavy trucks headed for the Hudson River docks always shook the space when they rumbled by. The coop had no outward signs of creativity.

There was never a way of knowing just what Jule would be doing. He wrote his music away from the keyboard, in his head, scrawling on yellow sheets, oblivious of the radio or TV sometimes blaring. He often worked on three scores simultaneously, miraculously keeping them separate. If he happened to be at the piano, seeming to attack it rather than stroke it, singing in a harsh but somehow appropriate tunesmith's voice, he was most likely trying a new piece on Sylvia or Dorothy.

So the inner office was seldom quiet, the other side of the moon from Alan Lerner's closet, where work was done in stillness at a child's desk. Jule couldn't endure silence or being alone. In fact, it seemed that he was subdued only when talking to bookies, and this he did daily. Though he went about it secretively, he was a direct contributor to Frank Costello's collectors. By this time in Jule's life, gambling had gone beyond mere vice and was now a near-terminal sickness. He won some races, but overall lost heavily, in very bad months up to twenty-five thousand. Sammy Cahn, in the Hollywood days, was always hoping Jule would lose, because the more money he lost the more music he wrote. A friend, Harry Crane, said, "Even when he was a kid, he was the only one on the merry-go-round with a racing form."

Comden and Green were dismayed by the gambling, but had no idea of the depth of Jule's addiction, nor the size of his debts. From time to time, they'd become peeved when Jule suddenly broke off work to place bets; stopped a creative burst to catch the results from the fifth at Hialeah.

But other than the fact that he was a talented composer who had not yet reached full range, and a charming, vastly amusing, affectionate man, Comden–Green knew very little about Jule Styne. Occasionally, he told stories of Chicago and playing piano in mob dives; about being vocal coach to the Ritz Brothers and Shirley Temple and Alice Faye at 20th Century-Fox; about writing for Westerns at Republic; the many Sinatra days and nights.

That year, at age fifty, brown-haired and quick-eyed beneath thick double lenses, Jule Styne appeared to be somewhere in his late thirties, a decided advantage in dealing with younger people of the theater. Few of his co-workers had any idea how old he was, and most who were several years his junior couldn't match his pace and energy, anyway. They simply took it for granted that he was late thirtyish, give or take a few birthdays.

Jule's lack of height, and a tendency to pudginess, had bothered him early in life, but he'd learned to compensate with an air of command, as small men are often forced to do. Now, he was seldom conscious of his size, and indeed seemed to grow physically as each production gained in intensity, particularly if it was shaping into a hit. Those who dealt with him steadily—lyricists, orchestrators, orchestra conductors or vocal arrangers—were seldom aware that he was only five five. They were very much aware that he could leap for the jugular over a creative matter or a trumpet's sour note. Where work was concerned he'd never been easy to deal with; height was of no consequence.

What had startled Comden and Green, and others before and after, was Jule's use of verbal shorthand. He spoke a language all his own, defying any known syntax. Words spewed out, sentences beginning mid-phrase and left dangling; subjects changing without pause; *non sequiturs* compounded. At full throttle, his vocal cords always lagged well behind his thoughts. "What the hell did he say?" Green asked Comden, on their first exposure to "Stynese."

Much later, Comden–Green contributed their definition of the Styne patois:

> **Stynese,** (or **Styne-ese**), *n.* language circa middle 20th century, spoken and understood by only one man. Noted for its incomprehensibility. Delivered in darting, unfinished, broken phrases. *Example:* (on the subject of Theater Dynamics) "What we in the theater call 'dynamics' is —well—fast . . . but not—you can't do that—a slower tempo would—together—that's not how, well, if two—not right away—but—Dorothy, let's go have a cup of coffee."

No one knew just when "Stynese" started, least of all Jule, but it had become an effective weapon: a machine-gun–style locution useful in production meetings. Once the listener learned to decode, it was often discovered that four ideas were being discussed at the same time. One of the four might be a gem with the potential of saving a musical. But it always took a while to unscramble "Stynese." No wonder Dick Rodgers was bewildered when Jule charged away with elaborate plans to restore the moth-balled *Pal Joey*.

Adolph Green put the telephone directory on Jule's desk back-side up, and said, "There it is." A pretty girl with all sorts of telephone wires plugged into her upper torso smiled out. She was the advertising herald for the new telephone answering services, something that Ma Bell said would revolutionize business.

Jule studied the photo and jumped up. "My God, that's a wonderful idea. A girl who meddles in everybody's business . . ."

That was exactly what Adolph and Betty had in mind. They also had in mind their former "Revuer," Judy Holliday, now a Hollywood superstar. After making several movies, winning an Academy Award for *Born Yesterday,* her initial stage success, Miss Holliday wanted to return to Broadway. The plugged-in telephone girl was to be the vehicle for that return. Within the week, Comden and Green were at work on the "book," as the libretto for the untitled musical comedy was called, and Jule had begun to scrawl music that might fit the story.

By early 1956, Comden and Green had their slim book sketched out: The "meddler" was appealing and slightly scatterbrained Ella Peterson (Holliday), an operator at Susanswerphone. Ella couldn't resist getting involved with her clients, principally a playwright, an actor trying to emulate Marlon Brando, and a dentist songwriter, each with his own vexing problem. Ella solved the problems handily, ending in the arms of the playwright at final curtain.

The libretto, even in its early stages, was fun and froth, bubbling with sure-handed Comden–Green cleverness, a zany whirl through a Manhattan populated with fascinating characters. Holliday read the book, heard four of the unpolished songs and clapped hands. Next, Jerome Robbins came in as director and choreographer, a huge step forward.

Robbins had begun his dancing career in the late thirties, and his first assignment as a choreographer was *On The Town,* indicating the arrival of a major talent. Since 1944, his dance direction credits had included *Look, Ma, I'm Dancin', High Button Shoes, Call Me Madam, The King and I.* He'd directed, as well as choreographed, *The Pajama Game* and *Peter Pan.* He'd already won an embarrassing number of awards, and though his first love was ballet, he directed drama with a sure and demanding hand. Jule said he was "The only true genius in the theater."

But the Styne–Comden–Green project still lacked both a producer and money to stage the show. It was by now early spring, and Jule suggested that the Theatre Guild, long dormant and hitless, might be interested. Within a few days Jule was at the piano, auditioning for the Guild's Armina Marshall and Lawrence Langner. Comden and Green performed their raw lyrics to a half dozen unpolished melodies. The entire project—book and songs, Holliday and Robbins, librettists and composer—had the tantalizing and distinct possibility of being a *hit.* It was a feeling as much as anything, but in less than twenty-four hours the Guild agreed to produce the new musical (eventually titled *Bells Are Ringing*) conceived from a phone book—not an unusual route, at that.

From birth to this point *Bells* had gone quickly and rather smoothly but no show in which Jule Styne was ever involved, from the ruins of *Glad to See You* to Merman's *Gypsy* and Streisand's *Funny Girl,* came easy. Periodically they all turned into writhing vipers, whether hits or duds. This was expected, it was part of the breathing body of show business.

But for a while *Bells* was a little more hell than most. Adolph Green was pushing his friend Sydney Chaplin, handsome son of the late Charles Chaplin, for the leading role of the playwright. Jerome Robbins definitely did not want Chaplin. Though Robbins liked Chaplin and thought he was most attractive, physically fitting the part, Sydney left much to be desired as a singer. There were three or four songs he could never handle. As usual, Robbins was thinking of the entire show, not just of personalities. But then Judy Holliday reacted glandularly. She fell in love with Mr. Chaplin, and announced she wouldn't do the show without him. Robbins scoffed and stood firm. Holliday, at first enamored of Jerry, now hated him. The production was in turmoil for several weeks. A compromise was finally reached: Sydney could open with the show, five days in New Haven. If he got audience response, he was *in.* If not, he was quickly out. Comden–Green and Jule Styne immediately lost five rather good songs. What dismayed Robbins was that Sydney wouldn't even attempt them. Rehearsals were six weeks away. The score was a third finished and the book was lagging along half finished.

Jerry Robbins said to the musical team, "I'm locking you in my house, then I'll know you're writing. I'll serve you lunch and you can go home at the end of each day." Comden–Green–Styne complied.

For three or four months Jule had been playing a simple melody, a two-note thing that reminded knowledgeable listeners of a half-note prelude, a tune based on half-steps. Half-step up or half-step down. Jule had played this tune for Comden and Green at least fifty times. He'd played it at countless parties: *La-la-la, la-la-la, lalalala* . . . The chromatic passage, as artless as a nursery rhyme, had been *la-laa*ing in his head for years.

There was no question but that the melody had great potential, yet title and words never seemed within anyone's grasp. They always eluded the sparse musical structure. Jule went over to Frank Loesser's apartment to play the tune. "We're in trouble with it. What would you call it?"

The composer-lyricist of *Where's Charley?* and *Guys and Dolls,* as well as dozens of hit songs, an old, old friend, answered that he had no idea what to call the tune but "keep on rolling it and the words will come up." Jule went back to Comden and Green with Loesser's advice, and within two days the lyrics to Jule's melody did come up, as well as a title, "Just in Time." It was a song for Chaplin, one that his limited vocal range could handle.

Comden–Green then gave Jule another title, "The Party's Over." Within an hour, Jule had set the beginning of the melody. Betty and Adolph went into another room, wrote the lyrics and returned to Jule's side. The song was completed in half a day, and within six more days most of the songs for *Bells,* including the five new ones, all within Chaplin's range, were finished. Sometimes the buttocks of Styne–Comden–Green were jammed precariously close together on the small piano bench as notes and words jelled.

One late afternoon in Robbins's fashionable East Seventies' house, drinks were being poured. The host was there, an amiable, relaxed Robbins, not the severe Robbins of rehearsals, as was Judy Holliday and Milton Rosenstock. The talk was of a song to end the first act. Restlessly moving about, Jule finally picked up the libretto and began scanning. He broke up the chatter. "Listen to this line. Listen. *I knew you before I knew you . . .*" He went over to the piano and began to play, improvising; stopping mid-chord and turning around for reactions. "Don't stop! don't stop!" Judy shrieked. The cocktailing ceased while Comden and Green put together a dummy lyric. The song, "Long Before I Knew You," went into the show.

There was never an exact, set pattern with any collaborator, a creative plus. Sometimes Jule arrived at the full melody, as in the case of "Just in Time," before the lyrics were written. Sometimes he had only a fragment of tune to play for the lyricists, sometimes the writers delivered all or part of the lyrics in dummy form. Other times, just a title. It made little difference. What mattered was that the right sound was there to go with the right words to express the idea—whatever the character was trying to say at the moment; what the show was trying to say. Jule freely admitted that the words were far more important than his music. The overture, usually a meld of the show tunes, and some of the dance or ballet music, came later, and was often more difficult to compose than the individual songs.

There was still another problem with Judy Holliday, thankfully not romantic, this time. She'd warned Comden–Green–Styne that she would not perform any ballads. She flatly said she wasn't capable of doing a ballad. Well, "The Party's Over" was certainly a ballad. So Jule began working with her, putting her at ease musically. He'd always had a knack for the unwinding of feminine vocalists. Betty Comden had told him that Holliday loved to sing obligatos over a melody, so he decided that the only way he could get her to sing "Party's Over" was to sucker the show's star. He taught her the song, claiming she'd be singing only the countermelody. She sang it almost to perfection.

After performing it more than a dozen times, Judy asked, "Now, who's going to do the ballad?"

Jule replied, "You, baby, you've been doing it for a week."

In early fall Jule went over to the Paramount Theatre, where Frank Sinatra was appearing in a limited engagement with the Tommy Dorsey band. Believing the songs were tailor-made for America's No. 1 male singer, Jule wanted to demonstrate both "Just in Time" and "The Party's Over." Buddy Robbins, of the Chappell Music Company, which had just set up a new subsidiary, Stratford Music Company (Styne–Comden–Green), went along, certain that Sinatra would accept the songs eagerly. That being true, they'd be hits before *Bells* ever tried out in New Haven, Connecticut. Hits, of course, meant box-office attraction as well as records, sheet music sales and ASCAP* royalties.

*ASCAP (American Society of Composers, Authors and Publishers) had been founded principally by Victor Herbert to protect his *Mlle. Modiste.* A café down the street had been playing all the songs from his show, cutting into box-office receipts, he maintained. Since 1914, ASCAP had been licensing the performances of songs, collecting royalties for composers, lyricists and publishers. The protective society was often the difference between solvency and bankruptcy for many composers and lyricists.

A Sinatra recording could provide hundreds of thousands of extra dollars.

When Jule and Robbins arrived backstage at the Paramount, Sinatra was in his dressing room, resting. A Tchaikovsky symphony was seeping from under the door. A few of the usual Sinatra cohorts, friends or employees, were around. Jule and Buddy waited patiently for almost two hours before the singer came out. Though they'd been close friends years earlier, there was little warmth in Sinatra's greeting. In that earlier period, Frank had affectionately invented a nickname for Jule—"Shtimp." This time, he didn't use it.

Jule said, "Here's a song I think you'll like." He did not say—*It's your kind of song. I wrote it with you in mind.* Why say the obvious?

Jule sat down at the small red backstage piano, the same piano on which he'd demonstrated songs for Sinatra in the forties. He played five bars of "Just in Time."

Sinatra interrupted. "It's obvious."

Then Jule said, "You liked 'Funny Valentine.' Just listen to this."

"The Party's Over" came from the red piano, lyrics from Jule's lips.

Frank commented, "It's nice. I'll be with you in a moment."

Jule and Buddy Robbins sat in the dimness of the Paramount for another twenty minutes. Meanwhile, Sinatra had ducked out of another exit. Jule got the idea that their own long-time "party" was definitely over.

That same day, feeling letdown, Styne and Robbins went to Columbia Records, telling Mitch Miller, "We want Tony Bennett for "Just in Time." We want his sound on this." The record was No. 1 within a week after it was released. In November, Nat "King" Cole recorded "The Party's Over" and it rose to No. 1 on the charts, remaining a King Cole signature until he died. Both songs, without Sinatra's help, turned large profits in records, sheet music and ASCAP fees.

Bells Are Ringing tried out in late October 1956 in New Haven, and Richard Rodgers, who had invested heavily in the show, unfortunately sat directly across the aisle from Jule, who was already suffering chronic first-night jitters. Throughout the overture, Rodgers was deadpan, arms folded. Jule felt himself sweating as he glanced sideways at Mr. Rodgers while Milton Rosenstock briskly led the orchestra into the opening curtain. As each new song came up, Mr. Rodgers made audible comments, though none could be taken positively. There were disconcerting "ums" and grunts; even murmurs of "Hmh, is that something?" What did that mean? Jule was thinking. Finally, when Sydney Chaplin finished "Just in Time" and the audience exploded, Rodgers said loudly, "Wow!"

Styne almost slid off his seat.

Much to Jerome Robbins's amazement, Chaplin registered big in New Haven, receiving much more applause than Holliday; this was a situation of immediate concern, both for the show and the still-hot romance. Chaplin wallowed in the curtain calls, while the females in the audience burnt their palms. What he couldn't do as a singer he made up in sex appeal. Crisis, nonetheless.

At a meeting called next day, it was mutually agreed that what Holliday lacked was an "eleven o'clock" song, a big song for the second act, just before closing. Robbins, Armina Marshall and Lawrence Langner all turned toward Styne–Comden–Green.

At the next stop, in Boston, Jule shared a suite of rooms with Chaplin. A suite was always needed to accommodate Jule's piano, and production money was saved by sharing it with Sydney, an agreeable man who was enjoying himself immensely as the "surprise star" of the show, throwing champagne parties almost every night for ten or twelve guests; celebrating his success even before the Broadway opening. Naturally, the love affair between Sydney and Judy was beginning to show signs of strain.

Sydney consoled Judy, who by this time had a strange look in her eyes, reportedly telling her, "Sweetheart, you're wonderful. And don't worry about an eleven o'clock song. They're all trying, but you don't really need it."

Comden and Green *were* trying, frantically. They'd been trying since the second performance in New Haven. Six or seven songs had been written, then discarded. Jule spent hours at the piano.

There were back-biting conferences at the Ritz Hotel. One ended at 3:00 A.M. with Jule and Adolph Green snarling at each other, screaming about "shitty music" and "shitty lyrics." Jule stormed into his bedroom, slamming the door. Robbins, Holliday, soft-spoken Betty Comden and Chaplin all sat in a state of momentary shock at what these good friends had called one another's work. Five minutes later Jule opened the door, wearing only a towel. He danced all around the room like a middle-aged nymph, flashing his nates at Green. The place broke up. Jule always had a way of releasing tension, some of which he'd surely built himself. The tempest was over—for that night.

Then, three days before taking the train to New York, Judy gave Robbins an ultimatum. She would not open on Broadway unless she had that "11:00 P.M." number. Robbins promptly sent the ultimatum down the line.

Catastrophe looming, Jule sat at the table in the living room of the suite. Chaplin slept soundly a few feet away. For several days, Jule had been considering something he'd learned from George Abbott during *High Button Shoes:* If you say something funny once, the second time you say it, if it's in the right spot, it'll be'll be even funnier...

Specifically, Jule was thinking of a part in the play where Ella Peterson was telling her life story, about how she'd worked for the Bonjour Tristesse Brassiere Company prior to joining Susanswerphone. Françoise Sagan's *Bonjour Tristesse* was then a best seller, and in one of those absolutely unexplainable audience reactions, the bra company mention got a large yock each time.

Jule wrote some music down, tried it out on the piano and then called for Comden and Green. They came down from their lyric labors and as they remember it, Jule said, "Look, we've got a situation here where everything is up for grabs. Ella's telling the truth about herself. She isn't a little old lady at the switchboard. She's an attractive but very frustrated girl. She's shapeless over those telephone wires." Jule began to pound the piano and sing raucously, "I'm going back to where I belong, to the Bonjour Tristesse Brassiere Companeee . . ."

"Yeah!" Adolph yelled, and the song was written within the next hour. Sydney Chaplin, aroused from slumber, was the first to hear Holliday's eleven o'clock song, and it went into the show that Saturday night, at the last performance in Boston. This time it was Judy Holliday who got the sustained applause, the curtain calls, and Chaplin stood in the wings, dumbstruck.

Bells went confidently on to New York for previews at the Shubert. A few nights later, on November 29th, the musical opened handsomely; the critics, melted by Miss Holliday, gave it a solid welcome. The New York company played 924 performances, Judy Holliday winning the Antoinette Perry Award (Tony) for the best female performance of the year and Sydney Chaplin landing on his feet again for the best male performance of 1956.

Styne–Comden–Green not only had a critical and financial success, but a pleasant bonus of two songs that are still considered vocal gold in the pop field. Most major recording stars have taken turns with "Just in Time" and "The Party's Over."

2

My father, shee said, is soone to be scene
The seely blind beggar of Bednall Greene
That daily sits begging for charitie
He is the good father of pretty Bessee.

—Ballad sung during reign of Elizabeth I

In 1957 Jule voyaged to London, place of his birth, to open the British production of *Bells Are Ringing* at the Coliseum. He had not been "home" in fifty-two years, and although he anticipated the return with some excitement he also dreaded it emotionally. Whatever his state of mind, the London cast of *Bells* was appalling. Without Judy Holliday, Ella Peterson was a caricature; the play was entirely lifeless, quickly sentenced to a short, unhappy run. Distraught, Jule now sought out 711 Ducal Street, his birthplace on December 31, 1905, in what had been the Jewish ghetto of Bethnal Green in London's East End. It was an immigrant slum only slightly less crowded and miserable than Southwark or Shoreditch, known in the sixteenth century as Epping Forest. It was a 755-acre area of ordinary street peddlers and exalted costermongers, filled with tiny, mean houses huddled roof to roof on narrow ways, alleys and dead-end courtyards.

> New Nichol-street, Half-Nichol-street, Ducal-street, Turvil-street: among its inhabitants may be found street vendors of every kind of produce, travellers to fairs, tramps, dog-fanciers, dog-stealers, men and

women sharpers, shoplifters and pickpockets. It abounds with young Arabs of the streets, and its outward moral degradation is at once apparent to anyone who passes that way.

—John Timbs, *Curiosities of London,* 1898.

Jule remembered that 711 Ducal, a two-story frame building that housed his father's butter-and-egg store and the cramped living quarters above it, was down a hill and up a street from Whitechapel Road. He recalled hawking eggs in front of the shop when he was four years old, his mother occasionally coming out to pick up the pennies. He eventually came to the bombed-out, half-roofed shell of a house, and said to his companion, Ruth Dubonnet, "I swear this is where I was born."

Gingerly, he went inside and found the front door to the house, with its 711 number plate and door knocker still intact. A wrecking crew was nearby and Jule, excited now, paid the foreman a pound to retrieve both the plate and the knocker. Bethnal Green had been one of the first targets of Nazi flying bombs in 1944; even before that, the *Luftwaffe* had cleared a good portion of the old slum, to which Samuel Pepys had fled during the Great Fire. Tributes to the "famed blind beggar and his dog," of ancient Bednall Greene still remained, in wood carvings and stained-glass windows. Jule remembered there had been a sweet shop and grocery store at the end of the street. The building was still there. Entering the shop, he identified himself and asked the old lady behind the counter, "Do you remember a couple who used to own a butter-and-egg store just up the street?" She'd been in the shop for more than fifty years but couldn't remember the Steins.

Momentarily, Jule was upset. Why couldn't she remember them? She'd been there all that time. He mumbled something and departed, moving away with a strange feeling. He'd had the same feeling earlier in Chicago, while trying to locate his mother's gravestone in the snow.

. . . that old woman's name was Cohen and she finally did remember my father and mother. She called me later at the hotel and said she'd talked to other people and they remembered a young couple named Stein, and so she recalled them, too. I got her tickets to Bells Are Ringing, *which was no big treat with that lousy company.*

The brothers of the family Stein—Jule and Maurice—view each other through different prisms and from varying distances, as does sister Claire, but all three see their late parents with a single eye: Isadore and Anna were loving and old-fashioned and duty-bound.

Isadore, the son of an Orthodox family of egg candlers, was born in Volochisk, Russia, in the Ukraine; Anna Kertman came from Sotonab, not far from Volochisk. Both orphans, they immigrated to England about 1900 and first met at a *landsleit,* a periodic social for homesick immigrants. Anna was smuggled to London by her brother, Hyman Kertman, who was also in the butter-and-egg business.

I was the first child, and my earliest vague memory was of when I was about three years old and I roamed around this little store on Ducal Street. My father was a very bad businessman, I learned later on. He'd sell the best, do a big volume and still lose money. Always a disaster in business. Always. My mother wasn't very good at figures, either.

Isadore was a powerful, square-jawed man who would have preferred to wrestle for a living. In Russia, in his teens, he'd been a middleweight champion wrestler, though Jews were not supposed to engage in the sport. Isadore was defiant until he died.

When I was four, my father wrestled the great Hackenschmidt, contender for the world's heavyweight champion then, and I saw that match at a sporting club. Some things you always remember. It was the greatest thrill of my father's life, and he was a hero to me. Hackenschmidt took on four men that night, in a challenge, and my father, at one hundred eighty pounds, was demonstrating speed. He took the German off his feet, even though he was outweighed thirty pounds. I'll never forget that night, in that smoky sporting club. My father was a tough Jew in days when Jews weren't supposed to be tough . . .

Anna Kertman Stein was a pretty dark-haired, brown-eyed woman, very much the opposite of her husband. She wasn't tough at all. She was tender and affectionate, and seldom complained about the fact that she was committed to a life of scrimping. Any luxuries were usually contributed by Uncle Hyman and Aunt Rose, Hyman being very successful.

Anna cried when she was happy. Something nice would happen to her and she would cry. Isadore would bend over to give her a surprise kiss and she wept openly.

Claire Stein was born in 1907.

Two years after me. They put her in a basket on a lower shelf in the store. I was often told I was very jealous of my sister. In fact, I tried to cut her head off with a saw, actually had it down in the basket. Can you imagine that? Well, my father whacked me good and I think I was very protective of her from then on. She became a beautiful girl, looked like an actress, the brainy one . . .

Mostly English was spoken in the Ducal Street shop. The Steins occasionally spoke Yiddish, but never Russian. The oppressive mother country was a bad memory, and they had no desire to return to the Ukraine, nor hear the language.

Anna and Isadore, learning English, picked up the Cockney dialect from their customers in Bethnal Green and spoke it until they died. Jule, similarly, spoke Cockney for a while. It was so strange, later on in America, he remembers, to hear his mother and father mix Cockney English and Yiddish.

Next to wrestling, Isadore's favorite entertainment was vaudeville, and he sometimes treated himself to the headliners, Harry Lauder in particular. Isadore placed Lauder on Hackenschmidt's sacred pinnacle, and in 1909 brought home five or six of Lauder's songs and taught them to Julius, complete with gestures and Scotch burr. The next year, Rose and Hyman Kertman bought tickets for the entire Stein family to a Lauder performance at the Hippodrome. Hyman always went first class, and their box was directly over the edge of the stage. Hyman had no idea that his five-year-old nephew would make use of the position.

While Lauder was performing, I jumped right over the edge of the box and down to the stage. Everyone began to laugh. I suppose they thought I was part of the act. Lauder stopped the orchestra and said, "Good evening, what's your name?"

"Julius Stein."

"Do you live in London?"

"Yes, I'm here with my father and mother."

"What do you do?"

"I sing songs."

"Would you like to sing one now?"

The audience began to applaud, more than ever believing that the precocious child in the sailor suit was an addition to Lauder's usual routine. (Anna could recite this scene in the Hippodrome word for word.)

"Yes."

"What do you want to sing?"

" 'She's My Daisy.' "

"What key?"

"Your key."

In the box, Isadore was horrified and had to be restrained by Hyman. He wanted to jump down, hoist his son up and run from the theater in disgrace.

Lauder tossed me his crook and I sang the song, imitating his gestures, and then jigged a little at the end. After that Lauder lifted me back into the box, while the audience roared. My father had to be talked out of hitting me, but my uncle and aunt were pleased, and my mother cried, of course. Ever the weeper . . .

After the performance, Isadore said he would not leave the theater until he had personally apologized to his idol. He wrote a note saying that the parents of the little boy would like to come backstage and explain that the rude interruption was not on purpose. Isadore was still livid.

A few minutes later, Lauder laughed about it. He told the Steins he hadn't had so much fun in weeks, then, turning to the boy, he said, "Never be an imitator. Don't do what I do. You're musical timing is quite good." To Isadore and Anna, he said, "Why don't you get him a piano and let him learn how to play?"

It was Anna who did precisely that the following year. Tightening the budget, she went to the London Conservatory of Music to enroll her son. Six-year-olds were not eligible to study at the Conservatory, but one of the teachers agreed to give lessons at her home. Unable to purchase a piano, Anna arranged for Julius to practice on a rented instrument in the back room of the music company.

So that was the very beginning. But after taking nine months with this lady I heard rumbles that we were going to America and the lessons stopped. I was glad. I wasn't performing, only practicing every day, like a ballerina at the barre. It was the practicing I didn't like, then and later . . .

With war threatening Europe in 1912, the Steins, Anna pregnant again, boarded a Cunard liner for New York. The Steins were in steerage, the Kertmans in first class. Julius discovered that by singing and jigging for the stewards he could buy his way into first class, a lesson to eventually bear melodic fruit in *Gypsy*'s "Let Me Entertain You."

Milton Rosenstock said, "It's so funny, but Jule can sound almost British when he's terribly angry. Otherwise, he's pure Chicago. He's definitely not a New Yorker."

Book

THE CHICAGO STORY

1

Listen, whatever music I write, whatever musical intuition I have, it was all made in Chicago. I've drawn on Chicago for show after show. The best black musicians who ever played were in Chicago and you'll never believe who else started there —Benny Goodman, Gene Krupa, Muggsy Spanier, Davey Tough, George Wettling, Frankie Teschmaker, Frankie Trumbauer, Art Hodes; then in came Louis Armstrong, Earl Hines, Bix Beiderbecke, Eddie Condon, Jack Teagarden, Glenn Miller, Wingy Manone, Charlie Spivak, Harry James. Between the blacks and whites, you have the whole jazz and big band hall of fame. The composer Victor Young was there, playing a fiddle; David Rose was there. Think about it: never before and never since has so much musical talent been gathered in any one spot on earth, at any one period. God, it was a feast . . .

—JULE STYNE, 1976

By deciding on the Midwest instead of New York, Isadore Stein unwittingly enrolled his often cocky young son into what was soon to be the finest popular music school in America—the whole of gin-soaked Chicago of the 1920's. The black music masters from New Orleans ran the rhythm classes in smoky dives and dance halls, and the white boys came to listen and worship.

In 1912, Alfonso Capone, a.k.a. Alfred Capone, a.k.a. Al Brown, a.k.a. Dr. A. Brown, had yet to be summoned by crime boss Jim Colesimo, via Johnny Torrio; yet to be seen around town in a cloth cap and cheap pants, mouthing spaghetti in Esposito's Bella Napoli Café or playing pinochle in Amato Gasperri's barber shop. And Towertown, between the Gold Coast of Lake Shore Drive and the Italian slum of Little Hell, was best-known for artists and poets, not gangsters. In 1912, Chicago wasn't quite ready to be called "The Jazz Baby," a later and fitting enshrinement by newspaperman and playwright Ben Hecht, but pianist Ferdinand "Jelly Roll" Morton, who often claimed he created the Creole-black improvised music in 1902, had already pioneered Crescent City ragtime at the Pekin-Theatre Cabaret and was this very year doing the blues at the Elite Café on State Street.

King Joe Oliver, Louis Armstrong, Kid Ory, Bunk Johnson, Baby Dodds, Jimmy Noone, Sidney Bechet and other immortals, were still down in the honky-tonks of Storyville, their beloved red-light district off New Orleans's Rampart Street, playing what they termed "rag" or "blues." But *jazz* was born, of record, before they could ramble up from Rampart, and ramble they did, to settle mostly in the heart of the Black Belt, Thirty-fifth Street between State and Calumet. Chicago's Lambs Club insolently named the new music "jass," a Windy City colloquialism for vagina; loosely, for copulation. The Lambs owners advertised a "jass" band rather than a "blues" band, and not unexpectedly packed the joint.

And so the feast began, on ivory keys and horns.

The night Maurice was born, a few weeks after the Steins arrived in Chicago, Anna could see the glow of a fire from her hospital bed, but had no idea that their apartment, in which she had not even slept, was burning. Up in flames went everything they'd brought over from London. The fiery night was appropriate. Maury did indeed become the family rebel.

Isadore located another ramshackle flat, third floor, rear, at 7 Frank Street, in the Jewish settlement on the West Side, near Blue Island and tough Halstead. A spread of railroad tracks was across the way. As a white-coated egg inspector at South Market, holding three eggs in each large hand and passing them before a candle in a can, Isadore was making exactly $19.80 per week. He could afford no better than the seamy, sooty walk-up in an area only slightly classier than Bethnal Green.

Hyman and Rose Kertman absolutely refused to visit Frank Street, shunning the ghetto and infuriating Isadore, but Anna finally persuaded her stubborn husband to accept Hyman's assistance so they could move to the more respectable Humboldt Park district. Isadore's pride was injured and he quarreled often with Hyman, feeling that he was continually being bought by his successful brother-in-law. A single tree was in front of 2617 Evergreen and Anna constantly marveled at it.

About six months went by, during which time the musical education of little Julius Stein was hardly mentioned. Then the Kertmans came to Evergreen for Sunday dinner, bringing as guests Max and Jenny Amsterdam. Max, violinist with the Chicago Symphony, arrived with a half-size fiddle, probably at Hyman's urging, and soon placed it under the boy's chin. Anna wept happily at the sight.

Hyman beamed. "Now, Julius, what are you going to be?"

The boy snottily replied, "I'm going to stand on the corner with this, with a tin cup and dark glasses."

Max Amsterdam, father of comedian and TV actor Morey Amsterdam, was insulted and Anna grabbed the violin away as Isadore howled with joy over the put-down of Hyman. That night Anna asked her oldest son, "Just what *do* you want?"

Jule replied, "I want what Harry Lauder said I should have, a piano."

The next week, Isadore bought a new Kimball upright, placing himself in debt for the next ten years. Such was the gentle persuasion of his wife. The piano was lugged up to the Evergreen flat and eight-year-old Julius Stein began taking lessons from Esther Harris, at the Chicago College of Music. Anna, who somehow squeezed the money from her house allotment, went to every lesson, sitting quietly in the room but listening intently to everything Harris had to say.

Anna was not at all musical; neither was Isadore. There had been a grandfather, on her side, who was supposed to be one of the great Russian-Polish cantors. She'd heard that he often improvised on the High Holy Days, never singing the same melody twice; that members of the congregation applauded him, even though it was considered to be sacrilegious to do so. Aside from the Russian cantor, there was no known musical skill in either family.

Yet, seven months after the lessons began, Jule appeared with the Chicago Symphony in competition with other pre-teen pianists. Dressed in a black silk Lord Fauntleroy suit, with lace collar and cuffs, his feet barely grazed the extension pedal of the grand piano. The anxious Steins, midway in the audience, were mystified when the boy began to carefully wipe the keys before playing the Rondo from Haydn's D Major Piano Concerto. Max Amsterdam and musicians closer to the piano readily understood and were amazed at Jule's composure. The preceding contestant had cut a finger and there was blood on the keys.

Jule won a silver medal that night and the Steins, in a happy daze, were told that they had a "child prodigy" on their hands. Within another year, he'd played with the Detroit and St. Louis symphony orchestras, and been publicized in such terms as "remarkable" and "extraordinary."

Years later Claire distinctly remembered "him up at those grand pianos dwarfed by them. It was frightening to watch and hear him . . ."

Naturally, Anna talked about having "another Paderewski" in the family, and increased the practice schedule to four hours a day, often looking in from the kitchen, always listening. "Curve your fingers, Yoilek [Julius]. You're playing with flat hands." The fingers were supposed to be curved, as if an apple were in each hand. "Slower, slower, slower, Yoilek," she'd yell, and then report the results of each session to Esther Harris.

It seemed to Claire that Jule was endlessly at the Kimball, and she resented her mother's "starring" him at home. Always a recital after Sunday dinner. Anything and everything for Jule. Butter for Jule. Steak for Jule. Ice cream for Jule. Claire asked, "Why, Mama?" He is "very special," she was told. Now, harmony lessons in addition to regular lessons. Where Anna got the money remains a mystery. Isadore rode a second-hand bicycle because he couldn't afford carfare.

Yet the boy wasn't all that enthused about practice, nor about the concerts, though he liked the attention, on stage and off. He wanted to be outside; wanted to play baseball. He could hear all that from the street—the timeworn story of the prodigy. Finding ways to cheat the alarm clock, he finally managed to reduce the tedious practice sessions to about two hours, and then performed nightly for his father after dinner. The last fifteen minutes of this recital were usually devoted to Jewish songs; sometimes Scotch and Irish songs. Twenty or thirty minutes of classical music was enough for Isadore. "My God, that's plenty of that . . ."

The impoverished egg candler was not much impressed with Mozart and Beethoven. He remained the tough Cockney immigrant of Bethnal Green, and became a ringleader of the West Side Jews who fought off Polish ruffians with rocks, sticks and fists. The Poles occasionally broke windows of Jewish homes and pulled the beards of rabbis in the market area. Even before Maury's time, Isadore enjoyed a good fight.

One late afternoon he brought home sheet music for a half dozen Yiddish songs he'd heard at a local theater, and said to his son, "I'll show you how they go." He went to the kitchen for his glasses, preparing to sing the songs for the boy. By the time he returned, Jule was already playing them. Isadore said, "Here, I'll sing them for you, so you'll know how they go . . ."

Jule said, "I'm already playing them. I can read music."

Isadore, trying so hard to be a part of the endeavor at the Kimball, insisted. "I was there last night. I'll show you how they go."

Jule replied, "I know how they go. I can see."

"All right, smart ass," Isadore said angrily, taking the music and stomping out of the room. From that night on he refused, in many ways, to acknowledge his son's success as a musician or composer. At least, he seldom acknowledged any sense of pride to Jule. Years later, Jule looked back upon the incident with regret. *One of those things you find hard to live with. He wanted so much to be a part of it, and I turned him down.*

Yet the following year the candler was responsible for a secondary musical education, one that indirectly led Jule Styne to Hollywood. Isadore said to the boy, "You know, you have a nice voice when you sing the Jewish songs. You should be in a choir with a good cantor."

That good cantor was named Josef Rosenblatt, and six weeks or so later Jule was rehearsing with the choir for the forthcoming High Holy Days in the neighborhood synagogue. Isadore had arranged it.

Suddenly, Rosenblatt said, "There's a wrong note being sung."

A chubby child soprano dared express an opinion. "Yes, the altos are singing F sharp and the sopranos are singing F natural." Cantor Rosenblatt might well have echoed Isadore's thoughts about a smart ass. "What's your name, boy?" he asked, none too gently.

"Julius Stein."

"Do you play an instrument?"

"Yes, piano."

Rosenblatt, who slightly resembled Sigmund Freud, surveyed the altos. "Hit your note." They hit F sharp.

"Now, sopranos." They hit F natural.

The cantor snorted and fixed it, but the same prickly scene, more or less, was to be replayed in orchestra pits and on rehearsal stages for the next sixty years. As late as 1974, in London, Styne was barred from rehearsals of the Angela Lansbury *Gypsy,* when British musicians threatened to strike. Jule kept hearing notes that weren't in his score, and said so, in a shout.

But the cantor of 1914 was sufficiently intrigued with the boy's "ear" to accept Sabbath dinner in the Stein flat, bringing along his own pots, even though he was joining a strictly kosher table. Anna wept, of course, and sent Claire to summon all the neighbors to the back door. They heard Cantor Rosenblatt singing the *Kiddush,* the prayer over the wine, and the Steins gained status. Jule sang with other cantors and in other choirs until his voice changed two years later.

Isadore finally got a raise. He was now making $24 a week, and did extra work on Sundays for another five dollars. Anna counted pennies, fifteen cents for that, twenty-four cents for this, scrubbed the floors and took in boarders when they moved to a larger flat on Potomac Avenue. Anna was determined to send Jule to Carnegie Hall, and was quite willing to sacrifice all but the basic needs of her husband and other children in order to fulfill the goal. Composition was added to Jule's lessons. By now, she'd also started Claire on piano, too, thinking that the daughter could play duets with Jule when she caught up. More than half of Isadore's money was going into music.

But along about now the elder Steins were also making a terrible mistake. Some Sundays, the family would go to the Kertmans for large dinners. As soon as the table was cleared, cards were played. If the limit was more than a nickle or dime, Isadore and Anna promptly dropped out and just watched. Young Jule was mesmerized when the poker pots of the Kertmans and their well-to-do friends went to forty or fifty dollars, almost twice what Isadore made each week. The Steins should have fled with their prodigy, telling him that God would strike him dead if he ever gambled; that horse racing, crap tables and five-card-stud were the evils of all evils.

Jule was now taking his lessons in the instruction room where Gita Gradova (Gertrude Weinstock), a brilliant young concert pianist, practiced almost daily. Occasionally, they took classes together. Gradova was the first to warn Jule of a problem: "The fourth finger on your right hand is weak. Until you strengthen it, you can never play the difficult pieces." Mozart and Haydn did not tax him, and he played their works sufficiently well to win a Mozart scholarship, then a liberal grant from the Strausses, a Chicago banking family. At last the financial pressure was off Isadore. Anna promptly started Claire on elocution lessons, as well as the piano.

And while Jule was coping, rather unsuccessfully with those "difficult pieces," Rachmaninoff themes and Scriabin études, the true saints of the blues were beginning to march away from Storyville. The United States had entered World War I. With twelve blocks of whorehouses padlocked by U.S. Navy pressure, there weren't many customers in the dance halls and honky-tonks. Ragtime had greedily fed off the barrelhouses, and now it began to roll north by river boat and boxcar. The subtle quarter tones of "jass" were headed for Chicago.

The same summer that heard "Over There" and "The Yanks Are Coming," Jule Stein became an ex-child prodigy, a former Paderewski hopeful, a nonentity at the age of thirteen. Anna almost went into mourning. Isadore couldn't believe it.

Concert pianist Harold Bauer was teaching several special students at the college, and listened intently as Jule played Rachmaninoff, where the octaves came very fast, with chords in between. Then he studied the boy's hands. Finally, Bauer said, candidly and unsparingly, "I'm sorry, but you'll never be a concert pianist. Your hands will never be large enough and strong enough to play certain things. I blame this on your teacher. You should have been stretching your hands all this time. You've been playing Beethoven and Haydn and Mozart. They don't stretch your hands. It's too late now. You're too old."

The child felt destroyed.

At home, a tearful Anna said, "Don't worry. You're young. We'll find a way."

A few weeks later, Jule went to a Paderewski concert and sat up near the virtuoso, watching his hands. They were huge and powerful. Jule looked down at his own tiny hands and realized that Carnegie Hall was attainable only in his mother's mind.

2

"Wang Wang Blues," "Milenburg Joy,"
"Froggie Moore," "Jelly Roll Blues," "Empty Bed Blues,"
"Didn't He Ramble?," "Chicago Stomp-Down,"
"Friar's Point Shuffle," "Wabash Blues."

—A LITTLE NIGHT MUSIC FROM CHICAGO, 1920'S

Jule lasted about six weeks at Lane Technical High School in that fall of 1916, afraid of hurting his fingers on the machinery, and then transferred to Tuley High. Physically, he was a mess. Short and pudgy, he was soon nicknamed "Fat." He had slightly long hair and was more than a little arrogant. The "Hey, Fat!" along the corridors and in the classrooms soon deflated some of his arrogance.

There was usually dancing in the Tuley gym at lunchtime, and the plump ex-prodigy strolled in one day, watched and listened for a while. The boy at the keyboard couldn't play very well, and when he'd finished Jule sat down without being invited and rendered some Chopin. The gym emptied in a few minutes and Jule immediately thought, What was all this about Chopin and Beethoven? Nobody except some long-hairs at the College of Music liked it. *I was still suffering from what Harold Bauer had said. I now hated anything classical.*

One Saturday morning, he went to Eller and Kogan's Music Store on Division Street, bought several copies of sheet music at a dime each, scanned them a moment and then sat down at the demonstration piano and got right into "Alexander's Ragtime Band."

Manager Jack Kapp, later to become president of Decca Records, walked over to express interest. Further, he offered a job. "Just keep sitting there and playing."

Jule took the first day's wages in sheet music, twenty-five songs, and on Monday returned to the gym at noon, awaiting his turn. Instead of Chopin, he opened grandly with "I Want a Girl Just Like the Girl That Married Dear Old Dad." He quickly became the permanent lunchtime pianist at Tuley and "Fat" was soon discarded. He was called by his rightful name.

A week or so later, he was offered a job for five dollars a night with a juvenile band that worked school dances. Anna and Isadore had no idea that their son had begun to play popular music. What's more, for pay. Jule kept a pair of long pants at a friend's house and lied about the source of the cash, some of which he turned over to Anna. However, a few dollars trickled to Big Jim Colesimo's horse rooms. *One of the kids in the band kept talking about how much money he made on the races. I placed my first bet on the ponies when I was thirteen and had the misfortune to win.*

The next year Jule felt grown up enough to join the musician's union, declaring he was sixteen, though he looked to be no more than twelve. A few days after joining, the union booked him as relief pianist at the Haymarket burlesque house. On the battered piano in the pit he learned grind music and how to play the strippers on; watched the drummer time the bumps and generally began another kind of classical education that served him well years later in two Phil Silvers shows and *Gypsy*.

The Haymarket strippers mothered him in a unique way. They got up over the lights and bumped straight at his nose. Backstage, they threw G-strings at him and flicked at his fly. Unquestionably, an education.

By the late spring of 1920, when Jule, not quite fifteen, was still in knickers and long brown stockings, a very different music was being heard in the seven-room Stein flat. Anna, alarmed at this new, strident, low-class sound, asked, "What is that?" A little of the "Twelfth Street Rag" and "Mama's Blues" was what it was.

"Just some music the kids are playing," Jule replied. The statement wasn't altogether true. Not many kids were playing the blues, and some of the new sound in the Stein apartment was direct from the Dreamland Café, in the Black Belt, where King Joe Oliver was blowing chorus after ragging chorus, fanning smoke and the smell of gin. Lil Hardin, later to be Mrs. Louis Armstrong, was at the piano, and the boy, edging around the mostly black audience, watched Lil's hands and listened to her two-beat Dixieland.

State Street awakened at midnight, flushing out the whores and pimps and gamblers and just plain joyfuls who were escaping daylight misery. The syncopated music was irresistible. Anna complained occasionally about the late hours her young son was keeping, unaware that he was prowling the gin mills and dance halls. She had little knowledge of the underside of his life.

As Jule turned a somewhat wordly sixteen, Chicago was fully entitled to Hecht's "Jazz Baby." Every righteous black sound, from the corners of New Orleans's Rampart and Tchoupitouslas streets was in the night air on the teeming South Side. The best white jazzmen, also up from Mardi Gras city, led by Leon Rappolo's clarinet and George Brunis's trombone, had settled in at Mike Fritzel's Friar's Inn. Jule subbed with the band from time to time.

In Storyville the bands had played mostly ensemble and solos were few, but King Oliver had made some changes. It was now ritual for his cornet to rip out a solo with the rest of the band backing him; then, after a chorus, each man took his crack at it. The choruses were sandwiched between the solos, but there was no exact pattern. It was freestyle, basic jazz.

The first course of the ragtime feast was on the Windy City buffet.

Henrici's Restaurant, hangout for politicians and assorted musicians, was already famous, and in the late winter of 1921 Jule began a Saturday noon pilgrimage to the sedate restaurant on Randolph Street. One such noon he stopped by the table of Rocco Vocco, who represented the Leo Feist Music Company in Chicago. Vocco was chatting with a boy about Jule's age and made the introduction. "Mike Todd, Jule Stein. Jule plays piano with dance bands."

Todd asked, "You write songs?"

"I guess I can," Jule replied.

Todd then invited the piano player to lunch, borrowing a dollar for the tip; on the way out he stopped at another table to borrow five for the lunch tab. Mike Todd's career began early.

Outside Henrici's, Todd said, "Come on up to my office. Let's talk some more."

Todd's "office" was on the top floor of the Oriental Theatre, which was located in the Masonic Temple, and Jule had the feeling that the Masons were unwilling landlords. A very temporary placard said, "Mike Todd Productions." There was a wall-type pay phone, hauled to Todd's corner. The "office" furniture was obviously borrowed from the meeting hall.

A bit bewildered, Jule sat down as Todd began describing an act he'd assembled. *Mike told me he'd have a girl in a cocoon. She was the moth. Then there was a guy who would be the flame. The moment he touched the girl he fell in love with her, catching her on fire. Then she stepped out, half-naked, but unhurt. Pure Mike Todd, even at the age of sixteen.*

Todd said he planned to sell the act to the Chicago Theatre and needed a song to dress it up. He gave Jule a title, "The Moth and the Flame," and then asked how long it would take to compose the music.

"Not long," Jule replied, "but who's going to write the words?"

Without hesitation, Todd said, "I will," and then guided Jule to a piano across the meeting room.

A few minutes later, Jule provided a melody and Todd ordered, "Stay here. I'll be back." He grabbed the single sheet and dashed off. Two hours later, the future World's Fair man and producer of *Around the World in Eighty Days* returned and began counting off ten-dollar bills.

Todd later hired Jule to write additional songs for his musical, *Peep Show,* but never got around to paying for them.

In early spring of this "moth-and-flame" year, Jule went along to the union hall, hoping for a club date. Thus far, he'd worked only with pick-up juvenile bands, still doing high school and college dances, occasional Jewish weddings. It was obvious that he could play good dance-band piano and hold his own with more experienced musicians; he thought he was now ready for clubs.

Apparently, so did another Stein, whose first name was also Jules. Some fifteen minutes after Stein No. 1 arrived in the hall, this second J. Stein, then twenty-six years old, a medical student, walked up to say that he'd heard good things about Stein No. 1; would he like to work a summer resort?

The Music Corporation of America had yet to be founded by the older Stein, of South Bend, Indiana, but already he was booking talent. He'd started by providing musicians for Jewish country-club affairs and was now expanding. Dr. Stein used fellow medical students and other musicians from the union to fill his dates. Away from opthalmology courses, he was a violinist and saxophonist of little promise.

Not unexpectedly, Anna reacted to the announcement of summer dance-band work with dismay and concern. She still clung to the hope that Jule would return to the classics. Isadore, however, seemed pleased. The years of lessons weren't wasted, after all. Jule played with the Stein band that summer at Miller Beach, Indiana, and soon learned what other musicians had known for several years: young Dr. Stein was a much better booker than he was a violinist. They couldn't wait to get him off the stand whenever he visited. Dr. Stein never improved his musicianship.

For "sweet" bands of this type, the main booker in the Chicago area in the early twenties was Edgar Benson, who took a third of the musician's earnings as his commission. Enterprising Dr. Stein had a theory that more money could be made; that the assorted horn, fiddle and piano players would be a happier lot if the agent only charged ten percent. Later on, Jule met him one night in La Salle, Indiana. The doctor, wearing a fur-collared coat, already looking successful, said, "Would you believe that that band made $30 thousand in thirty nights? I made three thousand." Mickey Rockford, a five foot two bodyguard, was with him, holding the money satchel. Mickey had a gun.

The following winter, Jule worked a series of one-night stands for Benson, playing one stag on the outskirts of Chicago with a musician named Jimmy Petrillo. Jimmy loathed Benson and firmly believed that musicians should have a union equally as powerful as the steelworkers' organization. If the band made $500, Edgar took $200, leaving the musicians $25 or $35 each.

Remarkably, and not only in Jule's case, age had little to do with professional standards. This year—1921—Benny Goodman was received into the union wearing "short" pants and knee socks, appropriate in that he was only twelve. The Austin High gang—Frankie Teschmaker, the McPartland brothers, Bud Freeman, Jim Lannigan—none of them over sixteen, could already play with most professionals, as could drummer George Wettling at Calumet High and Davey Tough at Lewis Institute.

What was so incredible about that period was that none of us realized what would happen. I played with Benny Goodman while I was still in high school, and so what? He was good but none of us knew how good he was. For seven or eight years these people came in and out of our house—Beiderbecke, Goodman, Milt Mezirow, Dave Rose, Bud Freeman, Davey Tough. Others. They were just kid musicians that you knew, nothing else.

In 1922, the Austin High musicians either graduated or dropped out, forming the Blue Friars, an astonishingly good jazz band, with Benny Goodman on clarinet. These particular jazz babies, along with Eddie Condon, Muggsy Spanier, Biederbecke, Art Hodes, Milt Mezirow and Gene Krupa, over the next years and in various combinations sculpted "Chicago-style" jazz, distinctive from the essentially black New Orleans import. Their music was edgy and harsh, with hot solo work. No piece was played the same way twice. Experts claimed it to be *the* pure jazz.

Jule graduated from Tuley High this year of the Blue Friars without a solitary honor. He did leave behind a reputation as being the best noontime pianist in Tuley's history, and the music for a song, "The Guy in the Polka-Dot Tie."

One of the first gigs he played after departing Tuley was in a run-down club on the South Side, memorable because of a banjo player named Blind Paul and a limping saxophone player. Jule took his six books of pop music to the club and awaited the arrival of the rest of the band. Eventually, Blind Paul came in with his dog. Then the drummer arrived; finally, the sax player hobbled in. On the second or third number, the sax player pulled up his pant leg and the drummer beat a rousing tattoo on the wooden limb.

These guys were all war veterans, much older than I was. Sometime during the night the drummer left the stand, then the sax player. A moment later, Blind Paul leaned over and said to me, "Why don't you go out and listen to the orchestra?" Without thinking, I did. One banjo! That was all that was left on the stand.

However, listening was better than ever in 1923. Satchmo Armstrong had departed Fate Marable's Showboat, joining King Oliver at the Lincoln Gardens, now and then daylighting at the Vendome Theatre with Erskine Tate's band. Some weeks, Fats Waller and Earl "Fatha" Hines got up to the Vendome pit piano for two-hour concerts. The Stein boy was often in the audience when they played.

Good boogie piano was available at the "house-shouts" or "calico-hops," those throbbing rent-raising parties of the Black Belt. For twenty-five cents, Meade Lux Lewis or Jimmy Yancey or Albert Ammons, all revered names of boogie, might be heard on any night. Jule went to several of the chitterling rags to listen to the bargain beefy-handed music. The whole building shook. Big Bessie Smith was singing the blues as if she owned all the indigo in the world. Ma Rainey was also around. Jule listened to Bessie singing "Empty Bed Blues" and marveled at her phrasing. The earthiness of some of Jule Styne's Broadway music surely dates back to 1923.

On April 24, Jule traveled to Davenport, Iowa, with the Benson Orchestra of Chicago, ten pieces featuring the C-melody saxophone of Frankie Trumbauer, another heady name in the jazz world. After the first set, an undersized, round-faced country boy in a baggy coat and pistol-legged britches, cuffs a good three inches above his scuffed shoes, approached Jule to ask, "Mind if I sit in sometime tonight?"

"What do you play?"

"Piano and cornet." The boy, Bix Beiderbecke, said he was better on cornet. "Better" did not adequately describe his brilliance on the instrument. He was, of course, to become legendary, but even that night the country boy startled the Benson band with his playing.

Bix had already been to Chicago a number of times, sneaking away from Lake Forest Academy to do what every other young musician was doing—haunting the dives. He'd played in a few of the joints, sitting in. And Bix did move to State and Wabash that summer, joining a band at the Valentino Inn, but it wasn't until December that he became a member of the original Wolverines, to begin the legend of the "man with the golden horn."

The feast continued.

3

More or less, musicians fed off the mob. They still do, to a certain extent, and before I got out of Chicago, I must have worked a couple of dozen mob joints. But those people always seemed to like musicians and I did my job and kept my mouth shut. That whole town was wild in the mid-twenties, as you know, the South Side a rat's nest. There was a beer war and a gambling war. Every place you turned there were local books. North Clark, Quincy, Dearborn. In cigar stores, basements, hotel rooms. Even aldermen were making book. Capone had the North Side. Ten thousand books, maybe. The gangsters were Italians and Irish and Jews. Capone and Johnny Torrio, the Genna brothers and the Aiello brothers. Nails Morton was a Jewish mob leader. Then I remember Dion O'Banion was shot up in his flower shop. That was sometime in '24. Guys were shot up all over the place during the beer war. Saltis gang. McErlane gang. Spike O'Donnell's gang. It wasn't just Capone. I was in a club one night when a guy started shooting. The intersection of Oak and Milton was called Death City. But as awful as it was, I think music came out of it, was part of it. Jazz was, I know.

—JULE STYNE, 1977

In 1924 Jule worked for a while in the Balaban & Katz theater chain, playing pit piano for the stage shows, a dull way to make a living. Then he became "Jules Kerwin" for a few summer months, leading the Benson Bluejackets at the Bismarck Hotel, with Benny Goodman on clarinet. At the time, there were few band "leaders." The stick-waving was for show, unnecessary with a small group. Whoever conducted, from his seat, was the boss; he contracted the musicians, selected the numbers. But it was apparent that the public liked the idea of a leader, waving the baton around and making introductions. As movies were soon to go from silent to sound, bandleaders were soon to become personalities in their own right.

Late that fall, baton-waver Arnold Johnson called Jule to ask about availability. Specifically, would he like to play Florida during the winter? There was little hesitation in answering yes. The Johnson orchestra was nationally known, and Jule had never been south of St. Louis.

The Johnson band had just finished at the Green Mill, a Capone place on Broadway near Wilson, playing dance tunes and backing the floor shows. Helen Morgan and Ruth Etting were among the innocents in the Green Mill show. The garish night club was about to gain lasting fame as a point of dispute between comedian Joe E. Lewis and the mob. Lewis had the capacity to make Al Capone laugh, and when Joe departed the Green Mill to joke over at the New Rendezvous, an opposition dive, "Machine-gun" Jack McGurn saw to it that the "joker" didn't leave laughing. Lewis was pistol-whipped; his tongue was gouged; his throat was slit. *But the musicians had to play these places or starve. The only good thing about them was that the gangsters paid well and bought the best talent. Not one of them ever welshed on me.*

The Johnson band, Jule alternating with Adolph Deutsch as pianist, opened January 5, 1925, at the Hollywood Golf and Country Club, performing for the rich. Half of New York's high society seemed to be in Florida that season, some just to sun and golf; others to sun and golf and buy cheap land. The boom was on, the Hollywood Land and Water Company selling lots for $10 a front foot.

Except in moving pictures, Jule had never seen a palm tree, nor had he seen the Atlantic Ocean other than during the crossing from London, and after twelve winters by Lake Michigan did not quite trust the warm breezes blowing over Palm Beach and Fort Lauderdale. It was such a playground that he quickly took up golf, taking lessons from the club's pro, Gene Sarazen. *Everyone in the band was on the greens each morning and I felt left out.*

Sarazen's lessons led to a fateful game with a complete stranger, one Moe Shapoff. As the afternoon went along, Jule learned that Shapoff was the trainer for Jock Whitney's Greentree Stables. After the eighteenth hole, Shapoff invited Jule to the opening day at Hialeah racetrack. *I told him I was going anyway because the Johnson band was alternating with Paul Whiteman that day, but I'd certainly be grateful if he gave me some tips on horses. I admitted I'd placed bets in Chicago, in the horse rooms, but I'd never been to the track.*

Shapoff quickly obliged and Jule put up two dollars on Quesada (he clearly remembers the name), then had the pleasure of personally watching it win. Jule located Shapoff down near the paddock, thanked him profusely, and asked for another horse. The second one came in, paying $23. *Actually, it was the worst thing that could have happened to me. I wish to God that the horses had wound up in the palmettos.*

Jule then began going to the track each day, playing very little golf, winning more than he lost; winning enough, in fact, to become partners in some Fort Lauderdale lots with Adolph Deutsch, who later won several Academy Awards for film scores. Deutsch orchestrated for the Johnson musicians.

At season's end Jule took the train north, but not before telling the bandleader that he'd be most happy to return to Florida the following year. Golf, horses, pretty girls; horses.

At home again, now Crystal Street, a better section of Humboldt Park, because the sons and daughters were contributing to Isadore's still meager income, Jule returned to the Balaban & Katz pits for the summer and fall, playing standards of the day, "I'd Climb the Highest Mountain," and "San" and "China Town, My China Town."

But I couldn't wait to get back to Florida. The gambling was creeping up on me so fast and just as soon as I arrived that next winter I found myself betting horses in the afternoon and sweating out blackjack at night. There was a place in Lemon City, between Lauderdale and Hollywood, that I went to just as soon as we buttoned up "Goodnight, Sweetheart." I was out and gone, betting twenty-five dollar blackjack. If you lost, and had any property, you'd get face value for your land deeds. I carried mine around in my hip pocket.

There was one lasting accomplishment by the warm sands that winter of 1926. One sunny afternoon Jule was on the beach with a pretty girl he'd met several nights before in the club. He began to hum a melody, one he'd idly fingered over the past weeks. Everyone in the band was attempting to write songs. However, there was another and more basic motive to the humming as they strolled along. One of the easiest and quickest ways for a musician to fill the empty-bed blues was to write something for the pretty girl.

The dialogue probably hasn't changed since Queen Elizabeth's *Virginals Book:*

"I haven't heard that song before, what is it?"

"Oh, just something I made up."

"Play it for me tonight."

"I'd have to orchestrate it."

"Oh, please play it for me tonight! It'll be our song and I'll stay with you."

Jule practically ran back to the empty country club, finished the half-done melody, feverishly made rough orchestrations and awaited the night. During the first set, he spotted the girl, nodded to her and then signaled to Johnson. Soon, the band segued into the untitled piece and even Johnson was impressed. Featured at the piano, Jule played it dreamily, milking every note. The number got a good hand and wide smiles from the girl.

At the break, lyricist Irving Caesar, of "Tea for Two" fame, made his way to the stand. He'd been sitting with Al Jolson, one of a number of celebrities in the club. Caesar asked Johnson, "That a new tune?" Johnson replied that it was, indicating his twenty-one-year-old pianist.

Caesar then approached Jule. He said, "I like that melody. Any lyrics to it?"

Jule answered that he'd just written it.

Caesar said he'd like to put words to it; furthermore, he was certain that "Jolie" would sing it. "Jolie" liked the tune, too.

Jule was so excited that he rushed off the bandstand and ran toward Jolson, momentarily forgetting the girl. She turned out to be a disappointment, anyway. In fact, Caesar and "Jolie" were disappointments, too. Caesar didn't write the lyrics and Jolson's infatuation with the melody went no further than a handshake and smile. Other adventures also fell apart as the season ended. Jule sold his share of the real-estate investment to raise cash for gambling, and Adolph Deutsch decided the boom was over. He sold the other half. Today, the property, standing in the center of Fort Lauderdale's business district, is said to be valued at around four million dollars.

Back in Chicago and broke once again, Jule played several months in Benny Krueger's band at the Uptown Theatre, now and then rendering "our song" from the sands of Florida. Krueger liked the tune, as did almost everyone who heard it, and finally said, "Jule, why don't you get that thing published. Take it over to Leo Feist and see Rocco Vocco."

After Jule had played about eight measures, Rocco, Mike Todd's friend, said, "That's a positive hit." He added, "I'm going to put Ned Miller on it for lyrics. He works for us."

Jule, of course, was delighted, even though he had no idea who Ned Miller was, and didn't care. He accepted the deal without question, signed the papers, and a month later "Sunday" was published, becoming an immediate hit, selling more than five hundred thousand copies of sheet music. The superb Jean Goldkette Band, from Detroit, recorded it, as well as such individual stars as Gene Austin and Cliff Edwards. Much later, Frank Sinatra made a "Sunday" single and the song is still performed by jazz groups.

Overnight, don't you know, I was a hit songwriter. Can you imagine that? Accidentally. Something I'd written for a devious purpose. People were saying, "Listen to how well he plays the piano. He wrote 'Sunday.' " You always get fame for the wrong reason. My playing hadn't improved a bit because of that song but that's how it works.

Jule also learned that he'd inherited his father's lack of business sense. Everyone in Chicago seemed to own a piece of "Sunday." Lyricist Chester Cahn took a fourth share for polishing Ned Miller's work. He changed one word. Fatherly Benny Krueger cut himself a slice as "contact" man. There was a partner that Jule never met. The creator of the song was getting less than a penny royalty per copy sold.

Yet thinly sliced "Sunday" and its ability to attract attention did persuade bandleader Ben Pollack to phone Jule at the Uptown and offer a job as arranger during a stand at the Chez Paree, a mob club soon to open. A jazzman, graduate of the New Orleans Rhythm Kings, Pollack was, without doubt, one of the best drummers in town, and his band was considered to be one of the finest in the nation. He'd just completed a successful California tour, recruiting Benny Goodman and a young trombonist named Glenn Miller.

Ben Pollack? Wow! Do you know what that meant? The big time. Here was a man who'd played with Leon Rappolo and George Brunis. He was trying to introduce jazz into the ballrooms but in a different way, a kind of semijazz. Benny Goodman later turned that same style into swing. I quit Benny Krueger that same afternoon and then Wayne Allen, Pollack's pianist, had to leave, so I took that spot, too.

When the Chez Paree opening was postponed because of license difficulties, Pollack quickly booked his men into the ballroom of the popular Southmoor Hotel, at Sixty-ninth Street and Stoney Island, to play "big band" jazz, a first for white musicians. Whites had previously played jazz in small groups. There were ten instruments on the Southmoor platform.

However, the Ben Pollack band of 1926 and 1927 became legendary from still another aspect. Gathered on one stand was Benny Goodman, Glenn Miller, Charlie Spivak, "Fud" Livingston, Gil Rodin and a future Broadway composer named Jule Styne, as well as other lesser known but equally good musicians. Very likely, no other bandleader of the time matched Pollack's talent for spotting instrumental brilliance. What became the drive and style of Miller's "Chattanooga Choo Choo" edged onto the tracks at the Southmoor Hotel.

A concert pianist has no sense of timing. You play freely. The symphony orchestra is supposed to follow you. So, with that background, Ben Pollack was a great influence when I needed it the most. He quickly taught me to keep time. He often hit my fingers with his drumsticks when

I speeded up. I know that the Pollack band was the first one that made real demands on me as a musician. Everyone in it was so good, so highly professional, that I was embarrassed when I loused up.

Other musicians visited the Southmoor to hear Pollack's music. No higher tribute could be paid. And caught up in this professionalism, Jule seldom thought about gambling; seldom placed a bet. He returned to haunting the Chicago dives to listen. On Monday nights, he occasionally took the train to Detroit to hear the Goldkette Band at the Graystone Ballroom. Bix Beiderbecke, the Dorsey brothers, Tommy and Jimmy; Pee Wee Russell, Joe Venuti and Russ Morgan, were among Goldkette's prize players.

On one of the band's shinier nights at the Southmoor, Meyer Marks, co-owner of the Granada and Marlboro theaters, occupied a table. During the evening, Jule met Marks, who casually mentioned that he needed a conductor for the Granada pit. He returned the next evening to make a flat offer. The Granada would pay more money and provide a different prestige; the Pollack band was closing at the Southmoor, heading for the Rendezvous, and Wayne Allen, Pollack's original pianist, planned to rejoin the band. Jule accepted Marks's offer.

The Granada, at Sheridan and Devon, was a big Moorish-flavored movie house with a high, domed ceiling. It had the usual stage productions, with vaudeville and specialty acts, between film runnings. Horses and elephants sometimes performed in the more lavish numbers. There was a chance to play both jazz and light classical. Jule would now have thirty musicians to supervise; be an official contact with the union on band matters, "the contractor." In the musicians' world of play or starve, it was a position of some importance.

I had all these plans to reorganize the band, get my sound into it, but within twenty-four hours I discovered that Mr. Jimmy Petrillo, down at the union, made the hiring choices, not me. And one man that Petrillo personally sent down was Bob Pacelli, a trombonist. We hadn't even started to rehearse when another musician said, "Be nice to Pacelli. His brother is alderman for the 20th Ward." That was Capone territory. So I quickly made Bob Pacelli the contractor. Forget the importance. I didn't want the job! Then there was Benny Meroff, who emceed the show and "led" the band. The audience thought Meroff was doing a Gracie Allen bit with his malapropisms, but they were for real. Once, I told Benny to ad-lib something and he said he couldn't do it unless I wrote it out. His comments to the audience destroyed the music: "We'll now play for you a cute little number called Faust." My God, I died. Or I'd be taking the orchestra through the Ilguarnia Overture and get into the andante passage which is big and flowing, and that son of a bitch would start pretending he was ice-skating, like Ben Blue . . .

The third irritant at the Granada was a telephone voice in the office. The voice belonged to Ethel Rubenstein, attractive, blue-eyed blond sister-in-law of Meyer Marks. Before they met, a minor matter arose and Jule thought that the girl on the telephone was most inefficient; the girl thought the rapid-talking man named Stein was most rude. Twenty-year-old Ethel Rubenstein was the youngest daughter of six in the family of Hyman and Fanny Rubenstein, affluent West Side kosher caterers. There was one son, Joe.

For many years, the Rubensteins had utilized their succession of huge homes for business, renting out space within the houses for Jewish weddings, bar mitzvahs and other events. Sometimes two or three affairs went on simultaneously. The family, close as a tongue-and-groove, lived on the third and fourth floors of such mansions as the Ashland or Wrightwood, listed as "clubhouses" in the yellow pages. The whole family cooked and served and quarreled and laughed and gambled.

Ethel was clearly a homebody, preferring to be around her parents and sisters most of the time. She wasn't at all like the tall showgirls Jule had been dating of late. She was quiet and observant and didn't particularly care for show-business people, bands or night life. Aside from the fact that connections were to be made through Ethel's family, Jule wasn't at all sure why he was drawn to this sensible blonde. She wasn't sexy, clever or witty. She was a "good, good girl" but an unlikely mate for Jule Stein. He did find her family great fun. They played poker or mah-jongg in the afternoons after setting up the night's parties. Gambling was often the main topic of conversation in the Rubenstein's living spaces. Then Jule discovered, of all things, that Hyman, Ethel's father, was a dedicated horseplayer, and always sought companionship for track visits. An immaculate, proper man who wore a diamond stickpin in his tie and a Panama hat in the summer, Hyman was happiest when he had a racing form in his hands, handicapping with three colored pencils. Son Joe also played the ponies regularly. It was one more step for Jule Stein into a gambling abyss.

Jule and Ethel dated throughout the spring and summer, and were married in September 1927, at the Wrightwood Club, the Rubensteins not only giving away their last daughter in matrimony but catering the event as well. Hyman and Fanny were not too pleased over Ethel's choice of a musician and the Steins weren't joyful about the merger, either. Isadore thought that Hyman and Fanny had inflated opinions of themselves; Anna was only happy that Jule wasn't marrying one of the *shiksa* showgirls he'd been courting. She cared little for Ethel.

Jule moved in with the Rubenstein clan at the Wrightwood, and began going to the track each day with Hyman and Joe.

A few days after the nuptials, a wide-smiling, triumphant Bob Pacelli said to Jule, "Mr. Brown wants us to play at the Metropole. He's throwing a big party the whole week of the Dempsey–Tunney fight."

Jule was about to say that he certainly couldn't take the band away from the Granada without the approval of Meyer Marks when Pacelli continued, "It's all arranged at the union. Another band will come in for the week. Mr. Brown wants *you.* He wants to see you. Right now. I've made the call."

Whatever "Al Brown" wanted, he usually got. He occupied about fifty rooms on two floors of the Metropole Hotel. As "Dr. A. Brown," he had smaller, more private syndicate offices at 2146 Michigan Boulevard. The Metropole rooms were mainly for casual visitation and entertainment: low-level business transactions. "Scarface" was very much back in town. Big Bill Thompson had been elected Mayor of Chicago in April, signal for Al Capone to return from nearby Cicero. Things were again flourishing at the Metropole, a Victorian-type hotel at Twenty-second and the Boulevard. An estimated two hundred Capone hoods were in the hotel around the clock, tending the private bars, manning the private elevators; making routine deals in liquor, gambling and prostitution. The place reeked of garlic and pasta sauces. High-level business usually occurred in the "Dr. Brown" suite two blocks away.

Jule went over to the Metropole, wishing his benefactor, Bob Pacelli, organizer of this unusual gig, had come along, too. Jule had seen Capone at the Green Mill and once at the Midnight Frolics but had never gotten close to him; had never met him. Furthermore, he had no desire to begin an association with Capone, other than playing in his clubs.

He saw that the lobby was full of gunsels, lounging around on red couches. Some faces were familiar. Within seconds, he was frisked and on his way to the fourth floor, via private elevator and under escort. The destination was a suite, 409 and 410, which overlooked Michigan Boulevard and was approached down a heavily guarded hallway.

Ushered past the anteroom palace coterie of about eight staring gunners, ripe with chest holsters, Jule finally saw his future employer. He was seated in a swivel chair with an armored back, beneath excellent oil portraits of Mayor Thompson and Abraham Lincoln. The gangster, dressed nattily, rose up and offered his hand.

Speaking in a low, soft voice, Capone then outlined what he needed for the week beginning September 16th: He was taking over the Metropole ballroom for six nights and would feature the Granada Orchestra, plus such headliners as the Duncan Sisters, Harry Richman and Sophie Tucker. A different star each night. Capone stressed that he would be host to many important people throughout the week, particularly the night of the Dempsey–Tunney fight. He wanted things to go smoothly. Finally, he asked Jule, "Does your band play Gershwin?"

A bit startled, Jule replied that the band indeed played Gershwin. Al Capone knew Gershwin's music?

The gangster nodded, and Jule was dismissed without further conversation, escorted back to the lobby and out to the street. Weak with relief that it was over, he hurried away from the Metropole and went straight to Meyer Marks who said, "I know, I know."

So the Granada orchestra opened for a very limited, exclusive engagement in the Metropole ballroom, playing for "Mr. Al Brown" and his dignified guests, including some forty senators and congressmen and their wives; a dozen or so federal, state and county judges, plus legions of local politicians. And by week's end, Jule had almost forgotten Capone's inquiry about Gershwin. But at the height of the gala party following Tunney's surprise decision over Dempsey, Capone walked up to the bandstand and said quietly, "Give me the baton. Have them play 'Rhapsody in Blue'."

Jule gladly handed over the stick, quickly instructed the orchestra and stepped down. For the next twenty minutes, "Scarface" conducted Gershwin.

Predictably, at finish, Capone received a standing ovation from the assorted senators, congressmen, judges and aldermen, as well as his beaming bodyguards. Even the orchestra members stood up, prompted by their leader, and saluted the gangster with applause. They did so more out of fear than approval.

Al Capone always rewarded or always punished. Late that night, before closing, he sent a representative to the stand with bonus envelopes. Each musician received $500; Jule's envelope contained $2,500, exactly enough to cover his losing fight bet. His man had been Jack Dempsey.

A few weeks after that memorable evening, while Jule still had the Granada band, a saxophone player became ill. Rather than replace him, Jule said to his brother, Maury, "I'll sneak you in. Just sit there and hold that horn. Don't you play, dammit. You don't have a union card."

So Maury, aspiring to be a musician, joined the theater pit band. Earlier, Jule had told his brother to learn how to read music or give up the saxophone. "That was the day he first caught me trying to play it. All I wanted to do now was hang around musicians, and I was improving. So I couldn't keep from playing a few notes. And Jule has ears like a bat. He heard me and gave me hell, but the other musicians said, 'Leave the kid alone.' And I got my union card early the next year and then Jule used me anytime he had a vacancy." Maury soon became a top sax player.

By now, the Rubensteins had sold the Wrightwood Club and had moved into the Embassy Hotel, taking along all six daughters and their husbands. There was much visitation along the corridors and up the stairs. Meyer Marks and his wife had rooms on the third floor, as did Jule and Ethel. On the fourth floor was drummer Bob Conzleman and his wife Lil, the fifth Rubenstein daughter. Conzleman had played drums for the original Wolverines band, the Bix Beiderbecke group, and was a third man in the Benny Goodman trio for a while. Jule and Bob certainly had a common ground—music—but Jule's visits to the fourth floor were usually for another purpose. He used the telephone to place bets. Unlike the other members of the family, Ethel did not approve of gambling.

Nineteen twenty-nine, the gaudy year the stock market collapsed, the year of the St. Valentine's Day massacre, the year music began to turn from jazz to sweet, was also the year that Jule quit the Granada to rejoin the Balaban & Katz circuit. He'd had quite enough of brother-in-law Meyer Marks and the malapropping Benny Meroff.

Nineteen twenty-nine was the year that Ethel gave birth to their first son, Stanley. The new member of the family did not appreciably alter Jule's hours and way of life. He found it difficult to "kitchy-koo," and had no desire to change diapers and walk the floors at night.

Nineteen twenty-nine was also the year that Jule, as a gasping bystander, was almost shot in the Granada Café. He was waiting to deliver special material to singer Mildred Bailey, standing a few feet from the Paul Whiteman bandstand, when a machine gun opened up. Jule wisely dove to the floor, as did almost everyone else in the restaurant.

Altogether, excluding the birth of Stanley, it was an unhappy year because Jule decided he didn't love Ethel; would never love Ethel. Some of it had to do with the tongue-and-groove Rubenstein family. Togetherness was dawn to dark in the Embassy, and Jule sometimes felt he was married to all the Rubensteins. Hyman and Fanny swooped down on baby Stanley, of course, extending their visiting time. Though it was seldom put into words, Jule also felt that Ethel did not approve of his occupation and his assortment of musician friends. Her disapproval of his fascination with racing forms was quite verbal.

In the summer of 1930 Ethel took the baby away for a month, visiting with her family at a lake resort in Michigan. Jule stayed on in Chicago, playing at the Uptown Theatre. Several days before Ethel's scheduled return, Jule called their live-in maid. *It seemed to be a good idea, get her there early, so that everything would be ready when Ethel got back. So she came to the apartment, a pretty young girl, and one thing led to another. Ethel came back early and there we were, sleeping like cherubs in the same bed. I told Ethel's family she'd have to divorce me. They said, "She'll forgive you." You know, I didn't want forgiveness, I wanted a divorce. She had the grounds, I didn't. The whole thing had been a mistake.*

In late summer, a man with a heavy Russian accent called Jule to offer him a job. The Spitalny brothers—Morris, Leopold and Phil—had been playing concert music as a trio in the Statler Hotel, Cleveland, but now Phil wanted to organize a dance band for a fall booking in Chicago's Edgewater Beach Hotel. Spitalny later became famous for his all-girl orchestra, featuring "Evelyn and Her Magic Violin."

Jule, fed up with the movie-house pits, soon became contractor-pianist for the new band, gathering together eleven musicians, including Maury, to play classical music between six and seven in the main dining room, then dance music in the ballroom between eight and midnight. Spitalny enjoyed the former and endured the latter. His musicians had opposite tastes.

On opening night at the Edgewater, Phil had the band play about a hundred choruses of "Moonlight and Roses" while he personally passed out a rose to each woman in the audience, kissing her cheek. When a band member attempted to help, speeding the rose distribution, Phil ordered him back to the stand, saying, "Denny, don't have such a good time."

On any given night, the band spent almost as much time laughing as it did playing. The gentle Russian was difficult to understand, an unintentional straight man with little respect for the abilities of his musicians. He often took pleasure in stumping the band, selecting some obscure piece for a rehearsal, knowing the orchestra couldn't play it. When the music collapsed, he'd throw the baton down. "Ah, you jazz musicians, you are nothing . . ."

The Spitalny band played at the Edgewater with amusement but never spectacularly until the night of November 22, 1930. That afternoon, Knute Rockne's Notre Dame football team beat their old rival Northwestern, 14–0, a fourth-quarter run by All-American Marchy Schwartz sealing the game. Usually a Northwestern hang-out, the Edgewater was invaded by a happy, boozed-up fighting Irish crowd shortly after eight. The celebrants were much too noisy for Spitalny and he lingered in the coffee shop after the break, telling Jule to take over.

A few minutes after the second set began, the Irish fans started to heave water-soaked hard rolls at the band. One hit the trumpet player; Maury took one in the shoulder. As the barrage continued, Jule decided to turn the orchestra around, so their backs faced the dance floor.

Then Spitalny walked up, startled at the sight of his band in a reverse position, he asked, "Boys, what are you doing? Julia, where is the band?"

Jule replied, "Phil, do you know what is happening here? They're throwing hard rolls at us. They about busted Bobby's lip. They hit Maury . . ."

The Russian said soothingly, "Boys, that is no reason to turn the band around. The customer is always right . . ."

At that moment, a roll bounced off Spitalny's ear and he yelled, "I declare war. Throw the rolls back. Wild Bill Davidson, you should blow the bugle . . ."

The battle of the buns ended the Edgewater Beach engagement. Phil Spitalny and his musicians were fired before another set could be played.

4

Everything was changing on me in these years and I remember being depressed a lot of the time. Even before Prohibition ended, things were changing rapidly. Jazz was still losing favor and the Guy Lombardo and Wayne King orchestras were gaining it. The big-band day had definitely started, and it looked as if New York, not Chicago, was the place to be. If you'll remember, this was the eve of the great Benny Goodman and Glenn Miller and Dorsey bands; Duke Ellington, Count Basie and Glen Gray. More than I can think of. Then along came the pre-Sinatra crooners like Russ Columbo and Rudy Vallee and Bing Crosby . . .

—JULE STYNE, 1977

The past connection with "Al Brown" provided a surprise in the spring of 1932, when elegant Eddie Leibensberger said, "Jule, I'm opening a new place soon and I'd like to have you form a band, a small band with plenty of class." Jule had already heard about the "new place" opening at 225 East Superior Street but hadn't known that elegant Eddie was involved. Reportedly, Al Capone and his chief henchman, Frank Nitti, were the owners of the "225" Club, a town house undergoing conversion. The gracious old Victorian mansion had belonged to the Potter Palmer estate.

Jule had met Eddie Leibensberger only once, and that had been a "how-do-you-do" occasion. He didn't learn until much later that Eddie was Capone's pay-off man to the district attorney. Management of the "225" was Eddie's reward for jobs well done, according to mob sources. Errant son of a prominent Chicago family, Leibensberger looked and talked pure Ivy League. It was said he'd become bored with the Midwest Four Hundred, deciding it was more fun to pal around with the underworld. In appearance, Eddie could have easily passed as president of the stock exchange.

About a week after the initial conversation, workmen were still hammering and sawing as Eddie and Jule walked around in what had been the living room of the palatial Potter home. Leibensberger asked, "You like the bandstand?"

It appeared to be too small, and Jule requested that two lips be built out, accommodating additional men. Leibensberger readily agreed.

Jule said he planned to have the orchestra in tails and white ties to give it class; then asked if the "225" could afford a harpist.

"Anything you want," Eddie replied.

The room was only partially completed and littered with remodeling debris, but already it was shaping up to be less than a quarter the size of most night clubs. "How many can you seat here?" Jule inquired.

"We're planning on eighty."

Leibensberger then ticked off the names of entertainers booked for the opening night and first month: Sophie Tucker, Joe E. Lewis; the Aber Twins, acrobatic dancers; Dario and Diane, an adagio team from New York, and to play during the orchestra break, smart-set pianist Dwight Fiske. An unbelievable show for just eighty people. Jule quickly estimated that it would cost at least $5,000 a week. "With only eighty people, how can you afford those names?"

Leibensberger lifted his eyes. "Gambling upstairs, of course."

Of course.

Jule estimated his needs, in view of the type of entertainment to be offered. "I'll need a very good band. Most of them will get at least $175 a week; two of them $250."

"Whatever you need," Leibensberger replied, money seldom being a problem when the Capone organization was involved.

After the Pollack band, this was a whole new dimension for me, a class band in a class place. A big break, and all resulting from that crazy week at the Metropole and the Gershwin thing. All I had to do was play a good audition for Leibensberger and I was in.

Jule began assembling his musicians, attempting to gather the best available still in Chicago, signing such notables as Benny Gill on violin, Jack Galter on drums, Earl Gaines on bass. Nepotism aside, Maury was quickly becoming a superior saxophonist and Jule selected his kid brother for sax. Still missing was the key to the final gloss, a harpist who could handle dance music and jazz. Maury went to work on that vacancy and soon located Pete Eagles.

The day that Jule selected to audition his group before Eddie

Leibensberger, complete with harp glissandi, was not exactly ideal. When Maury drove his coupe to the Oak Park section to transport Pete Eagles, the thermometer registered about ten degrees below zero. A problem immediately arose when Pete announced that his harp case had been stolen. Maury suggested that they wrap the expensive instrument in a blanket and place it in the rumble seat. Eagles would have none of that. The harp would ride with Maury in the front while Pete shivered in the rumble.

When the pair arrived at the "225," Jule looked at the harpist and said, "Good Christ, he's frozen."

The benumbed Eagles said he was all right; that he'd sat on his hands and could play his harp.

Jule said, "Okay, get that thing in tune with the piano."

A few minutes later, the new Jule Stein orchestra broke into "I Got Rhythm" for Eddie's benefit, Pete Eagles's warm harp adding that final touch of velvet.

The club opened on schedule the next week.

A discreet canopy, bearing only the numbers "225" marked the entrance to Chicago's latest, most sumptuous speak-easy, a gold-cord work of mob art. The first night invitational guests included Capone (out of jail on bond, because of income-tax problems), his kid brother "Bottles"; Frank Nitti, and His Honor, the Mayor of Chicago, as well as a covey of aldermen, plus assorted millionaires and their ladies. Between nine and ten that evening, in this bottom year of the Depression, the Superior frontage was filled with limos, mink coats and diamonds. Just the right flavor was added with the appearance of John Factor ("Jake the Barber"). Kidnapped by the Roger Touhy gang, he'd been released that day and was roundly applauded as he made his way into the club, tuxedoed and smiling.

The evening proceeded with Leibensberger, exuding charm, greeting the guests and then turning them over to Joe Spagot, the maître d', a long-time mob employee and converted confidence man. Spagot, a man about jockey size who was always deeply tanned, was a skilled operator, keeping special bottles of imported cognac in the broom closet of the basement "musicians' room" to dispense free to the mighty. An ex-prizefighter, Gentleman Gene Delmont, was stationed at the electronically controlled pushbutton door to the casino, which featured roulette and crap tables. No finer speak existed that year.

On departure, after the conclusion of the floor show, Messrs.

Capone and Nitti congratulated the bandleader on the performance of his musicians. It was the third and last time that Jule was to shake that infamous hand.

In the months that followed, full-page ads were run on Sunday mornings in the *Chicago Tribune.* They, too, were subtle. The copy simply mentioned that Sophie Tucker or Joe E. Lewis or Fanny Brice or Marion Harris were performing at the "225" Club. At the bottom of each ad was, prominently: *Dance to the Music of Jule Stein and His Society Orchestra.*

The other Jules Stein, the eye-doctor and bandbooker, had married a social kind of girl from Kansas City, Doris Jones, and members of their exclusive country club often kidded them about "Jules Stein's" band.

"Hey, Jules, hurry up. You're due on the stand in five minutes."

"Hey, Jules, you like your band?"

It was said that Doris Jones Stein burned a little each time she heard the digs. *There she was, married to a doctor who was head of the Music Corporation of America and that other Stein, me, was nothing but a piano player. Going into a dress shop, she might be told that "her husband had a terrific orchestra."* The Sunday morning *Tribune* ads did not help the situation.

About a month after the "225" engagement began, Jule was summoned to the MCA office by one of the executives, Charles Miller. Miller possessed an Alabama drawl. "You know, we got great plans for you. After you finish the "225," you can follow Buddy Rogers into the College Inn. Then we've got a tour for you in the South. Baker Hotel in Dallas; Forest Club in New Orleans. You'll make a lot of money. But first, you can't have the name of Jule Stein. It sounds too Jewish."

Jule was almost speechless. "Wait a minute, your boss is named Jules Stein and he *is* Jewish."

"That's different, he's a doctor," said Miller. Another executive was in the room and nodded his head in best agent style.

Jule mulled it over for a moment and then said, "I've never thought about changing my name, but if it means all that money, give me a few days. I'll think about it."

Miller said, "No thinking. We've thought it all out. We have a new name for you. Now, go over to that mirror."

There was a wash closet with a stand and mirror at the end of the room. Jule dutifully went down there, opened the door and examined himself in the looking glass. Then he heard Miller drawl, "Yoah new name is Dick Ford."

Jule whirled around. "DICK FORD? There's nothing about me that's Dick Ford."

"That's what your new name is."

Jule said, "Fellows, let me tell you something. I love my mother dearly and she is proud of me. She gets a thrill every time she sees my name in the *Trib.* How can she go into the kosher butcher shop and say, 'My son, Dick Ford.' " I don't look like a Dick Ford and I won't be a Dick Ford."

Miller replied, "Well, you can't be Jule Stein, either."

Jule remembers steaming and muttering all the way back to the third-floor apartment in the Embassy. There, he sat down and wrote out twenty or thirty names. The only one he liked well enough to write a second time was S-t-y-n-e. Anna and Isadore wouldn't be too upset and MCA would have to be satisfied with the slight juggling of letters.

The next Sunday's ad in the *Chicago Tribune* was changed accordingly.

Fanny Brice followed Marion Harris into the "225," and Jule not only accompanied her but wrote some special material for her act. She played the club for four weeks, providing insights that were used musically twenty-seven years later in *Funny Girl.*

One night during the Brice engagement a burly man with a glass eye walked into the club as if he owned it, brushing past Joe Spagot to sit down at a corner table. Very few of the "225" 's clientele came in alone, and the glass-eyed man stood out like a gargoyle. He sat quietly, ominously, staring around, a gun bulge evident under his left coat lapel. To Jule, the usually poised Spagot seemed very nervous, as did Eddie Leibensberger.

At the break, Jule asked Leibensberger, "What's with that guy?"

Eddie replied tersely, "Just do what he tells you. He's running the club now. His name is Winkler."

Spagot quickly provided background on Gus Winkler: Former and possibly current bank robber, supposedly the first to use an automobile smoke screen during retreat from an Omaha holdup in the early twenties, Winkler was a graduate of the Detroit Purple Gang; a loose associate of the St. Louis Egan Rats gang, likely imported by Capone for tasks unknown. His sudden appearance at "225" was also for unknown reasons. But he was to be treated with respect.

Jule soon determined that Winkler liked Polish songs and he added several to the orchestra's usual fare, endearing himself to the ex-bank robber but not to the customers. A casual friendship developed, and toward the end of the second week Winkler asked, "You play golf?"

Jule said that he did, and Winkler promptly made a date for the next morning. With several Capone men tagging along, Jule and Winkler played an outlying suburban course, the relationship cementing nicely. Then, without enthusiasm, but now trapped, Jule became the gangster's steady partner for two or three months. Gus managed to lose $50 a game for incentive. Actually, he took little part in the management of "225," leaving details to Leibensberger and Spagot, but showed up each night to patrol the casino with all the finesse of a walking shark.

Eddie was scared to death of him, so was Joe Spagot. So was I. Winkler didn't have all his marbles. But I was stuck with him and didn't know what to do about it.

Jule's engagement at "225" ended dramatically about nine months after it had begun, during the weeks that Marion Harris was again headlining the bill of variety acts, which included a return spot for the perennial Joe E. Lewis.

Each year since the pistol-whipping and knifing at the hands of Jack McGurn's hoods, Lewis had gone to the Mayo Clinic, in Rochester, Minnesota, for a checkup. This time, Winkler decided to accompany the comedian and undergo an eye examination by Mayo specialists. Lewis and Winkler were placed in the same room.

By coincidence, or otherwise, a bank in Minneapolis was robbed the next night. The vault was expertly blown. Lewis remembered wishing sweet dreams to Winkler and also recalled that Gus was in bed, or back in bed, at dawn. Beyond that, the comedian knew nothing. The pair returned to the Windy City and two days later unnumbered bonds from the Minneapolis bank began showing up on La Salle Street in Chicago. An arrest was made in the late afternoon and the bond salesman squealed early that night, admitting that the stolen paper had come from the "225" Club.

Three or four hours later, Joe Spagot went down to the musicians' room to get a bottle of his special cognac, which he always stored in several empty milk cans. Sticking his hand down in one, he touched a bottle but also discovered stiff paper—some of the Minneapolis bonds. Fuming over the stupidity of stashing loot in the musicians' coat closet, likely Winkler's work, Spagot wanted no part of whatever was going on. He knew that the Capone people were never bank robbers, nor did they deal in stolen bonds. This was trouble for someone. Perhaps Winkler; perhaps Eddie Leibensberger. Perhaps both. By now,

Eddie was doing whatever Gus Winkler told him to do.

Joe had been feeding Marion Harris's dog each evening, and in searching for an excuse to quit, went to Eddie to say, "Listen, Eddie, I'm tired of feeding that goddamn dog. Either the dog goes, or I go. I'm tired of this broad."

Eddie supposedly replied, "No contest, Joe. If you want to leave, leave. The lady's the star of our show." Leibensberger had seen Joe go to the basement and probably realized that Spagot had discovered the bonds. At any rate, he knew that the singer's dog had nothing to do with Joe's quitting.

As Joe hurriedly departed the "225," he stopped by the bandstand to whisper to Jule, *"Gei!"* In Yiddish, it meant, "Go!"

Jule watched Spagot leave and then went over to Eddie Leibensberger to ask, "What's going on?"

"What did Spagot tell you?"

"He said to go."

"Maybe you better take his advice," Eddie replied.

It was now almost 1:00 A.M. and Jule went back to the bandstand, had the orchestra finish the number, then said, "Pack up your instruments, and let's get the hell out of here. We're not coming back."

The "225" Club was raided by police and federal officers several hours later, and elegant Eddie Leibensberger committed suicide, after a fashion, about 8:00 A.M. Later it was said that Frank Nitti gave him a choice—shoot himself or be shot.

Gus Winkler called Jule about 10:00 A.M. to firm up the usual golf date. At the Olympia Fields course, Jule noticed that none of the Capone gunmen were around. This was a whole new cast, all strangers. In passing, Winkler said, "You hear about Eddie Leibensberger? Those sonsabitches made him do it."

The golf game seemed to last ten years. After it was over Jule drove to the Embassy, locked the apartment door and spent the rest of the day listening to the radio. *I wasn't involved in any of it, yet I was frightened. My heart was slamming all day.*

In forty-eight hours, Winkler was dead, too. The coroner reportedly counted 148 holes in his body.

About three weeks later, Jule was in Koppel's Restaurant on Western Avenue, when a call was received at the counter. A voice said, "Go to Room 434 of the Morrison Hotel and pick up your money. It pays off the "225" contract."

Jule went to Room 434, looked into the face of a man he'd never seen before, accepted the sealed envelope and went directly to the musicians' union. He handed the unopened envelope to Jimmy Petrillo, saying, "You pay the band off. I want all of us to share alike." Petrillo asked no questions.

Although there was a brief booking for the "society" band in the Prima Rainbow Gardens, and then one at the Chez Paree, another mob joint, Jule soon went back to the safety of the hotels. He played the College Inn of the Sherman Hotel, for a few months and then opened with the same organization in the Peacock Alley of the Congress Hotel.

He returned on one occasion to the Chez Paree, but as a casino customer, not an employee. In about an hour, playing blackjack, he owed $900 in markers. Coon Rosen, from Jule's old neighborhood on Potomac Avenue, was the dealer. Eventually, Rosen said to Jule, "You're stuck. I just got orders. You'll get even and then quit. Then get out of here and stay out. Understand?"

Jule clearly understood. The "225" incident and the unwanted friendship with Gus Winkler had tainted him. He did not frequent any of the mob casinos in Chicago again, and stayed away from the horse rooms though he still bet at the tracks. Hyman Rubenstein supported Jule, Ethel and young Stanley about half the time. Jule was making good money but the tracks consumed it.

Maury Stein wasn't too much in need of cash now. He'd quit Jule's band. Guy Lombardo had heard him play and had signed him at $750 a week, more money than Jule had ever made as an orchestra leader-contractor. *I couldn't help but be jealous. I looked on Maury as a kid and here he was with Lombardo.*

During this year of 1934, the marriage was no better. There was continual bickering about the gambling and late hours; about Jule's failure to be more of a father to Stanley. Jule's counterattacks included Ethel's lack of interest in his work and the ever-present interference of her family. But in his spare time Jule had coached a singer, Mary Bell, and now had a tentative offer to teach other singers in New York. Talent agent Jack Bertell was involved with ambitious girls who sought show-business careers and wanted Jule to prepare them. Meanwhile, Claire Stein, grown-up, of course, with a high-boned beautiful face, had married Robert Bregman, from a wealthy Chicago steel family. Her life had completely changed, from one of comparative poverty to one of ease. The Bregmans had a yacht and an airplane; they wintered in Palm Springs. Claire made certain that Anna had luxuries once in while.

In early summer, Claire came into the Peacock Alley with her husband, took a table and watched her dejected brother for a while. He was "like a little mummy at the piano," she remembers. His playing was lifeless. His face was almost expressionless. She said to her husband, "I can't stand this. Jule has to go to New York."

"Why can't he go?" Bregman asked.

"He has no money, you know that."

"I'll pay his way," said the steel man.

Claire got Jule to the table eventually, telling him he had to leave.

Jule replied, "Yes, I know."

"Even if Ethel won't go, you have to."

In about two weeks, Jule took the bus for Manhattan, with thirty dollars over and above his ticket.

THE HOLLYWOOD STORY

1

By now, Fifty-second Street in New York was the home of jazz, and the big bands, playing hotels, were about to take off. As I remember, Benny Goodman was at Billy Rose's Music Hall when I got to New York but wasn't attracting much attention. He didn't hit, I don't think, until he opened at the Pennsylvania Hotel. But all the good musicians were headed for New York.

JULE STYNE, 1977

Jule had called Manhattan to inform Joe Rubenstein, who was living at the Hotel Edison, of his imminent arrival, and of his plans to become a vocal coach for Jack Bertell's stable of girls. Joe thought it was a splendid idea. In fact, he seemed quite anxious to have his brother-in-law take up residence in New York, quickly offering to book him a room at the Edison. Jule accepted, hoping that Joe might offer to pick up the tab for a while.

Ethel's flashy brother, usually in a snap-brim hat, a good-looking, gregarious guy, greeted Jule enthusiastically at the bus station on Forty-second Street, whisking him off to the hotel where he was given royal treatment at the desk. The management fawned over him, going far beyond the usual, "Sir, we hope you'll be happy here" routine. Jule was baffled about the red-carpet reception until they reached the privacy of the room. Then Joe laughed. "I owe 'em a thousand. I told 'em my famous orchestra-leading, song-writing brother-in-law was coming to town. We'll put everything on your tab for a while."

Joe was definitely down on his luck again, having had six or eight disastrous months at the track. He was down to playing pinochle for food and smoke money, making about ten dollars a day on cards, budgeting seventy-five cents for his wife's breakfast, fifty cents for his; fifty cents to feed their poodles; three dollars for dinner at any cheap Broadway café. Anything left over was for entertainment and two-dollar bets. Joe never appeared to be broke, but the fifty-cent "Havanas" he was smoking were actually five-cent Phillies dressed in authentic Cuban wrappers. If he had twenty dollars, a ten-dollar bill covered the roll of ten ones.

His current defunct condition was a complete reversal from the previous year, when he'd staged a very successful "Idaho Potato" contest. Claiming that he wanted to help the nation's depressed farmers, Joe had rounded up $6,000 to finance ads in farm journals; also rent space in Grand Central Palace, the exhibition hall in Grand Central Station. The ad stated that "thousands" of dollars would be awarded the best ten sacks of Idaho spuds. A careful line at the bottom of the ad stated that the sponsors were not responsible for the return of the sacks. There was no limit per farmer on entries. About 7,000 bags of potatoes arrived at Grand Central Palace, and on judging day Joe selected ten sacks, not even bothering to look inside, sent wires to the "winners" and then called in buyers from the wholesale market. Within two days, Joe had sold off both winning and losing entries. He made a fine profit after paying off modest prize money and left the New York Police Department in a quandary. The scheme had been perfectly legal. Unfortunately, Joe had blown the potato money at the tracks.

I really learned quite a lot from Joe and I've always tried to find a musical where I could use the potato scam. He used to tell me the facts of life. The conferences were sometimes held in Joe's bathroom at the Edison, Rubenstein immersed in the tub, smoking a long cigar, racing form handy on the ledge.

Joe spent hours trying to tell me how to operate in New York, but most of it had to do with swindling of one type or another. Yet it was an education. Joe said he wouldn't go to work for a thousand a week but would gladly go to Africa for a scam. He enjoyed conning. For Broadway, you write music to character and I used Joe a number of times, beginning with High Button Shoes. *But he wasn't all phony. He'd taken Rudolph Valentino on the road and also promoted an Admiral Byrd appearance in Jersey City. Byrd thought Joe was the greatest.*

The Jack Bertell job hadn't materialized, and Jule went to Meyer Davis and got on the roster to play piano for any of the Davis society bands. For the next seven or eight weeks, he worked out-of-town engagements on Friday and Saturday nights, earning $70 to $80, enough to keep afloat at the Edison.

Then he met Al Siegel, a transplanted Chicagoan, vocal coach and pianist for Bea Palmer and a bright new talent, Ethel Merman. Ill with tuberculosis, Siegel was headed for a sanitarium stay and asked Jule if he'd take over coaching six girls.

I knew enough to do it. I chose the right range, the right song. How to phrase a song by learning the meaning. Most beginning singers phrase the music instead of the lyrics. People listen to the lyrics, not the melody. I also told them how to use their hands, what hairdo to use, and what make-up to apply. Some girls accentuated the lip-lines and looked grotesque when they sang; others used too much mascara; even wore the wrong type of shoes. This all detracts from delivery. I'd learned all this in Chicago, beginning with the synagogue choirs, and then watching singers from the orchestra pits. Sophie Tucker and Marion Harris had talked about things and I'd listened. I could tell a lot of the flaws immediately.

One night, Jack Bertell, Jule's original contact in New York, visited a vocal session, watched Jule work for a while, then said, "Why don't I open a studio for you at Steinway Hall?"

Several weeks later, the name of Jule Styne, Vocal Coach, was gold-stripped to the glass door of a small studio on the fifth floor of Steinway Hall. Jule hadn't made it to Anna's dreamland in Carnegie but there was a certain prestige to Steinway. The girls were charged $25 a lesson.

Soon Bertell began to send up girls who were booked by Fefe Ferry, a mob-connected producer of night-club shows. Ferry himself dropped by one day to say, with marked amusement, "Some can sing. Some can't. But if they're taking lessons from you, their boyfriends will know they aren't in bed. You look harmless."

The exterior appraisal was correct. At twenty-nine, Jule appeared to be in his late teens. There was a clean-cut, handsome boyishness about him, a Princeton-Cornell smack. The collegiate look plus his small size did not add up to threat, especially when he sat down at the piano. The roster soon grew to about twenty girls, now at $50 a lesson. About half of them were provided by Fefe Ferry.

But Jule viewed the coaching, from the start, as only a way to make a living and gain contacts in New York. At the same time, he had no idea what he wanted to do. He thought about organizing another band; thought about calling Benny Goodman to ask if he needed a pianist. A few times he thought about dropping out of music altogether. He did not think about writing songs, still believing that "Sunday" was a fluke.

And Ethel, understandably concerned about Jule's "girls," surely remembering the baby-sitter episode, had changed her mind about coming east, and arrived in early fall with five-year-old Stanley. They joined him at the Edison, Stanley playing in the corridors and on the roof of the hotel.

The arrival of Jule's family made little change in the pattern of his night life. He was on Fifty-second Street almost every evening, listening to music, seldom with Ethel, usually with one of his students. His friends, at the time, were invariably female. Males talked business and he couldn't listen to the new tenor sax or the new fiddle player at the Open Door or Club 18. Ethel was lonely and called Chicago every day. Her brother Joe wasn't much comfort. Mainly, Joe visited to borrow a few dollars. Within three months the Stynes had moved to an apartment on Central Park West, and the bickering between Jule and Ethel was less frequent, though there were many periods of silence. They had little to talk about.

Two years later, Jule was still unhappily on the same treadmill, the vocal coaching still a stopgap. Worse, all around him musicians were beginning to become household names via late-night radio shows from hotels and ballrooms. The big-band era had finally begun. Goodman was now a smash in the Manhattan Room of the Hotel Pennsylvania, star of a Saturday-night radio show. The Dorsey brothers were making big-band sounds. Guy Lombardo, Eddy Duchin, Paul Whiteman, Wayne King, among others, were as well known as movie stars. Trooping back and forth to Steinway Hall each day, grooming the would-be singers, most with little or no ability; in reality, baby-sitting for hoods, Jule began to doubt his own abilities.

But there were occasional assignments that were fun. The Ritz Brothers—Al, Jim and Hal—hot comedy team of the day, needed special material for their act at Billy Rose's Casino de Paree, and Jule wrote an operatic oratorio based on the novelty song, "The Music Goes 'Round and 'Round." Performed with great dignity by the Ritz ensemble in the style of Verdi's *Requiem,* the number drew howls from the Casino audience.

Then Andrea Leeds, the only girl that Jule thought had any chance of moderate success, was booked into the Beach & Tennis Club in Miami Beach. Jule prepared her for the engagement, made arrangements of the songs she did best, and sent her on the way, second-billed to Harry Richman, the glamour boy of the musical-comedy world. He'd starred in George White's *Scandals of 1927,* with Frances Williams and Willie Howard. He'd joined Helen Morgan, Ruth Etting and Jack Pearl to star in *The Ziegfeld Follies* several years later. His latest Broadway appearance had been in *Say When,* costarring a newcomer, Bob Hope.

The night that Leeds opened in the Beach & Tennis Club, movie executive Joseph Schenck, president of 20th Century-Fox Studios, was in the club. Schenck had founded 20th Century in 1933 with Darryl F. Zanuck as partner, later merging with the Skouras brothers' Fox company. After Leeds sang, Schenck asked his table guest, Harry Richman, to find out who'd coached the girl and made the arrangements for her.

Richman contacted his agent, George Woods, and eventually the Broadway star summoned Jule Styne—but not to discuss Andrea Leeds. Richman's pianist and conductor had resigned and the singer asked, "Who have you worked with?"

"Fanny Brice, Sophie Tucker, Marion Harris, Bea Palmer, Andrea Leeds and you."

"Me?"

"Metropole Hotel. Week of the Dempsey–Tunney fight. I had the band."

Richman whooped. "That week. I thought you looked familiar."

George Woods then said, "Harry is going to do the new Lux radio show and needs someone like you to conduct and accompany him."

Jule auditioned for the man with the wavy, pomaded hair and signed a year's contract within a week. Between rehearsals and the airing, the Lux show occupied less than two days a week, and Jule continued his coaching stints at Steinway, though dropping most of the girls.

Now, for the first time, Jule got a taste of the musical stage. Richman didn't talk about Goodman, Lombardo, Duchin or Whiteman. He talked about such Broadway figures as George M. Cohan and Ed Wynn and Victor Moore and Bert Lahr; Mae West and all the beautiful women in his life.

I soaked it all up. We got along well. He was happy with the way I played piano for him, happy with the way I conducted and handled the orchestrations, and was fascinated with my gambling, though he didn't gamble himself.

Jule began traveling with Richman, playing Detroit first; then the Mayfair Casino in Cleveland, where the young publicity man, Lew

Wasserman, was excited about joining MCA. (Wasserman now heads MCA-Universal.) A few months later, Richman received a bid to attend the coronation festivities for King George VI, following the abdication of King Edward VIII.

Plans for the joint trip to England continued until Jule received a surprise phone call from Lou Irwin, liaison man in New York for Joseph Schenck. Irwin said that Mr. Schenck hadn't forgotten the performance of Andrea Leeds in Miami; that Fox was in trouble with its musicals; that a good vocal coach was needed to assist such stars as Tony Martin, Alice Faye and Shirley Temple. Irwin said that Fox was prepared to offer $350 a week plus travel expenses to the West Coast.

Jule went to Harry Richman to discuss the offer. The singer unselfishly said, "Take it. You may have a future there."

Ethel was pleased, of course. Any place would be better than New York City.

A few days later, Jule received a personal call from Mr. Schenck, which in terms of the movie world, was comparable to talking to the White House. The film mogul advised, "You don't know anything about Hollywood, so just don't jump in. When you get to the studio, take a couple of weeks to familiarize yourself. Visit the sets; go to the music department; the dance department. Tell them I said not to rush you into anything." Jule remembers being in a happy daze during the call from Schenck. Lou Irwin had already dropped those heady names —Tony Martin, Alice Faye and Shirley Temple. It was miracle time.

When the train bearing the Styne family pulled out of Grand Central Station, bound for Chicago and Los Angeles, Jimmy Dorsey was playing the Terrace Room of the Hotel New Yorker; Artie Shaw was in the Blue Room of the Lincoln; Guy Lombardo was in his usual home at the Roosevelt Grill. Tommy Dorsey's band headlined at the Paramount Theatre. Duke Ellington was settled at the Cotton Club.

For the first time over several years of open envy, Jule didn't give them a thought.

2

Shirley Temple? Listen, I was afraid of that kid.
I didn't want to get in the middle with her.
From Schenck and Zanuck on down, everyone humored her.
I'd have to play games with her to get her to rehearse.
Games, games and finally we'd get down to work.

—JULE STYNE, 1977

With Stanley and Ethel temporarily living in the Hollywood Roosevelt Hotel, Jule reported to the music department at 20th Century-Fox, which sprawled over many acres facing Pico Boulevard, across from the Hillcrest golf greens, on the edge of Beverly Hills. Simply because he'd been hired in New York, and by none other than Joe Schenck himself, Jule was immediately viewed with some suspicion. Whose job was to be pirated by this unknown vocal coach? Was he a spy with a hot line direct to Schenck? Even worse, to Darryl Zanuck, head of production? Had he been sent out, in fact, to take over the entire music department? Hollywood never trusted New York, and vice versa, and insecurity lurked behind most welcoming smiles.

The only people on the lot that Jule knew were the madcaps from Manhattan—the totally insane Ritz Brothers. So the first visit was to the stage where Al, Harry and Jim were making their second film for Fox, a quickie called *Pigskin Parade.* Any Ritz set was riotous, camera running or not. The trio had little regard for the screenplay, the director, or even Zanuck, who wisely stayed away from the stage. The brothers did Cossack dances contrary to the scene; pratfalls and imaginary sword fights that had nothing remotely to do with the script. Mostly, they were beyond human control. They were also avid horse-players and had three phones in their bungalow dressing room. Work sessions were constantly interrupted to catch race results. The studio assigned a unit production manager, Ben Silvey, to stay with them throughout the working day as a "keeper."

Awed by it all that first morning, Jule stood around the set gazing at the narrow, wooden chain-hung bridges holding the arc lights, watching the technicians, the property men and the grips and electricians and soundmen, taking it in. After a while he felt a sensation in his right foot, as if it had been tapped. Yet there wasn't anyone within six feet of him. (He had not seen the quick movement of a long stick held by a technician.) A moment later, there was a sensation in the other foot. Everyone was deadpan. He went up to the Ritz Brothers and said to them, "Look, I don't know what's happening here but I'm getting funny sensations in my feet. It feels like someone is tapping them."

Harry, the Ritz who could roll his eyes, said, "You're not wearing the right shoes."

Al added, "You have to wear tennis shoes, Jule. It happens to all people who are new on the lot. With all these arcs around, you have static feet. Go to the doctor and then wear sneakers for two weeks."

The studio doctor examined Jule's feet and said soberly that the Ritz Brothers were absolutely right. Static feet was common to newcomers. He then coated both feet with Mercurochrome and advised the wearing of rubber soles until the entire body could adjust to the high voltage of the arcs.

I did that, you know. I walked about that lot for two weeks in tennis shoes and every night or so painted my feet up to the ankles. That's how sophisticated I was. Big threat from New York going around with red feet.

Assigned a bungalow at the lower end of the lot, behind the sound stage complexes, Jule's next-door neighbor was a Russian named Sam Pokrass, a composer and arranger who worked for the Ritz Brothers. Pokrass, who once wrote an opera based on *Cyrano de Bergerac* and had been a stage stooge for comedian Jack Pepper, could butter the keys of a piano and still play it well; he could drape a tablecloth over the keys and make music; he could even play backward. He was a perfect associate for the zany brothers. Unlike Jule, miserly Sam lived in his bungalow night and day, doing his laundry and hanging it out to dry; cooking goulash on a hot plate. Across the street was Shirley

Temple's bungalow and the sound of the child's temper tantrums occasionally disturbed the quiet. Jule didn't look forward to coaching her. Actress Barbara Stanwyck was on the lot and MGM star Robert Taylor, her fiancée, often brought his cello to an empty sound stage and played for an hour or so while awaiting Miss Stanwyck's lunch break. It was all very different from Chicago and New York, to say the least.

At the end of two weeks, Jule drew his first assignment, a Jack Haley picture entitled *Wake Up and Live.* Buddy Clark, a top vocal artist at the time, was called in to dub—substitute Haley's voice on the sound track. *I frankly didn't know what I was doing, but went through the motions and tried to sound as if I really understood what was going on. I listened to Clark rehearse a few times, made several vocal suggestions, and then we did a take. I was sweating from ignorance when I walked away from that recording stage.*

The vocal coaching began a few days later with whatever star was scheduled to sing in whatever upcoming picture. The assignments were made by the music department. Players under contract included Linda Darnell, Arleen Whelan, Shirley Temple, Tony Martin, Alice Faye, Jane Withers, Joan Davis, Joan and Constance Bennett. The Ritz Brothers, of course. *I'd work a half hour or an hour a day with one or another of them if they were scheduled to sing in a picture. In that area, I now knew what I was doing.*

But almost daily Jule was instructed "not to make waves." Further, he was told "you fellows from New York just don't understand. This is how we do it out here; this is how it should be done; this is how it's always been done. The system functions, let it alone." But the temptation to buck the system was irresistible. It doesn't matter what rules you have, Jule thought. Good is good. Bad is bad, Hollywood or New York. Talent is talent. No talent is no talent. Almost from the start, he was not very well liked in the music department at Fox. He made the mistake of saying too often, "That doesn't sound right to me. I'm sorry to tell you that is a wrong note."

At his first meeting with Zanuck, regarding vocalists, Jule remembers the studio chief saying, "Don't tell me that a song has to be sung more than one chorus. When you sing a song once, why sing it twice?" Zanuck was correct, in Jule's opinion. The screen never begged for encores.

Zanuck said, "They [the singers] go into waltz time. They parade all around the set. This whole song thing is screwed up."

Jule then learned from Zanuck that there was another reason he'd been sent out by Joseph Schenck. Songwriters demonstrated their songs for a producer or director but it was almost impossible for those creators to determine, unless they had long experience, whether or not the song was good or bad for a particular picture; whether or not it could be sung by the star or stars. Time and money were continually lost because of the choice of wrong material; then the picture's production values suffered. Zanuck wanted Styne to begin monitoring the song demo sessions.

Then Zanuck yelled to Jule, "They do ballads around here for five minutes. You can't shoot a song that long. It won't hold. You shoot it through the harp, through the violin, then what? People in the music department will hate your guts but I want this song thing straightened out." As often occurred, Zanuck then went off on a completely different tangent. "If you can make Arleen Whelan sing, it's worth fifty thousand." The figure alone was enough to linger in memory.

Jule replied that he might as well be requested to climb the Eiffel Tower.

"You can do nothing?" Zanuck asked.

Jule answered, "I can do nothing to help her."

Zanuck said he appreciated the honesty, and so ended the brief, one-sided conference.

Yet it was all working. I was learning and learning. I had to write all the chorus parts for a Ritz picture. Like writing for an entire choir. I'd never done that before.

Jule was afraid of Shirley Temple, for good reason. Zanuck had inherited the curly-haired, temperamental moppet from the old Fox company. Dating back to a one-reeler, *War Babies,* in 1932, she'd put together a string of films that now earned her more than $300,000 a year. *Little Miss Marker,* in 1934, had made her a star with an audience far and beyond the knee-pants clan. By 1937, she was America's cute "movie-show" darling, and even won a special Oscar. Shirley Temple was a solid, sure-fire money maker for 20th Century-Fox and the child captain of the "Good Ship Lollipop" was in full sail when Jule began the unenviable task of polishing her voice and making her arrangements. The only people who could reliably handle her were dance director Nick Castle and the great black dancer, Bill Robinson, who had paired with Temple in *The Littlest Rebel,* 1935. But she stole scenes from Robinson as well as she had from such expert thieves as Lionel Barrymore.

Shirley's bungalow had been built by the studio especially for her, and in some ways resembled a playground. The only things missing were fairies with glittering wands. Jule hated the walk across the street to prepare her for such pictures as *Heidi, Rebecca of Sunnybrook Farm* and *Little Miss Broadway.* There was never a way of knowing what mood she'd be in. Her father or mother were always with her, and she didn't appear to have much respect for them, though her mother, Gertrude, seemed to have the most control.

The studio once sent Jule to Shirley's Palm Springs home to rehearse. Usually, no one from the studio came near that house. The morning started off with badminton, and Jule played in the hot sun until he almost dropped. *She was tough as nails, stamina of a steam engine.*

Finally, he went to her father, George, a Pennsylvania Dutchman, to say, "We should start rehearsing soon."

George than said to his daughter, "Honey, you have to stop playing now and start rehearsing."

She screamed at him, "Look, I earn all the money in this family. Don't tell me what to do."

Jule was embarrassed and walked on into the house, staying there until she decided she was ready to work.

Writing songs at Fox during this period were such notables as Mack Gordon and Harry Revel; Harold Spina and Walter Bullock, highly paid hit-makers. Gordon, a huge man who wrote in a bookkeeper's ledger, and whose hit songs included "Lull in My Life," "Love Thy Neighbor" and "Sitting on Top of the World," was under contract at $3,000 a week, and while Jule envied the money he had no idea of trying to emulate Gordon or Revel. "Sunday" seemed so far back, and his salary had now risen to a respectable $750 a week. Aside from Temple, coaching the various stars was easy. They cooperated; they wanted to sing passably well. It was luxury, in fact. Into the studio at 9:00 A.M., work for two or three hours; play some poker or go to the track; kibitz with Nick Castle or visit the sets. Then composer Lew Pollack died suddenly and his lyric writer, Sydney Claire, needed music in a hurry for a John Barrymore low-budget film, *Hold that Co-ed.* Zanuck said, "Get that what's iz name, that Styne fellow, he can write music."

So Jule knocked out a collegiate type song, "Limpy Dimp," in a few hours; Claire put lyrics to it, and the tune slid smoothly into the film. Zanuck saw the rough cut and said, "See, I told you that guy could write music."

There was no offer of extra pay from the front office. *I didn't ask for it, either. I was already on the payroll. But I think the fact that Zanuck noticed the song was enough.*

For one reason or another, perhaps purposeful forgetting, Jule claims that he wrote no songs between "Sunday" in 1927, and "Limpy Dimp" in 1938. ASCAP records, however, list Jule Styne as the composer of "In a Canoe" in 1930, and "It's the Words, Not the Music" in 1933. In fact, there were two other published efforts in 1927, and "Little Joe," for Mildred Bailey, became a standard in 1928.

At Fox, Jule's gambling became an addiction. The atmosphere was conducive. Practically everyone played the horses; there were poker games at $2,000 a card. Constance Bennett, for instance, was as sharp as any male player, and Joe Schenck often bought part of her game. Mack Gordon's brother, Harry, handicapped horses for the entire studio personnel, and produced a daily tip sheet for the lot.

Often, at lunchtime, the guys from the music table, the table in the commissary where everyone in the music department ate, would park a car outside the back gate. We'd all look like we were going off the lot for lunch, but then we'd drive like hell for Santa Anita, and leave at the end of the sixth race, come back to the studio and go home. My constant companion during this period was Walter Scharf, now an eminent composer and conductor.

These were the crazy good-times thirties of film, with carloads of starlets coming to the lot each day, plenty of work on the casting couches; stupendous, colossal, searchlighted premières and big money rolling into Fox from such pictures as *The Grapes of Wrath, Jesse James* and *Alexander's Ragtime Band,* and the Temple shows. The years of Zanuck genius. Even the B-units of Saul Wurtzel flourished, with such secondary stars as Jane Withers and Joan Davis.

By now, Joe Rubenstein had arrived on the West Coast. With wife and poodles, Joe stayed with Jule for a while. He would borrow $20 from Jule to place his bets at Santa Anita; then borrow $20 from Ethel to repay Jule. Most of Ethel's family had moved to California and were around quite a lot, to her great satisfaction and his grief.

Twentieth Century-Fox was also the beginning of the "other women" in Jule's life. Ethel knew about an actress, with a velvet voice and thoroughbred looks, former singer with a name band, under contract to the studio. Jule began dating her secretly in 1937 after some coaching sessions for a Tony Martin film. For a while, the romance was mutually serious.

The girl finally told Jule she knew that he'd never divorce Ethel, and then married an agent. *So beautiful and so gentle, she was the only thing that happened to me for real for many years. I was madly in love with her.*

As he grew up, Stanley Styne, with affection, called his father "the playboy-composer." Jule did "play." Yet the actress was just another symptom of the Styne marital problem. Jule socialized on Sunday mornings with the Hollywood crowd, sometimes inviting forty guests to brunch at their home on Foothill Drive, in Beverly Hills. Ethel was pleasant but stayed uncomfortably on the fringes. Or sometimes she'd just disappear inside the house. She was just as unhappy, just as frustrated as Jule, yet neither moved toward divorce. Ethel certainly had the grounds. She also had their second son, Norton, in 1939.

In the last months of that year, Alice Faye signed for the Chesterfield cigarette radio show and insisted that Jule be brought in to arrange and prepare her numbers at $750 a week, over and above his Fox salary. He'd coached Faye for a half-dozen musicals and they were close friends. In turn, Jule brought along Walter Scharf as an assistant and orchestrator. An accomplished pianist, Scharf had played with the Vincent Lopez and Rudy Vallee bands.

Jule's weekly take was now $1,500, of which a good half was running away on the dirt at Santa Anita or Hollywood Park. *That was big, big money for 1939, but I thought nothing of losing a thousand one week; next week, I'd win $1,200. That's how you get hooked. The week after that, I'd be down $2,000. It was insanity but I really gambled. Ethel's brother-in-law, Ruby Schwartz, once lent me $10,000 to pay off a bookie. I gave $9,000 to the bookie and went to the track and lost the other thousand. I can talk about it truthfully now. It was a sickness but I didn't know it. But with all that money I was making at the studio and with Alice, not much got home. Ethel raised hell but what could she do?*

In early 1940, after writing another unpaid song for a Fox picture, Jule was caught in a Zanuck purge. The studio chief announced that no more musicals would be made for at least a year and that the music department would be pared by three-quarters. Within a few days, Jule was called into Zanuck's richly paneled office on the second floor of the administration building. He was told two things: No. 1: You shouldn't be coaching singers. You should be writing songs. I'll get you a job at Republic. No. 2: You've got eight months to go on your contract and there's no work. So I want you to go on the road with Constance Bennett.

Connie Bennett was one of Zanuck's favorite actresses, a poker companion and close friend. Jule had little choice in the matter, anyway.

Along with the Countess di Frasso, the beautiful Constance Bennett had founded a beauty-product firm. Now she was going on a nationwide tour to promote her creams and oils, talk to lady-laden groups and sing a couple of songs. She couldn't very well do a dramatic scene as a solo; had no desire to do "readings." Jule was first to teach her how to sing, then play piano for her from Portland and Seattle to Dallas and New Orleans and Chicago and New York, with twenty stops between. Eight weeks of touring. On completion, she'd open on Broadway in *Easy Virtue.*

Within a week, Jule was spending three or four hours a day at the sumptuous Bennett home. A lovely, chic woman exactly Jule's age, Connie Bennett had considerably more class than any of Jule's previous vocal students. Most of her clothes were made in Paris. She dressed simply but stunningly. Jule remembers one plain black dress. With it, Constance wore a tiny gold maid's apron. Jule found it difficult to take his eyes off her. They got along famously from the first hour. He then announced to Ethel that he'd be on the road for eight weeks with the famous Connie Bennett. Her reaction was to ask if the Fox paycheck would be mailed to the new Elm Drive address, where the required swimming pool had just been installed. Jule assured her it would be.

On the plane, a drafty DC-3, to Portland, Oregon, the initial stop on behalf of the beauty enhancers, Jule was petrified. It was his first plane trip and the twin-engined aircraft bounced all over the sky. Connie covered him partially with her voluminous fur coat and then said, "Sweetheart, just relax," and promptly went to sleep. Miss Bennett was nerveless at more than poker.

She'd been divorced from a rich marquis and several other attractive men, and after about a week on the road, Jule saw no good reason to sleep alone down the hall. Connie did complain occasionally about Jule's lack of preparation for romance. He explained that from long habit he always showered and shaved in the morning, not on the occasion of presleep or anything else.

All in all, it was a workable and happy relationship. Jule was attendant on all occasions, handling the hotel affairs as well as playing piano; portering, ordering the meals and wine, acting as cashier and liaison with dry cleaners and French laundries; amusing and entertaining Miss Bennett. He was introduced everywhere, and fondly, as "my fiancé."

The arrangement continued happily for almost eight weeks, Connie finally proposing that they be married as soon as Jule could shed Ethel. She promised to take care of Stanley and little Nortie as if they were her own.

Though Miss Bennett was most appealing, Jule thought about his new starting salary at Republic as a full-fledged songwriter. Darryl Zanuck had indeed fulfilled his promise. He'd arranged for a job at the San Fernando Valley studio at a beginning scale of $145 weekly, quite a drop from the thousand plus in Beverly Hills. But Mr. Herbert Yates, head of Republic, believed in worn shoestrings, not silver rope. Jule then envisioned many difficulties on his $145 a week versus her several thousands per six days. Nor was he quite sure that he was "madly" in love with Miss Bennett. He finally and diplomatically declined the generous offer of matrimony by saying he could not bring himself to divorce Ethel for many reasons. It was as good an excuse as any.

The romance ended abruptly though the business end went along as usual. Jule wrote some special material for Connie to open in the appropriate *Easy Virtue* and they settled into separate rooms in Jack Warner's luxurious apartment on the thirty-sixth floor of the Waldorf Towers.

Jule had his own bedroom, but Bennett warned forcefully, "You are not to bring any dames up here."

Jule said, "That isn't at all fair."

Connie replied, "The hell it isn't. I won't permit it."

A British actor then settled into Connie's half of the suite. The first night the new occupant was in residence, while Jule was reading in bed at about 2:00 A.M., very much alone, there was a subdued knock on the door.

The actor stuck his head in to ask, "I say, old man, could I borrow your razor?"

"By all means," Jule replied.

Three weeks later, having learned another aspect of show business, Jule returned to Hollywood to finish out his Fox contract. He was loaned to Paramount to coach Mary Martin for her first film, after which she went to Broadway, becoming an overnight sensation with the rendition of just one song, "My Heart Belongs to Daddy."

Jule was back on the lot no more than a few days when Zanuck sent a cryptic message: "Gloria Vanderbilt will be coming to you for singing lessons." Wondering if the studio was about to sign the fifteen-year-old, Jule discovered that it was for quite a different reason. The shy heiress was coming out as a subdeb and needed to be coached for the singing of "Rose of Washington Square." The variety of work was becoming remarkable.

Jule then worked on two Barbara Stanwyck films before reporting to Republic, just over the Hollywood Hills from the rich film folk of Paramount and Columbia. Horses were kings and queens out there.

3

I wrote five or six songs for each picture. I wrote country-and-western music. I wrote music for cattle and mules and pigs and dogs. I did just about everything I was asked to do.

—JULE STYNE, 1977

On February 2, 1941, several months after Jule Styne checked in to begin his new career, *New York Times* reporter David Hanna termed Republic Pictures "Hollywood's Flea Circus," a most unkind remark and not totally accurate. Republic did have a lot of fleas and ticks around, as well as tons of horse droppings, but no studio in town made quicker, cheaper or better Westerns, serials and other action flicks.

Located at 4024 North Radford Avenue, North Hollywood, site of the old Mack Sennett Studio, bordered by the trickle of the Los Angeles River, Republic was founded in March 1935, by Herbert John Yates, who'd made a fortune in tobacco-dealing by the time he was thirty. He also owned a film-processing laboratory, which led him to the position of movie magnate, a role he immensely enjoyed. The very first Republic release, on August 19, 1935, was *Westward Ho,* starring a big former football player and ex-grip named Marion Michael Morrison. The name was later changed to John Wayne.

In addition to Wayne, the contract list included Roy Rogers, George "Gabby" Hayes, Smiley Burnette, Tom Tyler, Gene Autry, the Weaver Brothers and Elviry, James Gleason; Bob Nolan and the Sons of the Pioneers. From time to time, other talents such as singer Frances Langford, comedienne Judy Canova; comedians Joe E. Brown, Phil Silvers and Jimmy Durante; dancers Ann Miller and Johnny Downs. Even Bing Crosby did a few camera turns on North Radford.

Though scoffed at as the best-known tenant of Poverty Row, Yates's busy "Flea Circus" was also the finest movie-making school in Hollywood. Feature films were often shot in six days. The sets were "lit" in twenty minutes, whereas the majors took a leisurely, expensive three hours. Mute extras were paid $7.50 a day while those who spoke received $25. So sign language was used as much as possible. "Which way did they go?" The mute extra pointed and saved Mr. Yates $17.50.

Such writing talents as Welles Root, Isobel Lennart and Nathanael West did scripts at Republic; no one in town wrote better chase music than William Lance. Composers Victor Young and George Antheil spent time with the fleas and ticks. Directors, cameramen, property men, electricians and wranglers were all thorough professionals. They had to be.

Once or twice a year Republic reached for the "A" class and in 1939–40 proudly announced that the works of Sinclair Lewis, Vicki Baum, Whit Burnett and Jack London would be produced, in addition to "six Autrys," "seven Roy Rogers" and four "Higgins Family" films (the answer to MGM's Andy Hardy series). And, of course, the now classic Saturday afternoon serials—*The Lone Ranger, Dick Tracy, Drums of Fu Manchu, Adventures of Red Ryder* and *King of the Royal Mounted Police.* In 1940, the studio announced sixty films at a total budget of $9,000,000.

At one time Clark Gable used Republic for another purpose. He fancied up a station wagon for Carole Lombard in a slab-board shed just outside the main gate. Cowboy actors and wranglers often rode their horses to work from nearby homes and ranches. Most of the exteriors used in Republic films were buildings on the lot, and Mr. Yates would gladly lend his Cadillac for use in a scene, charging himself no rental.

No matter what anyone said about stingy little Republic, with its largely unpaved streets and one decent sound stage—the Mabel Normand, tribute to the Sennett star—the studio had a definite flavor and flair all its own and is now the object of film cultists. Who but Republic could take a former railroad telegrapher named Gene Autry and make him into a valley version of Fort Knox? Autry's first film cost $20,000. Yates also signed Roy Rogers at a reasonable rate: $75 a week. Raises came painfully slow.

In addition to the horse operas and action shows of one kind or another, Republic, always the copier, did its share of pocket musicals, which was one reason why Jule Styne had been happily accepted by Yates and music department head Cy Feuer, now a successful theatrical producer. *Hit Parade of 1940,* starring Frances Langford, produced by Sol Siegel, was a good example of these cinematic songfests, with a story line as thin as the budget. Langford had starred in the first *Hit Parade* in 1937, along with smiling Irish singer, Phil Regan. The *Hit Parades* went on successfully until the mid-forties.

After talking with Cy Feuer, Jule made his way over the dirt street, avoiding dung, to his "bungalow," which was often used as a set. There was a "Hay & Feed" sign over the entrance, and it had a regulation Western front but not much of a back. Rough-boarded, interior and exterior, full of cracks, the bungalow could be utilized for the camera any day or night simply by removing Jule's upright piano, his desk and lumpy chair, and replacing all with the sparse furnishings of a grain merchant's office. Oats and barley were ground into the floor.

Cy Feuer, former trumpet player with the Roxy and Radio City Music Hall orchestras in New York, envisioned Jule as a "general music guy." When there was vocal coaching to be done, Jule was vocal coach; any choirs, he was choral director; he could play piano for rehearsals, too; conduct an orchestra, if necessary. And, oh, yes, he could also write songs, all for $145 a week. Co-head of the music department was Raoul Krashaar, and his special domain were the Westerns, which were often "tracked" from the library—previous scores pieced together. Feuer seldom dealt with the cowboy singers. He confessed that he didn't like them, nor their horses.

So Jule's first assignment was handed out by Krashaar. "You just watch Gene Autry to make sure he stays in 'sync' tonight," said the Hungarian. Autry would later record the song but for the moment would mouth it for the camera, listening to a recording of the music, attempting to stay in synchronization. "Tonight" began at 7:00 P.M. on the freezing banks of the Los Angeles River at the edge of the Republic lot. There were bonfires and horses and wranglers; boots and sheepskin coats. Jule almost froze in a light parka from Beverly Hills. His ulcers couldn't take the cups of bourbon the cowboys were drinking, and he settled for coffee cream and began to wish he'd gone looking for work at MGM or Paramount.

Several days later, Jule was again required to watch "sync" for a Smiley Burnette number. A character actor, comedy stooge for Autry and others, Burnette nonetheless achieved Western stardom at Republic, joining the list of "best oater money-makers." He had a wide fan following. *Smiley's hat was pulled damn near down over his mouth and I couldn't see a thing. It didn't matter. That song had four lines and the hat took care of whatever he was doing.*

Then Krashaar said, "See Joe Kane. We need a song for a Rogers picture."

At last, praise God, Jule thought, something creative. He went to Joe Kane, a big, crusty but very capable director, *the* director for all the Roy Rogers films, and Kane, viewing the fashionably dressed Jule Styne as something strayed from the accounting department, said, "Roy is going to be walking along this Western street with Trigger. He's going to be eating watermelon at the same time. He's feeling good. He's happy. I've even got a title for you. 'I Love Watermelon.' "

For an astonished moment Jule didn't know what to say. He finally ventured, "It might be hard for the lyric man to rhyme watermelon. What about singing something happy about the beautiful day, the blue skies above . . ."

"Bullshit," said tough Joe Kane. "He's eating watermelon. That's what the song has to be about. When a man is sewing a boot and singing, I want him to sing about sewing that boot. That's what I want."

Jule nodded and went over to Cy Feuer's bungalow where there was another upright piano and said to Cy, "That crazy guy wants a song about eating watermelon." Feuer, having been on the Republic lot for several lively years, veteran of gunshots and hoedowns and songs about "punkins" and crows, did not even blink. He said, "Give it to him."

While Feuer got busy on the phone with larger, more pressing problems, Jule sat down and wrote "I Love Watermelon." The lyric writers were most often Saul Meyer and George Browne, who usually split $50 to provide words to songs about boot-stitching or fruits of the cucurbitaceous vine.

I was present in the sound booth when they scored that picture, heard my music and have never been able to look at watermelon without thinking of Roy Rogers. However, Joe Kane liked the song, Roy liked it, and so did Yates. Then Cy Feuer rewarded me with Sing, Dance, Plenty Hot, *which starred a dwarfish little girl named Ruth Terry. I can't even remember the songs I wrote for that picture, but they were bummers and so was the picture.*

Bummers aside, another part of the foundation for a lifetime of composing was laid there by the banks of the Los Angeles River, midst the whinnying of horses and thumping of tin washboards. Jule learned the feeling of Westerns, and more importantly, just how far his own previously sophisticated terrain of Haydn and Mozart and Connie Bennett and Darryl F. Zanuck was from the reality of millions who cared more about Gabby Hayes and Elviry than they did about *The Razor's Edge* and *The Snake Pit.*

It was an awakening, and I wrote five or six songs for each picture. Wrote music for cattle and horses and dogs; pigs, mules and chickens. I helped with orchestrations. Sometimes I conducted. Swallowing pride, I did just about anything they asked me to do. Play piano for Trigger? Sure . . .

One night Jule stayed late with Cy Feuer to see a rough cut of a film about to be flown to Herbert Yates in New York, to be screened for a convention of European theater owners.

They'd worked on it during the day but it hadn't been fully dubbed or scored, and somebody had fouled up. The musicians were gone. No one was there except a few men in the dubbing crew, and thank God, the film editor. The sound-effects cutters were long gone. No one had gotten the word that Mr. Yates, in his gray suit and black tie, was waiting for it. So we ran it, and the biggest fight scene in the film had no sound effects, no crashing and bashing. The fight lay there, dead. Just a bunch of guys bopping each other and breaking chairs, silently.

Cy Feuer yelled, "Christalmighty, Yates will kill us all."

So Styne and Feuer brought in bottles to break, chairs to smash; pounded fists into open palms; "ughed" and grunted as belly punches hit, while the dubbers recorded. Then came a quieter moment in the film, when the girl lead returned from England to a Western ranch for a harp recital. She stroked the strings on-screen but again, no sound. The musicians' large instruments were still on the stage, on call for the next day. Feuer remembers asking Jule, "You ever play a harp?"

Jule replied, "Nope, but let's open that one up." He began plucking it, following the scene, hitting chords.

It didn't really make a damn what I was playing. I did glissandi, like Harpo Marx. To tell the truth, it was great fun and Cy almost rolled on the floor. But it was this kind of thing that was so valuable at Republic, a make-do challenge. It was the last place on earth for any prima donna.

Any picture budgeted at around a half million dollars was considered a major undertaking at Republic, and *Sis Hopkins,* to star Judy Canova, Bing Crosby and Jerry Colonna, qualified in both budget and stars. Soon after it was posted on Republic's 1941 production schedule Cy Feuer assigned the film's seven songs to Jule.

Feuer remembers that Jule immediately asked for a top lyric writer. "He begged me to get him someone who was really good. I thought for a moment and then suggested Frank Loesser, who was then at Paramount and just beginning to stride out."

Loesser had written "Says My Heart," music by Burton Lane; he'd written the lyrics for two huge hits, "Small Fry" and "Two Sleepy People," music by Hoagy Carmichael.

Jule asked excitedly, "Can you get him?"

Feuer answered that he'd try, and then called Louis Lipstone, head of the music department at Paramount, saying he'd like to borrow Loesser. "But I can't pay a premium. What'll he cost?" Poverty Row seldom paid premiums for anything.

Lipstone said that Loesser was under contract at $350 a week but his loan-out rate was to be $500. The deal was finally made at a lesser figure, with some kind of option that involved the future services of John Wayne. At the time, Wayne earned little more than Loesser.

Frank was wild when he heard of it. He came steaming over to North Radford and yelled at Feuer, "You son of bitch, I'm writing for Hoagy Carmichael now. I'm not coming here to work with some half-ass piano player who is really a vocal coach." Loesser and Styne had met briefly at Paramount while Jule was coaching Mary Martin and the meeting had been very friendly. In fact, Loesser had urged Jule to take the Republic job and try his hand at composing; stop the silly vocal coaching. They hadn't seen each other since that time. Conditions had changed.

Loesser raged profanely at Feuer and the pair retired to Eaton's Restaurant across the street, where the argument continued for another two hours. Finally, Loesser begrudgingly agreed to at least see the "half-ass" piano player but did not agree to work with him. Feuer pointed out Jule's hay-and-feed bungalow and then retreated to his office.

Frank Loesser had been a process server, food taster, jewelry salesman, waiter in a Catskills hotel, newspaperman, night-club entertainer and press agent before taking up lyric writing for the Leo Fiest Music Company. He had a monumental temper, the frothing kind, and was not known anywhere for holding his tongue. Feuer recalls that both of Frank's feet could leave the ground when he was really angry. He had also been known to use his fists.

He roared into Styne's bungalow, yelling at the nervous occupant,

"You have demeaned me by asking for me. You have no respect for my talent, not that I can't understand why you'd want me. But Jesus Christ, every big picture at Paramount they've been giving to Johnny Mercer. Now, goddammit, who writes the hits? Me!" He then reeled off, "Sleepy People," "I've Got Spurs That Jingle, Jangle, Jingle . . ."

Jule sat quietly.

"Now, this pile of shit, Republic. You've destroyed me forever."

Jule still sat quietly, he remembers. He couldn't edge a word in, anyway. He was also concerned about Loesser's fists. They'd already pounded the desk.

Loesser ranted on for a few minutes and then exhausted himself. "Listen, I'm going to write these fucking songs in four days, but you're not going to hand them in for three weeks. I'm going to Palm Springs and sit on my butt. You understand that?"

Jule said he clearly understood.

Frank circled around the small room, with its dusty, bouncing floor, a half-dozen times, taking tiger steps. Then he ordered, "Play me something."

Jule, at last, had space and nerve to talk. He said, "The reason I wanted you here is because I wanted to do something very good. I've watched horses whinny in sync. I've written arrangements for coyotes. I've written songs about watermelon and grits and gravy. So please don't tell me about your sufferings with Johnny Mercer."

Jule distinctly recalls that Loesser replied, "I don't want your history. I hate your guts right now."

Jule said, "Okay, I'll play you something." He sat down at the scarred upright and hit the notes to a melody he'd completed the previous week.

Five bars into the song, Frank raced to the door and slammed it shut. "Sssssh. Stop!" he said. "Don't play that here. Never play that here again. Don't you ever play that for anyone else. We'll write that song at Paramount."

Styne and Loesser began collaboration on *Sis Hopkins* the next day, but not before Loesser drew big signs and tacked them on the hay-and-feed door. *No Cowboys Allowed. No Horses Allowed. No Gunshots.*

Feuer and Styne were not the only people that Loesser tangled with during his three weeks at Republic. He did not go to Palm Springs. He came to the bungalow each morning, ready to work, though grumbling about his fall to Poverty Row.

Jule soon wrote a melody in three-eighth time for a Loesser lyric entitled "Oh, Henry." The scene: A girl goes into a theater with a guy whose name is Henry, and there's a long verse built around "Oh, what you do to my heart." The girl's punch line is, "Oh, Henry, you're my favorite candy bar."

Herbert Yates heard the song and instantly said, "It's out."

Loesser demanded to know why. The song had satisfied Cy Feuer as well as the director.

"I'll tell you why," said Yates. "I sell O-O You candy bars in the concessions I own, not Oh Henry! bars. All through the South I sell my O-O You bars. Now, I'll just be goddamned if you're going to push Oh Henry! bars in my own picture. Change that line to *O-O You.*"

"O-O You?" Frank screamed back, at his very loudest. "How the fuck do I make that rhyme? The character's name is Henry, not O-O You."

The conflict went on for days until the legal department settled it by telling Mr. Yates he could not plug his own confection in a Republic picture. Yates never forgave Frank Loesser.

A month later, Republic loaned Jule to Paramount for *Sweater Girl,* at the request of Loesser, and then Jule began to learn what Frank was all about. There was no pressure to do seven songs in three weeks on the Marathon Street lot. Loesser took his time, writing lyrics in his head, except for long patter things. For five weeks Jule played the "smuggled" melody from Republic while Loesser walked around, smiled and drank coffee. At times it appeared he was ready to say something, but then he'd just smile and amble away.

I was going out of my head, spending hours alone with him in that little room, playing the melody again and again. I must have played it for him five hundred times, maybe more.

One day, Loesser walked in to announce, "I'm now going to sing you the lyrics. Every eighth note of your music I've treasured, because it should grace a strong word."

When he sang the lyric, as Jule played, the unexpected happened:

> I don't want to walk without that sunshine—
> Why did you have to take away that sunshine?
> Oh, baby, please come back or you'll break
>   my heart for me.
> I don't want to walk without you, baby,
> No, siree.

No rhymer this lyricist. He was a craftsman working in silence and loneliness. The five silent weeks took "I Don't Want to Walk Without You, Baby" to twenty weeks on the Hit Parade. A second song, a novelty number, "I Said Yes, She Said No," was on the Parade for almost a dozen weeks. Shortly thereafter, Loesser joined the Army and wrote, "Praise the Lord and Pass the Ammunition"* but not before advising Jule, "Don't ever write with smart-ass rhymers. Write with people who have something to say with their words. Fellows who are thoughtful and literate, and have wit."

Cy Feuer soon joined the Army, too, and his replacement as head of the music department at Republic was Jule's old friend Walter Scharf, late of 20th Century-Fox.

Scharf said, "If you think about it, Republic was where Jule got his start in theatrical training. Broadway began right there. I wasn't aware that he was learning that much, but he was always so careful that the music would fall in with the lyrics. He developed a great knack of being cognizant of the lyrics at Republic. When the high notes came, the right vowel would be on them. He'd never have a high note on a closed vowel, even that far back. He married the music to the words."

Herbert John Yates had fallen in love with a Czech ice-skater, Vera Hruba Ralston, runner-up to Sonja Henie in the 1936 Olympics. She'd later been featured in a touring ice show, and now, in 1942, Yates had signed her to star in *Ice-Capades* and had built a special stage for her. Love had finally loosened Yates's tight pockets. Mr. Yates and Vera Hruba often skated arm in arm on Stage 9 to the sound-track music of Borodin and Tchaikovsky. They made a fascinating pair on the white surface of the empty stage. *I sometimes watched them just to keep reminding myself of the acknowledged insanity of making movies.*

Jule was soon assigned to do the songs for the Ralston skate shows. *I pulled every trick I knew to satisfy Yates. I didn't give a damn about that Czech skater but I knew who was signing my check.* The check was now $350 a week.

And, at last, a Gene Autry picture. *I plotted for that one. I thought I could pilot myself a hit record again. Anything big with Autry sold about 500,000 copies. But Bob Nolan and The Sons of the Pioneers*

*Among Loesser's other hits for films were "Moon of Manakoora," for Dorothy Lamour and "See What the Boys in the Backroom Will Have" for Marlene Dietrich.

wrote many of Autry's songs. He was their bread and butter and they guarded him like Tiffany's. It's a whole different world, that of writing for singing cowboys. Accordions, harmonicas and fiddled saws. So I sat down in the bungalow and wrote something I called "Purple Sage in the Twilight." I'm not sure I'd ever seen purple sage, but it sounded like Autry. I took it to him and demonstrated it myself.

Autry said, "Jule, boy, I think I like that song."

Campaigning hard, Jule said, "Well, Mr. Autry, I go back to Chicago when I used to listen to you on WCFL. I've always been a great fan of yours. I love Western music."

That pleased the former telegrapher, of course, and he said, "I shouldn't let you write this song. I have my own boys, The Sons of the Pioneers, and they're sittin' right out in the front office, breathin' down your neck. They can come in here and write this in five minutes and I'm home. But, you know what, I'm going to teach you how to write a Western song."

"Gee, that would be terrific," said Jule.

Autry said, "You got a lot of good stuff in that melody but you waste time, too. You see, you got to get me somethin' to do on those seventh and eighth bars. I just can't keep standing there waitin' for the music to fill in. You make me wait too long. I got to keep my mouth movin'."

Jule said he could fix it, there and then. He could almost feel The Pioneers stalking him, and it took but five minutes to adjust the melody to Autry's liking. Then he called Walter Scharf. "I want to lay a song down for Gene Autry."

Scharf was surprised. "You mean he's going to let you write for him?"

"He is, and there are no waits on this. It goes right now. I've got The Pioneers on my tail. Set me up."

From his desk, Autry advised, "When you write the piano copies for printing, they belong to my company. Anything I sing is for my company."

Jule said he'd rather write for Autry's company than any other. "You sell copies."

In another few minutes, Jule and Gene Autry trooped toward the recording stage with The Sons of the Pioneers following a few paces behind, lugging their instruments. Jule "laid" the song down, played the melody. The recorder rolled, and then The Sons of the Pioneers, gathered by the piano, began to accompany him, following the lead sheet. Jule accepted the different chords The Pioneers were playing.

Autry's nodding head indicated that they were the ones he wanted to hear.

So I learned how to write a Gene Autry song. Different rules, but successful.

"Purple Sage in the Twilight," which became the name of the picture, sold 700,000 copies. The Sons of the Pioneers guarded the cowboy star more closely ever after and Jule never again wrote for Autry. Years later, he met Gene in a hotel lobby and said, "I bet you don't remember me, but . . ."

Autry grinned and broke into "Purple Sage in the Twilight" . . .

About that time, lyricist Sammy Cahn, who'd written the words for the Andrews Sisters' hit, "Bei Mir Bist Du Schoen," and several other top songs, severed from his partner, composer Saul Chaplin, and was rather frantically looking around town for a job and a new melody man. A New Yorker with a touch of mustache, thick spectacles and quite a little chutzpa, Sammy was a kindly, energetic man with large ambitions. He was also very fast and very good with a rhyme, working exclusively on a typewriter.

In search of a collaborator, Sammy had approached Al Cohn, producer of *Sis Hopkins,* and a known soft touch for almost anyone with a hard-luck story. Cohn then summoned Jule and suggested an alliance. Sammy was practically weeping, Cohn said. He needed work; he needed a good composer. Cohn said he thought Sammy had great, untapped talent.

Remembering what Loesser had always advised, "Write only with the big ones," Jule agreed to meet with Cahn, and then said honestly, "Look, Sammy, you've had some hits but I just came off two big ones. I've got to write at that level now."

Sammy said, "Give me a chance. If you don't like it after a week, at least I'll have had the chance."

So they went to the hay-and-feed bungalow and the only thing that Jule could think of was a song he'd written for Loesser. Frank had never gotten down to the lyrics.

Jule played, "Da-da-da-da-dah-dah-dah . . ."

Sammy snapped it up. "It seems to me I've heard that song before . . ."

Jule slammed his hands on the keys angrily. "Wait a minute. You've never heard that song before. I only played it for Loesser. What the hell are you, a tune detective?"

"No, no, forgive me," said Sammy. "That's the title of the song."

They finished it before midnight and "It Seems to Me I've Heard

That Song Before" went into Al Cohn's new film, *Youth on Parade,* and then lasted for ten weeks on the Hit Parade. Harry James's recording of it spun on almost every jukebox in the country.

It was all falling into place now without my even knowing it. I was finding I could write with any good lyricist and Sammy was very good, after all.

Among the more than fifty songs Jule Styne accomplished at Herb Yates's studio, with one lyric writer or another, eighteen were published and recorded for other than screen purposes. Such serviceable numbers as "Down Mexico Way" and "Pepita, Rosita, Juanita Lopez," lyrics by Herb Magidson, are still spun by disc jockeys.

One of the last films that Jule did at Republic was *Hit Parade of 1943,* starring the perennial Frances Langford and svelte dancer Ann Miller, borrowed from MGM. Scharf then borrowed lyricist Walter Bullock from 20th to complement Jule's music. Within a day, they'd written "A Change of Heart" for Langford.

4

Harry Cohn was every man's son of a bitch but he was still a genius in many ways. Sammy Cahn could make him apoplectic.

—JULE STYNE, 1977

Over a period of eight years, the song-writing team of Sammy Cahn and Jule Styne was one of the most successful in film history. *At one point, in the mid-forties, we were writing so many hits that it became embarrassing.* Styne remembers them tossing a song into the office of the Morris Music Company and dashing down the hall, whooping with laughter. Or they'd approach Edwin "Buddy" Morris soberly, "May we say, sir, another hit." And so it was.

From Republic, Jule and Sammy shifted to Paramount for a few months, writing songs for pictures that likely made money in those war years but are distinguished for little else. Those months in the venerable studio on Marathon Street were actually a letdown for Jule after the diverse cracker barrels of Republic. He was, however, beginning to learn much about his partner and vice versa. Sammy by now knew that there'd always be a pause during the day, perhaps several pauses, for Jule's communications to the bookies.

Sammy, a bachelor until 1944, began his day about 9:00 A.M. and often did not end it until 3:00 or 4:00 A.M. He was not at all attractive physically, but was a gifted conversationalist and acquired a string of girls that he shared freely with actors, other movie-set cronies and assorted workers in the studio music departments. If anyone needed a quick date, a sure-fire bed prospect, Sammy's black book had ample numbers.

In the mornings, Jule would drive over to Sammy's apartment, pick him up, and head for whatever assignment might be in the works. Sammy, often exhausted and red-eyed beneath the thick lenses, a kindred soul in suffering from ulcers, would never say much on these morning rides. However, he would often pass over a slip of paper about the size of a short laundry list. On it would be a title or more developed verse. "Kiss Me Once, Kiss Me Twice."

At the next stoplight, Jule would examine the title and stuff it into his pocket. He once saved up titles or sets of dummy lyrics and then wrote the music for all eight at once. They were published and became hits. The usual procedure, starting from a title or dummy lyric, was for both Sammy and Jule to rewrite their individual efforts, and then polish. They sometimes worked in the studios, or in the living room of Jule's home in Beverly Hills—Jule at a desk, scrawling notes, then trying them on the grand piano; Sammy in another room pecking at a typewriter.

I swear to God that Sammy must have been thinking all day and all night. Even when he had a girl in his arms, he must have been thinking about a lyric. He could write things in a minute. He was incredibly fast. Sammy wanted to stay in action, not sit in creative loneliness like a Loesser or Alan Lerner. Sammy would be bent over the typewriter, answer the phone, "Yeh, I'll have the broads tonight," hang up and go right on with the lyric, usually a good one. Incredible man. He never wanted to leave me without an idea for a song. So out came the laundry slips, any time of day or night.

Young Stanley Styne often listened outside the door to the living room where they worked. "The music seemed to come easy for my father. The words seemed to come easy for Sammy." The piano was near the front window and Sammy often sang his lyrics, in nasal New Yorkese, while Jule played.

Ethel got along well with Sammy Cahn, and he liked her. Sometimes it seemed that she talked more often and more easily with Sammy than she did with her husband.

Ethel Rubenstein Styne is not around to tell her story, but from sons and friends and relatives it appears that she was always in love with her husband no matter what he did. She'd clearly married the wrong man, but could find no way to cross over his bridge. Ethel had taken piano lessons as a child and had played concerts in her teens but never, in anyone's memory, did she sit down at the keyboard after marrying Jule.

Yet there were rare moments of warmth. There was a Saturday night ritual during the mid-forties at the Elm Drive house. The entire Styne family sprawled out on the floor to listen to The Hit Parade and wait for Jule's songs to come up.

But on some nights, when Jule came in excited over a new melody, Ethel would fall asleep while he was playing it. He'd look over, stop in mid-note, and go on off to bed.

Jule and Sammy were contracted by Columbia Pictures in mid-1943 on a seven-picture deal—$15,000 each for the first four pictures; $20,000 each for the fifth picture; $25,000 each for the sixth film, and $30,000 apiece for No. 7. They only finished three.

When the deal was offered, Jule said to Sammy, "Let's take it." Any money from records of the film songs would be theirs; any money from sheet music, and performance money from ASCAP was to be Styne–Cahn. It appeared to be a very good arrangement.

Columbia Pictures—graying, aged buildings on the corner of Sunset Boulevard and Gower Street, not far from Paramount and RKO—was also where dwelt Harry Cohn, studio head. By some, or most, he was viewed as a tyrannical monster. By some, but not many, including Jule, he was seen to be part genius. While Cohn headed Columbia, the studio made money and contributed such films as *It Happened One Night* and *Lost Horizon.* If he had little respect for actors, actresses, writers and directors, he had great respect for the paying public. By whatever means he determined audience acceptance, he was quite often right.

Jule purposely did not become friendly with Harry Cohn but Sammy Cahn became oddly coupled to the studio head. Harry liked to play gin rummy with Sammy, and the game occurred three or four times a week, one half cent a point. Sammy never played "lose to the boss." He often dined at the Cohn mansion in Beverly Hills, tuxedoed and on relatively good behavior.

Jule pleaded with his partner, "Just for business sake, Sammy, lose to him now and then."

"Fuck him," said Sammy. "He's paying for the pleasure of my company."

During this period of pleasure, Cohn would write IOU's when he lost and Sammy saved them up. Finally, he took them to Miss Missick,

Cohn's trusted secretary, a woman with great patience and endurance. She got on the phone to say to the boss, "Sammy Cahn is here with some slips. They add up to three hundred ten dollars."

"What are they?"

Miss Missick intoned such figures as $5.58; $7.40; $3.88; $11.20. "They must be some kind of gambling debt, Mr. Cohn."

"Send him in," ordered Cohn, in a frosty tone.

Sammy went in as if taking the last twenty steps to the electric chair.

Cohn said, "You're a fine son of a bitch. You just let my secretary know you beat me in gin. For Christ's sakes, I don't need you around here, you crumb. I allow you into my house and you eat my food and then you have to demean me. Why didn't you come in here and get five or ten dollars a week instead of waiting until it got to be three hundred ten dollars? You saved it up on purpose."

"What's three-ten to you?" asked brave Sammy.

Those words traveled around the studio, etched in glee, Sammy feeding the fire at every opportunity.

Jule watched in pain from the sidelines as his coworker self-destructed at Columbia. The IOU incident was one of many. Sammy would walk into the executive dining room before Cohn arrived. "What is Mr. Cohn having for lunch?"

"Well, they've flown in some special corned beef from New York."

"I'll have some of that," Sammy said.

Then Cohn would rage on spotting his delicacies atop Sammy's plate. "Your partner is a crude son of a bitch," Cohn told Jule.

"Why do you have him at your house?" Jule asked.

"Because I like to beat him in gin," Cohn answered.

There was a candy dish near the table where they played, and when Sammy would select a piece Cohn would slap it out of his hand. "You'll get the cards sticky," said the head of Columbia.

"What's the candy for?" asked Sammy.

"Looks," replied Cohn.

The attraction between the two men was at best curious and dangerous—for Styne–Cahn.

Meanwhile, Jule and Sammy gave Columbia its first big song hit from a picture, a flimsy Kay Kaiser (of the Kollege of Musical Knowledge) vehicle entitled *Carolina Moon.* "There Goes That Song Again" was another long-time Hit Parade resident. A second hit song for Columbia was "Poor Little Rhode Island."

The inevitable downfall of Styne–Cahn on the Gower Street lot was a huge birthday affair for Mr. Cohn, celebrating fifty years on earth, most of them battle-scarred in one way or another. By now it was known at Columbia, and elsewhere, that Sammy and Jule could write very special material for very special gatherings. Sammy was a master at parody.

So for this gala fiftieth anniversary, to be held in Cohn's mansion, his wife, Joan, requested the team to fashion a super tribute, something that would both please and amuse the studio head. This was a formidable task, since Harry Cohn's sense of humor was never predictable. However, the eighty-page script that they wrote was, in the opinions of those present, good enough to open on Broadway.

The stars included concert artist José Iturbi to perform on the piano; Phil Silvers to portray Harry Cohn; Al Jolson to play Al Jolson; Janet Blair, object of a bitter recent Cohn feud, and others. Sammy Cahn, naturally, cast himself as Sammy Cahn, gin player; Jule elected to portray Sidney Skolsky, the gossip columnist, complete with raincoat and hat. Both men were about the same size.

Styne–Cohn combed over the past and labored hard on the future and present. There was a skit about the gin games and Cohn sat on the staircase next to his wife, roaring with laughter, as Silvers (Cohn) slapped Sammy's hand away from the candy bowl.

Jule, as Sidney Skolsky, who was to produce *The Al Jolson Story* for Columbia, said to Silvers, as Cohn, "Harry, I've got the guy for the Jolson story. Finally got him. This guy is absolutely Jolson to the T."

Silvers (Cohn): "Don't tell me about Jolie. I used to plug his songs. I know what the guy was. Bring him in."

In walked Al Jolson in an off-white suit. He sang "Rock-a-bye, Your Baby" to Harry and Joan Cohn, exiting to audience tears and thundering applause.

Silvers (Cohn): "Ah, that's pretty good, kid. We'll be talking to you."

Blackout.

The entire evening went that way, two hours of the tempestuous life and times of Harry Cohn.

The next day Harry Friedman, Jule's agent at MCA, called to say, "I had a very unusual talk with Harry Cohn this morning. He wants to renew you both for five more pictures, but he doesn't want me to tell you about it."

"What does that mean?" Jule asked.

"Well, he wants to renew you for five more at the same money."

Sammy, who was in the same room, listening, said, "You tell Harry Cohn we'll work out our contract or not work it out. But from now on, we start at $35,000 per picture. Fifth picture, $75,000 each. If this displeases him, we'll leave the lot now."

Jule shrugged and agreed. Five additional films at the same money was a bad deal.

The following Sunday, Jule got a call from Miss Missick; Sammy also got the same call. Mr. Cohn would like to see them at his home. Now!

The pair truly felt that Cohn would put it all on a friendly basis: You can have your own unit; produce your own pictures. You'll do great things here!

They went to Cohn's splendid residence, both expectant and a bit nervous, and walked into a scene reminiscent of *Sunset Boulevard.* Mr. Cohn was at the far end of his long pool, clad in a black silk robe. The sun was out and birds chirped. No Italian production could have staged it better. Cohn yelled, "Stay where you are!"

The team froze, quickly understanding that it was hate time.

Cohn shouted, "You ungrateful people. You want to take advantage of me. I wanted to show how nice I was. Before your old contract was finished, I wanted to sign you up again."

Sammy yelled back, across the length of the pool, "You wanted us to sign to give blood. I've given you four days a week out of the best years of my life. I could have been out banging broads instead of playing gin with you, and eating your food, which I don't particularly like. Another thing: We care for you and Joan and knocked ourselves out to give you the greatest night of your life last week."

Cohn literally screamed, "Get off my grounds before I call the police."

Sammy trudged off, shaking his head.

Jule lingered a little longer. "I haven't opened my mouth, Mr. Cohn. I'm a little more conservative than Sammy. I just wanted to tell you something. It's tough for me to say, but, gee, we had such a swell party planned for your fifty-first birthday."

Then Jule trudged away, too, as Cohn shouted, "Get off my grounds."

Tonight and Every Night, starring Rita Hayworth, and another thoroughly forgettable film, were the entire Styne–Cahn contributions to Columbia, aside from the Kay Kaiser picture. Hayworth was having weight problems and studio personnel, on orders from Cohn, were watching her every ounce. Jule smuggled quarts of ice cream to Rita, chuckling every time he opened a carton.

There is a span of time in the life of Jule Styne that is best identified as the "Frank Sinatra period." *Well, I used to go to the Hollywood Palladium in 1941 to hear all the big bands, especially Harry James and Tommy Dorsey, and I was wild about Frank's voice when he was singing with him. I think he was on the Basin Street radio program when I first heard him, singing something with Dinah Shore. So one day that year I said to Sammy, "Introduce me to Frank Sinatra. . . ."*

Sammy Cahn had known Sinatra well before the crooner split away from Tommy Dorsey's band in 1942, beginning the years of the "Great Swoon," when teen-agers mobbed "The Voice" after shows at the Paramount Theatre. The bobbysoxers squealed as Frank finished "I'll Never Smile Again" or "All or Nothing At All"; some fainted dead away when he fought his way out the stagedoor entrance. His style, his misty eyes and deceptively fragile appearance, also had a marked effect on older female followers. He opened at an obscure Manhattan night club, The Riobamba, and promptly put it on the nitery map. Sinatra was suddenly multimillion-dollar merchandise to be sold in stage shows, night clubs, over the radio and in movies. Records, of course.

Jule was in the Riobamba the night Sinatra opened, and stayed with the singer until dawn. About 11:00 A.M., a messenger knocked on Styne's hotel room door to deliver a small package from Cartier's. Inside was a solid gold I.D. bracelet inscribed, "To Jule, Who Knew Me When, Frankie." Sinatra had little reason to doubt what would happen to his career.

Apparently, the first Styne–Cahn song executed by Sinatra was "I've Heard That Song Before," the Republic Pictures tune, performed before a packed Madison Square Garden audience in 1942. The evening honored Russian sailors who had come to the United States to crew lend-lease warships, and marked the last public appearance of Mayor Jimmy Walker. Now, in 1944, Sammy and Jule were signed by RKO Pictures to write songs for *Step Lively,* Sinatra costarring in this feature with George Murphy, the future politician; impeccable Adolphe Menjou, and Gloria De Haven. The screen story is of no importance. Neither were the four Styne–Cahn songs for Sinatra, though "Come Out, Come Out, Wherever You Are" had a certain lilt.

What was important was that Sammy and Jule "hit it off" with Frank Sinatra. No other factor was as crucial. Sinatra liked the breezy, energetic pair; they could laugh and joke with him, amuse him, and both men scattered ideas as if they had bottomless bins. Frank also seemed to recognize that Styne was an accomplished musician; that he *knew* music. The Styne "ear," ever outraged by off-keys, was appreciated by Sinatra, whose instincts for good and bad were already highly developed.

There was reciprocal respect. Jule knew that Sinatra understood orchestration and the importance of the lyrics. *He had a native musical intelligence that was remarkable. He not only chose the right songs, the right melodies, but was smart enough to realize that the real pay dirt was in the lyrics. The words were what counted, and no one has ever phrased better than Frank Sinatra.*

Howard Barnes, movie critic of the *New York Herald Tribune,* discarded *Step Lively,* as did other assayers, but none could deny the bedlam in the movie houses when Sinatra did his numbers.

Thus began, in the war years, the long and often tenuous professional and personal relationship between Styne–Cahn and Frank Sinatra.

Long before the "Rat Pack," we had a certain small clique and if you weren't fun, you couldn't belong. Myself, Sammy; Axel Stordahl, Frank's arranger-conductor; Phil Silvers; actor Bill Goodwin; that fine musician, Paul Weston; Harry Crane, top comedy writer for Jackie Gleason and others; Frank's manager, Hank Sanicola. The essence of this clique was stories and jokes. Laughs. We went to the fights together. We saved the latest funny stories for Frank. We went to his performances. It was fun and games.

Jule, as well as Sammy, enjoyed being a part of the clique and often gave priority to a Sinatra chore, perhaps a piece of special material, a musical parody, putting aside paid studio work.

5

Acting is a lot of things to a lot of people but I'd like to think it is more than just "questions and answers." Yet that's how Sammy defined it.

—JULE STYNE, 1977

On and off, over several years, Jule and Sammy had talked about doing a Broadway musical. Jule, in particular, wanted to attempt a musical and Sammy was also inclined to try his luck *on the street.* Neither man had actively sought material but both were interested when David Wolper, a cousin of the current documentary-maker of the same name, approached them with an idea: a USO show that toured military bases in the South Pacific. Wolper said that he'd all but cast fiery Lupe Velez and Danny Thomas; had a libretto by Eddie Davis and Fred Thompson; Valerie Bettis would be the choreographer. None other than famed Busby Berkeley, of the MGM musical spectacles, would direct.

Wolper's initial appearance as a producer on Broadway had brought forth *Follow the Girls,* starring Jackie Gleason and Gertrude Neisen. The book for *Follow the Girls* was a shambles, but the show became a hit, and a producer with a hit has some credentials.

Sammy and Jule first began work in Beverly Hills on *Glad to See You,* originally intended for Phil Silvers, but 20th Century-Fox would not permit Silvers to attend Broadway and second choice to costar with

Miss Velez was Danny Thomas. Then Thomas dropped out to do a radio series and Lupe Velez committed suicide.

Right then, we should have stopped. Ill-fated is an understatement for what happened to that show.

The pair went on to New York to continue work on the songs, while producer Wolper looked around for a Danny Thomas replacement. At Leon & Eddie's, a popular restaurant and night club on Fifty-second Street, Eddie Davis (not the librettist) was drawing servicemen crowds, packing them in nightly. The show couldn't afford an Eddie Cantor but needed charisma, and the other Eddie had it, in big decibels. He'd slap the piano on a high note; he captivated, or at least overpowered, the audiences. Jule went to the club several times and then suggested to Wolper that they sign Davis. For years, Eddie Davis, a Fifty-second Street fixture, had wanted to star in a musical on his own Great White Way. Here was the sweet dream within his grasp. He grabbed it, making nightly announcements that he'd soon be toplining *Glad to See You,* all about a touring USO group on the islands where the men were in battle.

One Saturday night, while the musical was taking shape, Sammy was alone in Jule's suite at the Gotham Hotel. Jule was out on the town, as usual. About 7:00 P.M., Sammy's sister Florence, and her husband, Jules, rang from the lobby and then went on up to the suite. They were surprised to find Sammy alone. No girls. No guys. They asked Sammy if he was feeling all right. If so, why was he in a robe? Why alone?

Sammy replied that Saturday night was for "civilians." They always went out Saturday night. Show people stayed home. He said that Saturday night was the loneliest night of the week for show people.

A little later, Florence and her husband departed and Sammy sat down at Jule's piano. Every lyric writer has a dummy melody in his head, according to Sammy Cahn. It is "da-da-la-da-da-la-da" and can fit almost any set of lyrics. The dummy melody is often used as a starting point for songs, and was utilized this night. Sammy tapped out about eight bars and then scribbled down some words. "Saturday night is the loneliest night of the week . . ."

Jule came home about eleven, and Sammy said, "Listen to this for an idea . . ."

Jule took the eight "dummy melody" bars and continued. The song was completed in an hour, and then both men got on an elevator. The penthouse suite of the Gotham was occupied by Manny Sachs, president of Columbia Records, and Saturday night was always gin rummy night in Manny's apartment.

Cahn–Styne walked in and Sammy said, "You fellows ready?"

The team played and sang the song. The moment they finished, gin-player Jonie Taps, of the Shapiro–Bernstein Music Company, said, "I'll give you $5,000 for it."

"You got it," said Sammy.

The next day, Manny Sachs called Sinatra in California. "Your fellows gave away a song last night. It's great." Sachs thought that the song was worth more than $5,000.

Sinatra called Cahn within a few minutes and the "giveaway" was reversed. Jonie Taps retired from the bidding action and "Saturday Night Is the Loneliest Night of the Week" was recorded by Sinatra's company, rising to No. 1 on the Hit Parade.

To replace the late Miss Velez in *Glad to See You,* director Busby Berkeley and producer Wolper chose June Knight, a very attractive girl who had starred in Cole Porter's *Jubilee.* She was no bombshell like Velez, and in Jule's opinion, couldn't sing very well, but she seemed to be the only available choice.

Later on, discussions about the songs, and the show in general, were usually conducted in a smoke shop next door to the Shubert Theatre, in Philadelphia. Wolper enjoyed playing the pinball machine in the cigar shop. *Those balls were binging-banging all over the place while I tried to talk to him about the music. He'd use body English and the lights would flash. Ill-fated, that show?*

And from Jule's point of view, Mr. Berkeley did not seem too much concerned about the libretto and score of *Glad to See You.* His interest seemed to lie in the costumes and scenery. At one point, Berkeley said to Styne, "When it's all cut together, it'll work, baby. You just see."

"Cut together?" That was film talk; that was editing talk. *Good Christ, Berkeley was talking about making a movie, not staging a play. I knew that movie people talked in movie terms but here he was thinking in movie terms. Frightening.*

Jule went to a morning rehearsal where Berkeley had two singers, a boy and Jane Withers, the ex-child star, doing a ballad up against the back bricks. Even without an absorbing audience, their voices couldn't be heard. Jule yelled up to Berkeley, "Those kids have to come down near the lights. I can't even hear them. I'll have twenty-five musicians in the pit and the audience won't hear a word."

Berkeley yelled back, "Don't worry about it. I'm panning on this. I'm coming in on a crane."

There he goes again, Jule thought. He has to be on dope. He's freaked. Using a crane? He thinks he's still at MGM. Jule ran out of the Shubert and into the smoke shop where Wolper was pinballing. "Our director has lost his mind," Jule shouted. "He's talking about using a crane."

Wolper answered soothingly, "He's only kidding you, Jule," and the lever unleashed another steel ball.

Jule went for a walk.

The night after dress rehearsal Eddie Davis drove his automobile too close to a moving streetcar. The resulting crunch broke his collar bone. No Eddie Davis would ever appear on his beloved Broadway. *God said to close the show, close it now. No one listened.* Forty thousand in Styne personal money was invested in the musical; he wasn't even drawing per diem. *Sammy Cahn was walking around as if he was chained and drugged. Worse, we both felt helpless.*

A post-midnight production meeting was held in the Bellevue-Stratford Hotel, headquarters for the company. Mr. Berkeley forthwith announced, "I'll play the lead. I'll replace Eddie Davis."

Jule asked, "What do you mean? We need a modern entertainer for that part. He's a USO show guy, a song-and-dance man."

"I'll play it like Jack Buchanan, the great British entertainer."

"What in hell does Jack Buchanan have to do with this show?" Jule asked.

"I can do it," Berkeley insisted.

Jule said, "Busby, it'll take you three months to learn these songs. This show has ten songs. There is also patter. Who's going to be directing while you star in it? We're in trouble already."

Then Sammy Cahn spoke up. "I'm the only person who can play the lead."

Jule's heart almost stopped beating. There was a deathly silence in the room. Jule recovered to say, "Sammy, you have a point. You're the only one besides me who knows the songs. But there is acting in this. It's the star's part you're talking about."

Sammy said confidently, "I'll do it until we get a star. We have to open."

Jule felt weak. He said, "I'm telling all of you we need an actor."

Daylight finally entered the Bellevue-Stratford room. Sammy said, "Listen, I'll tell you about acting. It's only questions and answers." Sammy stood there, Jule remembers, bleary-eyed and wan, but speaking with great conviction. "They'll ask me questions and I'll give them answers."

Jule was appalled. "Oh, Sammy, acting is only questions and

answers but what happens when a guy feeds you a statement?"

"I'll ask, 'What did you say?'"

Jule suddenly realized that his playboy, song-writing partner very much wanted that lead part. He wanted to make a Broadway debut as a full-fledged star; have his name up in lights.

Sammy looked around for approval.

There was an actor in the show of the Shakespearean school, a man of great dignity. He arose to about six feet three and said of Sammy, in a deep, rolling voice, straight out of *Hamlet:* "I will coach him for the part. I will personally apply his make-up."

Sammy, already transported, looked at the *Hamlet* man and replied, "Thank you."

Jule thought, God has absolutely doomed us.

Samuel Cahn went onstage the first night in Philadelphia resembling Groucho Marx's uncle, the baggy one. He wore Eddie Davis's costume, which did not fit; he wore horn-rimmed glasses. He appeared to be about eighty years old while doing his "acting is only questions and answers" routine, and the notices in the papers next morning were total kills, both for Sammy Cahn and *Glad to See You.*

Meanwhile, veteran song-and-dance man Eddie Foy had been lined up to replace Cahn as the star of a flop. Foy notified Wolper that it would take him three weeks to learn the part, so it was planned that Foy would open at the next stop, Boston.

Most of this period Jule Styne was in his hotel room, occasionally sobbing. *This was my first Broadway show and I took it very seriously. The name of Jule Styne was on the music and here we were being dumped on before the first act ended. The exact word is humiliation.*

Up the street in the Forrest Theatre was a Kauffman–Hart musical, *Seven Lively Arts,* a highly sophisticated, glittering production. It, too, was having problems but they did not compare to the daily horrors unfolding on Wolper's show. Then, miraculously, a writer named Cy Howard, married to a girl in the cast of *Seven Lively Arts,* ventured across the street, watched and heard *Glad to See You* and said flatly to Busby Berkeley, "I know what's wrong with your show."

Cy Howard was kidnapped that very night. He was wined and dined in Berkeley's suite, given caviar and champagne as he spouted out solutions. The ideas sounded good. In the early-morning hours, he told the principals of the show, "I'll have to rewrite from page one." Page one or page fifty, little difference insofar as Jule was concerned.

A few days later, Jule visited Cy Howard's hotel room and saw that every page of the libretto was tacked to the walls with glass pushpins. *It was like a game he was playing, put the infantry here; take the cavalry over there. But I thought there was no way to hurt that script. He could have shredded it for pulp and not hurt it.*

Cy Howard finished in ten days, delivered the new script to Berkeley and the company entrained for Boston. Over the weekend, the disheartened, battered cast had to learn new scenes, new lines; four new dances. Styne and Cahn provided two new songs.

The show reopened in Boston on a Wednesday not long before Christmas. Snow was on the ground and the sky was bleak, Jule remembers. Sammy Cahn played the first dress rehearsal still looking like Groucho's lost uncle, and then Eddie Foy mercifully took over, retiring Sammy. When Foy performed his individual numbers, there was life and response. Otherwise, the show remained a graveyard, and if the Philly critics had done a kill job, the Boston reviewers went for complete slaughter.

After reading the morning papers, Sammy said sadly to Jule, "You have a family. Why don't you go on back to the coast?" Jule, out $40,000 in addition to being lanced by the critics, was thinking of that; thinking how nice it would be to jump in his pool and forget that Wolper and Berkeley existed. He quickly agreed.

Sammy and Jule went to the train station together and Sammy saw his partner climb aboard. Seconds before the train began to move, Jule yelled from the boarding platform, "Sammy, I saw George Abbott for a moment last night. He said, 'Open with the closing.' "

Sammy shrugged. George Abbott had a reputation for making hits. Few people were as knowledgeable as Mr. Abbott, theatrically. His *On the Town,* the Comden–Green vehicle, was already a big hit. This was George Abbott, at full creative power, giving free advice.

Sammy yelled back, "Okay," as the train chuffed off, and then immediately went to Busby Berkeley with Abbott's suggestion.

Two nights later, *Glad to See You* opened with the closing. It did not seem possible that anything could harm this whimpering collection of words and music, yet the exchange of material produced an effect similar to that of a ship turning upside down. The forever curtain dropped soundlessly the following night. Closing notices were tacked up.

Meanwhile, Jule Styne was crossing the country toward the land of orange blossoms and swimming pools. He got off the train only once, debarking in Chicago to buy a paper and call a bookie.

However, the initial try at Broadway was not a total loss for

Styne–Cahn. "Guess I'll Hang My Tears Out to Dry," recorded by Sinatra and Ray Charles, became a standard. Another song from the show, "B-postrophe, K-postrophe, Brooklyn," was used in *West Point Story*, a James Cagney–Doris Day film.

Sammy and I were doing a score to a Danny Kaye movie in early 1945 at the Goldwyn studio and Sammy said, "Why don't we write a popular song here?" I said, "Goldwyn told me specifically that he doesn't want a hit song. He wants a class song." So we started to work on a sixteen-bar song in our little bungalow. That day there was a house painter in there doing the ceiling, working on a low scaffold. Sammy always lifts his head up when he's rhyming, and he was looking up at the painter and the ceiling, mumbling "true" and "flew" and "you," trying to get a line. Suddenly, the painter looked down at him to say, "Blue?" We broke up. Jesus, even house painters were writing songs.

The scene quickly shifted to MGM, where Sinatra had been signed for *Anchors Aweigh*, costarring Gene Kelly. If *Step Lively*, at RKO, had been largely junk, *Anchors Aweigh* was easily forecast as a smash, not only for Messrs. Sinatra and Kelly but for Messrs. Styne–Cahn as well.

MGM had great plans for Frank in signing him to a three-picture deal, and decided to provide Sinatra with the very best musical talent on the lot. They said, more or less, "Now, we have Jerome Kern and Harry Warren and Arthur Schwartz, and we'll even get Cole Porter for you, Frank, if you want him."

Sinatra, typically straightforward, loyal to those who were loyal to him, was said to have replied, "Gentlemen, you don't understand. If Jule Styne and Sammy Cahn don't do this picture, I'm out of it, too." For those few words, no matter what happened later on, Sinatra can do no wrong in the collective memory book of Styne–Cahn. It was at that very moment that they most needed push and support in the back-stabbing alleys of the studio. They were fresh from a Broadway debacle, and taking ungentle ribs from fellow songwriters.

In turn, Jule and Sammy provided Sinatra and Kelly with such memorable songs as "I Fall in Love too Easily" and "I Begged Her" and "The Charm of You." *Anchors Aweigh* was indeed a solid smash. Gene Kelly's dancing enchanted both audiences and critics. The latter also took note that Sinatra was much more than a singer. He could act, too.

Despite the success of the picture, the slow disintegration of the Styne–Cahn team likely began at MGM. Jule already knew that Sammy wrote like a skip-hop tornado; that his lyrics could be brilliant and often were. Yet Jule often had the distinct feeling that Sammy did not like to rewrite his words; that they became "set" too quickly.

It was thought around town that Sammy Cahn was the tougher of the pair. He always had more lip; seemed pugnacious at times. But Cahn himself knew that Jule had the ultimate knife, that Jule would wait quietly and then drive to the bone. One memorable day at the MGM musical table, when the partners were being ribbed about *Glad to See You,* Jule arose to say generally, "You fellows sit on your ASCAP and go home to your goddamn Beverly Hills pools and don't have the guts to take a chance. You write songs about Scranton and you've never been to Scranton. You write songs about ghettos and you've never seen a ghetto. I was born in one. That show was rotten but we tried and we have our self-respect."

Then he regally departed.

6

I once suggested to Jule that he should go see a psychiatrist who might cure him of his gambling. Several days later I saw him and asked, "Did you go see that shrink?" Jule answered, "Well, I went to his office but didn't go in. I saw the hours posted on his door, nine to five, and didn't like the odds."

—HARRY CRANE, 1977

In the mid-forties there was a very select group of musical greats who gathered one Monday night each month in the home of Jerome Kern, the dean of them all. These gatherings often included Ira Gershwin, brother of the late George, lyricist of *Lady, Be Good!* and *Porgy and Bess* and *Of Thee I Sing.* He'd also written *Lady in the Dark* with Kurt Weill.

Then there was composer Harry Warren, who'd come into prominence in 1922 with "Rose of Rio Grande," and had since contributed such timeless songs as "Cheerful Little Earful" and "Jeepers, Creepers" and "Shuffle Off to Buffalo" and "I've Got a Girl in Kalamazoo," plus the Glenn Miller sensation, "Chattanooga Choo Choo." Harold Arlen, a dapper New Yorker, sometimes attended. He'd written the music for *The Wizard of Oz;* "Blues in the Night," with Johnny Mercer and the Broadway hit, *Bloomer Girl.*

Mercer often came to these affairs, as did Hoagy Carmichael, all to talk about what was occurring on the musical stage, in Hollywood and New York. If anyone had written a new song, it might be played that night. There was no more exclusive popular musicfest anywhere on earth.

Of course, the dean himself held the stage, and deservedly so. Jerome Kern had entered the theater in 1905, with five songs in a Broadway musical. His first complete original score, for *The Red Petticoat*, played the Great White Way in nineteen-twelve. One song, "They Didn't Believe Me" from *The Girl from Utah,* written in 1914, is still a standard. When Victor Herbert heard the melody that year, he said flatly, "This man will inherit my mantle."

Then came the Kern scores for *Show Boat* (1927), with lyrics by Oscar Hammerstein, *The Cat and the Fiddle* (1931), *Roberta* (1933) and *Very Warm for May* (1939). Kern moved from New York to Hollywood in 1939 to concentrate on films and his score for *The Last Time I Saw Paris,* lyrics by Hammerstein, had won the 1941 Academy Award—his second Oscar.

One summer day in 1945, music publisher Buddy Morris, earning considerable money from the Styne–Cahn hits and elated with all their progress, said to Jule, "I'm going to take you to that exclusive club of ASCAP leeches. I called Kern and he said he'd like to meet you." Jule was thrilled and could hardly wait for the weekend to pass.

He was nervous Monday night when Morris picked him up on Elm Drive, but then slightly embarrassed by Morris's introduction in Kern's living room: "I want all of you to meet Jule Styne, who doesn't sit on his ASCAP. He writes songs every week, sometimes every day. He'll eventually have a bigger ASCAP rating than you, Harry [Warren]."

Jule knew everyone in the room except Kern. Hoagy Carmichael was there; Ira Gershwin. Harold Arlen.

Kern said, "I've heard a lot about you. You've got a No. 1 song now. Please play it for us."

Still nervous, Jule rendered "It's Been a Long, Long Time," a song written specifically for the girls left behind by servicemen. "Kiss me once, and kiss me twice, and kiss me once again, it's been a long, long time . . ."

When he'd finished, Kern said, as Styne recalls, "Listen, that's the hardest kind of song to write. A sixteen-bar song. It feels like it's thirty-two. Musically, it's a fulfillment. I had the same trouble writing 'The Siren Song.' It took me forever."

Good God, Jule thought, I'm actually talking to *the* Jerome Kern.

Harry Warren requested "Time after Time." Someone else asked for "I Fall in Love Too Easily."

As the evening wore on, Jule was invited to become a permanent member of the Monday Night Music Club. He went home feeling as if he'd been anointed by the Gershwins, living and dead.

The next night, at a friend's dinner party, the phone rang, and the hostess said, "Jule, there's a call for you."

Jule replied, "Find out who it is, and I'll call later."

The hostess said, "Jerome Kern."

A hush settled over the table as Jule rushed to the phone.

"I'm sorry to interrupt your party, but I go to bed early," said Kern. "Could I see you tomorrow morning for breakfast? About ten. It's important."

Jule said, "I'd be delighted."

Most of the talk at the dinner party the rest of the evening was about Jerome Kern. Was Jule going to do a musical that Kern didn't have time to write? Was it possible that Kern wanted to collaborate; wanted some special material for his own show, whatever that might be?

Jule didn't sleep much that night. He'd been invited to share breakfast with the great Kern. The speculation continued: Has Kern suggested me for a movie? He has an idea and wants my opinion. Does he think, in fact, that I'm the best musical dramatist around?

Jule arrived promptly at ten at Kern's Beverly Hills mansion and the composer himself answered the door. "Are bacon and eggs all right?"

Toast and coffee would have been fine. Just coffee would have been enough. Jule was not thinking about food.

During the leisurely breakfast, Kern asked about Styne's musical background; how he wrote; when he wrote; what made him write; where and with whom had he studied? What were his immediate plans? He certainly should not be discouraged by one Broadway flop. The best remedy was to immediately launch another show.

Jule was now ready for the "important" news.

Breakfast finished, they went into Kern's library and Jule looked at dozens of awards on the walls as Kern opened his desk drawer. The hand was destined to draw out a script, Jule thought. Instead, it extracted a daily racing form.

Kern looked over and said, "I hear you're the greatest handicapper in town. Ira Gershwin told me."

7

Jule was always distracted by the good life. One time he was working on an MGM picture with Sammy Cahn. Producer Joe Pasternak was impatient and wired Jule in Palm Springs, asking "Where is the score?" Jule wired back, "Have been working seven days a week. Will now try eight."

—HARRY CRANE, 1977

Sammy and Jule had been charting the progress of the war in music. During hectic 1944, they'd written "I'll Walk Alone" for a Charles K. Feldman film, starring Dinah Shore. Walking alone was waiting for the guy to get back from Iwo Jima; from Sicily. Shore sang it beautifully and it became a hit. Sammy suggested doing that song, a takeoff on Loesser's "I Don't Want to Walk Without You, Baby."

The clang of celebration bells after V-E Day, in May 1945, had barely cleared the air when Styne–Cahn wrote "It's Been a Long, Long Time." All the shooting was over in Europe. The girls were waiting. What better way to strike the romance chords again?

Then on a very, very hot day in the late summer of 1945, the partners were at the corner of Hollywood and Vine, waiting for a red light. Sammy said to Jule, "Why don't we go to the beach?"

Jule replied, "Why don't we write a winter song?"

So they went to the Morris Music Company on Vine Street, and Sammy used a spare typewriter to dummy-up lyrics for "Let It Snow, Let It Snow, Let It Snow." Jule sat down at a nearby desk to scrawl the notes. They polished the tune on Elm Drive that day. The song was another winner, one that fills the airways each and every Christmas.

Jule's melodic structure, as usual, was very simple. *There's an interesting thing about my popular songs: Harmonically, they all have a Bach line. They are pure. In a Bach theme, all you have to hear is the base line and the melodic line. You don't need the in-between.*

In the fall, well after V-J Day, the pair wrote "The Victory Polka," tapping that cult as well as the general audience. The song sold several million Bing Crosby–Andrews Sisters records. It remains a polka standard, and is again evidence of the commerciality of Styne–Cahn. Aside from the songs created specifically for film stories, they trended with events and the national mood, with seasons, returning to the songwriter's stock in trade of romance when the headlines were bare of inspiration.

In 1946, Sammy said to Jule, "Remember how lucky we got with that winter song last year? Let's do something for summer." This time they were rewarded on The Hit Parade for "The Things We Did Last Summer." About the same time, one of Sammy's laundry slips appeared with a scrap of sentence on it, "Give me five minutes more, give me five minutes more . . ." A few last kisses on the doorstep. The song went into *Earl Carroll's Sketchbook,* a Republic picture, and became an international hit.

By now, Sammy Cahn was well on his way to becoming a millionaire and Jule Styne was still teetering around the edges of bankruptcy, giving his all to the horses and cards.

"Win big, lose big, the man was possessed," said his brother, Maury. Once they went to Arlington Park together, while Jule was in Chicago, visiting his parents. He was either en route to New York, or returning to the coast. "Jule was betting five hundred across the board, a thousand across the board that day. All kinds of wild bets. So he bets on number seven and when the horse came down the track, it was running inside, right up against the stands. We never even saw him. Then Jule, in a fit of rage, tore up the tickets. He'd bet two thousand across the board. Well, that horse that we couldn't see actually finished second and we got down on our hands and knees to pick up the pieces of tickets. We spent an hour with the stewards getting the payoff. One day in California I saw him win sixteen thousand. Another time I saw him drop fifteen thousand without batting an eye. My brother could never get it into his head that he was a reckless gambler, not a good one."

Jule did try to keep in touch with his parents, though he often felt he wasn't doing enough for them. At one point, when Jule had three songs on the Hit Parade simultaneously, Isadore phoned him on the Coast with a request to come to New York for a convention of egg-candlers, a union-sponsored dinner-dance affair. "You'll do me much good by coming," said Isadore.

There was other business in New York to be conducted so Jule made an appearance at the ball, playing and singing his hits. Isadore wore a large badge that said, "Entertainment Committee, Father of Jule Styne." Yet, on such visits, Isadore would say, "When are you going to stop all this free-lancing and get a permanent job at the studio? Maybe conduct the orchestras. Play good music like you used to."

Isadore's ambivalance continued to baffle Jule. On a stopover in the Windy City, Jule said to his mother and father, "Look, I'll take you to dinner and then to *Pal Joey.*" A tour company had revived the 1940 Rodgers–Hart musical.

Isadore said, "We don't want to see *Pal Joey.* We want to go to the Yiddish Theatre."

Jule said, "I got you a gold pass to that theater. You can go anytime you want."

Isadore said, "We've been to the Yiddish Theater nine times already, and thank you."

"Well, why do you want to go tonight?" asked Jule.

Anna said, "We've been nine times already but not with you."

"You are important," said Isadore.

So they attended the Yiddish Theatre. *It was a terrible company in the Douglas Park Auditorium, with wooden chairs, and before the show I said, "Would you like to go backstage?" They said they would. So I took them back there. Has-been Jewish actors. Costumes falling apart. There was such drabness. Such feeling of despair. The man who ran the show was Ted Wallenstein, and he called the cast out. These little people crept from the shadows. In a loud voice, Wallenstein said, "This is the famous songwriter, Jule Styne. He makes more in one day than you do in a year." And do you know what happened? My father applauded loudly. I wanted to run.*

But the mid-forties, when such stratospheric personalities as Sinatra, Victor Young, Axel Stordahl, Jo Stafford, Tony Martin and Oscar Levant went in and out of the Elm Street address for attendance at dinners or parties, were really the "Sinatra" years. The Stynes—battling Mama and Papa, and the boys—frequently went to Frank's home in the swank Toluca Lake area.

Earlier, Jule and Sammy had traveled across the country by train with the entire Sinatra entourage—Frank's children as well as conductor-arranger Stordahl; managers and "gofers" of one category or another. These were hysterical trips, but Frank, at the height of his bobbysoxer appeal, seemed to love every minute of them. Sammy and Jule often wrote special material for him. One trip, when Frank, taking over an entire Pullman, was headed for New York, he detrained fifteen miles out of Gotham because an estimated 12,000 fans awaited at Penn Station.

However, Sinatra was having marital problems of his own with quiet and stable Nancy, and his close friends did almost anything to keep him at home. For a while, there were theatrical productions at the Sinatra address, full-scale shows with some of the most expensive talent on earth gladly participating, entertaining each other. Wives appeared in the sketches, frequently written by Harry Crane. Guests sometimes numbered a hundred at the black-tie affairs.

Jule wrote music for the shows; Sammy wrote patter and lyrics. They would often stop paid work at a studio to hurriedly get something together for *the show.* Jule on the piano and Maury on sax, backed as "orchestra." Frank, preparing for them enthusiastically, became a carpenter and electrician, as well as producer. He sawed lumber; hung lights; borrowed costumes from MGM and other studios.

The late Richard Whorf, actor and artist, fashioned a revue curtain for the home entertainment. Comedians Phil Silvers and Rags Ragland, actors Peter Lawford and Bill Goodwin performed; Danny Thomas was onstage; music men such as Stordahl and Paul Weston played. Anything to keep Frank home; anything to keep him amused. The shows often had complete scores; intricate sketches, based on character, affording intimate glimpses of the stars; glimpses never to be seen or heard in public. One evening, Phil Silvers's wife sang, "I'm the Wife of the Life of the Party," a devastating personal satire. The performance that Danny Thomas would give at a Sinatra show was quite different from a Thomas performance in Vegas or on the air. Once Frank appeared in blackface to do his version of "Mammy." For one New Year's Eve show, the production, talent alone, would have cost a million dollars in Las Vegas.

One show was unforgettable for Jule, and it was on a night, ironically, when there wasn't a show. Guests were there, but no sketches had been put together. Each of the guests was required to do a solo thing, off-the-cuff. Jule's turn came, and he whispered to Frank, "Just ask them, 'Has anyone heard the new score to *Annie Oakley,* by

Jerome Kern?' " (Eventually, *Annie Get Your Gun,* completed by Irving Berlin after Kern's death.)

"What's that?" Frank frowned.

"Just ask, that's all."

Jule hadn't heard the score, either. Kern hadn't finished it. But there was a half-formed melody in Jule's head and it sounded, to his mind's ear, almost pure Kern.

Jule sat down at the piano, turning to the guests to lie, "I've only heard a couple of the songs . . ." Then he built the few notes of the unfinished melody into a full song, ad-lib composing as he went along.

After he finished, there were "oh's" and "ah's" for the "Kern" melody. Requested to play other songs from the same score, Jule confessed that he "couldn't remember them." In fact, Jule almost forgot his own ad-lib composition. Later on, Sammy remembered it and they collaborated on "Time After Time," first performed as a gag in Sinatra's home.

Eventually, Sinatra organized "The Swooners," a softball team with regulation uniforms and scheduled games. Young Norton Styne served as bat boy. The players included Sinatra, actors Anthony Quinn and Barry Sullivan; writer-director Don McGuire, a former major leaguer; Jule and son Stanley; Sammy Cahn, Harry Crane; other assorted friends and business associates. They played Saturdays and Sundays on the Beverly Hills High School field against such opponents as Les Brown's band; pick-up teams from NBC, CBS or the studios. Once, "The Swooners" challenged a Marine team from San Diego and were demolished.

"Christalmighty, that's humiliating," said Sinatra. "What can we do?"

Jule called his old friend Coon Rosen, the former Chicago blackjack dealer and now the nation's No. 1 softball pitcher. The Marines were challenged again, and Rosen, imported from Phoenix, was paid $175 to pitch a shutout. It was all for laughs.

The home theatrical productions and the weekend softball games ended just as suddenly as they had begun, like a match flaring and burning out, with little or no comment.

Styne–Cahn were then signed by MGM for Sinatra's *It Happened in Brooklyn,* filmed early in 1947, directed by Richard Whorf, with a screenplay by Isobel Lennart. Singer Kathryn Grayson, Peter Lawford and Jimmy Durante co-starred.

A slight rift between Sammy and Jule had occurred several years previously. Jule had suggested that both men acquire a mutual agent. Eddie Traubner had been Sammy's close friend and agent for years, but Jule didn't want Traubner to represent them as a team, figuring Eddie would always favor Cahn.

Cahn had replied that if there was a choice between leaving Jule or Eddie Traubner, Jule would have to go. The words had not been forgotten, though both men continued to be good friends and to collaborate very successfully.

Now, on the set of *It Happened in Brooklyn,* Traubner walked up to Sinatra, unaware that Jule was standing behind a flat several feet away. Traubner said to Frank, "You know, Sammy would like to do your next picture with Harry Warren instead of Jule."

Frank eyed Traubner and said quietly, "Jesus, Eddie, I don't know how to tell you this but I've already set my next picture. I'd like Jule to write with Ira Gershwin."

That response was typical of Sinatra, who loathed back-dealing of any kind, and had no love for Traubner, anyway.

Sammy called Jule at home within the hour. "Hey, what is all this shit about you and Ira Gershwin writing for Frank?"

Jule answered coldly. "You're the most ungrateful son of a bitch I've ever known. You put this up behind my back. Frank said that to make schmucks out of both you and Eddie. If anybody writes his next picture, it'll be you and myself. But I'm shocked to think that you allowed Eddie to do that . . ."

Things were never quite the same between Jule Styne and Sammy Cahn after that day, yet they continued to fashion such hits as "Time After Time." They also did another Broadway show; other films. But there was a cloud over the relationship.

Looking at, and listening to, Sammy Cahn, it did not seem possible that this brash New Yorker, who squeaked through public school, could create the lyrics for some of the most beautiful popular songs ever written.

The Christmas Waltz

Frosted window panes, candles gleaming inside,
Painted candy canes on the tree:
Santa's on his way; he's filled his sleigh with
things—
Things for you and me.

It's that time of year when the world falls in love,
    Every song you hear seems to say—Merry Christmas!
May your New Year's dreams come true.
And this song of mine, in three-quarter time,
Wishes you and yours the same thing, too.

They were songwriters but they liked the fights, too, which was a good sign.

—JOSEPH KIPNESS, 1977

Sammy and Jule had been smarting over *Glad to See You* since the winter of 1944, and had been story-searching for several years. Jule had also asked MCA to find another Broadway property for them. *I simply could not take the crushing defeat of that Wolper–Berkeley thing. It sat like a rock in my belly.*

One Sunday morning in the early spring of 1947, *The New York Times Book Review* section carried a half dozen paragraphs on Stephen Longstreet's semi-autobiographical *The Sisters Liked Them Handsome,* a story about his family in New Brunswick, N. J., a period piece with ample chuckles. Jule thought it might have a chance as a musical, and on Monday he bought a copy of the book, read it and liked it, then took it over to Cahn. Sammy's reaction was also favorable but he had some reservations about ever trying a Broadway show again. That foundering Busby Berkeley ship turning upside down in Boston still haunted him.

Styne–Cahn discussed the project with Longstreet, who wanted to do the libretto. He'd done about everything else in the way of writing, and was an accomplished painter as well. Styne–Cahn were leery of Longstreet's capabilities as a librettist, but it seemed the only way to acquire the story. They agreed he could do the show book.

Then Jule went to MCA to ask for a leave of absence from their representation. The agency had been vainly searching for a suitable vehicle for three years. *I knew the show would have to be put together in New York, not Hollywood. So Sammy and I went to a small agency headed by Howard Hoyt, and he eventually packaged Jerome Robbins to choreograph, Oliver Smith to do the sets, and Miles White for costumes. We'd seen Robbins's talent in* On the Town *and decided we had to have him.*

Sammy and Jule went to work on the score in Hollywood, chiefly on Elm Drive, and then Jule heard that Broadway producer Herman Levin was in town. Jule lured him to Elm Drive to hear the score, six songs at that point. Then they gave Levin the first draft of the Longstreet libretto.

Levin later said, "I had certain reservations about it. The character of the swindler, played by Phil Silvers, vanished at the end of the first act. I said to them, 'Fellows, he's the most interesting character in the play, and I think you should keep him all the way.' The libretto was then changed but they never got back to me."

The play, set in 1913, is about a couple of swindlers, Harrison Floy (Silvers) and his assistant, Mr. Pontdue (Joey Faye), who arrive in New Brunswick to sell swampland real estate and fix the upcoming Rutgers–Princeton game. They become involved with Papa and Mama Longstreet, an unmarried daughter, and little Stevie Longstreet himself.

Of the fifteen songs in the show, Jule believed that two of them, "Papa, Won't You Dance with Me?" and "I Still Get Jealous," had great possibilities, both for vocal execution and dance. With the right girl singer, they could be show hits, he thought.

The team went on to New York with their completed score and libretto, having been summoned by George S. Kaufman and Max Gordon. Messrs. Kaufman and Gordon listened to the songs and read the libretto, making a quick decision. No thanks. Sammy and Jule swallowed the rejection and went off in search of other producers. At the same time, Monte Proser, owner of the Copacabana night club, and a ladies' garment manufacturer, Joseph Kipness, were looking for a show.

A burly man with a slight accent, native of Odessa, Russia, Joe Kipness could have passed as a bouncer of a waterfront dive. He'd worked as a sideshow man on Coney Island at the age of fourteen; became a trucker's helper in the garment district and then headed the

Garment Center Trucking Association when he was twenty. Off and on, Joe Kipness had admittedly been a strong-arm man. Other enterprises developed from his trucking group. Despite his appearance and tough talk, Kipness had a deep love for the theater and angeled shows. As partner with Alexander Cohen, he'd co-produced three on Broadway, all flops. Cohen had selected these properties and now Kipness wanted to choose one of his own.

Kipness said, "I hung out in the Copa lounge about five o'clock, and took care of business—ladies' garments at that time—and decided to do something with Monte Proser. A show, a café. Something. Then he introduced me to Jule and Sammy, and I learned they liked fights. So I took them to Madison Square Garden. Then I found out they had this show. Well, I liked the songs they did . . ."

A few days later, Styne–Cahn were walking down Madison Avenue, still in search of a producer, when Proser spotted them and treaded toward them, saying, "Let me make a call and then come on to the club."

Some fifteen minutes later, they entered the stale and darkened Copa and there sat Kipness. He tossed twenty thousand-dollar bills on the table and said, "Take them. That's your option money." Neither Styne nor Cahn had ever seen a thousand-dollar bill until that day.

Kipness said, "I often carried a lot of cash on me but had gone down to the bank to get the thousand-dollar bills. I didn't think those fellows could refuse them. They didn't. Then I took the show to Alexander Cohen and had him read the script. He called me to say, 'Forget it, Joe.' At that moment, I knew I had a hit."

The team first played the score for choreographer Jerome Robbins, who was among the already signed staff members. He'd read the libretto. He listened to the music and said he'd always wanted to do a cops-and-robbers thing onstage, a wild ballet. He envisioned it as being very long, perhaps eight or ten minutes. He talked about a Keystone Kops approach. Both Sammy and Jule were intrigued with Robbins.

Kipness soon added more expertise to the project. "I had a second apartment in the Park Central Hotel, a place to entertain girls, and had a piano put in there. Then I brought George Abbott up so Jule and Sammy could play and sing the score. He listened and said, 'You have a deal.' So Mr. Abbott became director of what was soon titled *High Button Shoes.*"

To all but a very few close friends, George Abbott was always "Mr. Abbott." He displayed few emotions. He was cold and hard and dry from the first meeting with Styne–Cahn. He'd earned his "Mr. Abbott" and knew it. His answers were usually "yes" or "no" and not much between.

Robbins has said, "I've been fortunate enough to work with two masters in the theater. Each is named George. One is known as Mr. A (Abbott); the other as Mr. B (Balanchine)."

Jule was wary of both Abbott and Robbins. *Not so much physically but in terms of their personalities, I felt like a grape between two sheets of steel. Both Abbott and Robbins could chill you with a single look.*

To conduct the orchestra for *High Button Shoes,* a large, bluff but congenial man was signed: Milton Rosenstock. He'd just finished a flop, *Barefoot Boy,* after conducting the successful *Finian's Rainbow.*

Not yet thirty years old, Rosenstock had been in *Who's Who in America* since the age of nineteen. A Juilliard graduate, he'd conducted a symphony orchestra in Brooklyn at the age of eighteen; he'd conducted the 110-piece orchestra for Sunday concerts in Central Park when he was twenty. Drafted into the Army when he was twenty-two, he'd been Irving Berlin's conductor for *This Is the Army.*

Mr. Rosenstock firmly believed that he knew more about music than did Mr. Jule Styne, whom he first met in a hotel room in Manhattan. He came up to listen to the score and was greeted by Phil Silvers with his usual toothy, cheery "Hello, hello, hello." It was in that room that Rosenstock first heard Jule's barrelhouse way of playing piano.

Not many weeks later, in rehearsal, they clashed. Rosenstock was not accustomed to being screamed at by any composer, and this little man from the Coast was undeniably screaming during a chorus rehearsal. "There's something wrong, I tell you," Jule yelled at Rosenstock.

"Where?" Milton asked.

"Right there," said Jule, tapping the music. "A chord is off. A LOUSY chord."

Milton ran through the music again, and could hear nothing wrong. He walked away, holding his temper, had a cup of coffee, and returned. Jule was still by the podium. "I tell you something is wrong."

"Do you want to bet?" asked Rosenstock, now angry.

"You're damn right I do," yelled Jule.

So Rosenstock took the section, looked again at the music, played it on the piano, and it sounded perfect; exactly as written. He said, "All right, kids, let's sing it now."

The chorus began and Jule suddenly yelled, "There . . ."

Milton stopped and ran it again. He knew immediately what was wrong. Clearly, a chord was not balanced. But he said to himself, Could it possibly be that that little bastard can hear so much? The chord was there, all right, but wasn't strong enough. The third of a chord is very important. Otherwise, it cannot be determined whether it is major or minor.

Yet Milton wasn't all that sure that Jule really knew what was wrong with the chord. Perhaps he was just guessing. So he went to the singer, a hefty Irish boy, and whispered, "Go to this note."

Jule asked suspiciously, "What did you do?"

"Nothing," replied the conductor.

Then Milton ran the section, and the Irish singer strengthened the note, as instructed.

Jule frowned. "It sounds right now."

Milton went back to the singer. "Take it out now."

They sang the piece once again and Jule screamed, "Goddammit, it's wrong again."

Milton grinned, "Yes, it is," and they became the best of friends.

Veteran Broadway star Vivienne Segal had been signed for the part of Mama Longstreet but then Jule saw Nanette Fabray perform in *Meet the People.* She was sensational, he thought; would be much better than Segal in the Mama Longstreet role. There was a problem —Segal's contract was for the run of the play. There were no forgiving clauses or loopholes.

Jule said to Kipness, "I'm the only one who can get her out. I'll do an audition and not play 'Papa' or 'I Still Get Jealous."

Kipness then arranged for Segal to attend an "angel" audition in Jule's apartment at the Gotham Hotel. As soon as the potential backers were gathered, Jule played the score, purposely dropping the hit numbers. He watched as Miss Segal ran out of the room to phone Joe Kipness. "What happened to 'Papa' and 'Jealous'? My big numbers."

Kipness said, "They're out. The boys are writing new material."

"Then I'm out, too," said Segal. "The only reason I took the show was because of those numbers."

Kipness said, "Sorry," and then with Monte Proser immediately sought out Nanette Fabray. She was signed within the week. Jule's treachery was "for the good of the show," he maintains. As it turned out, he was correct.

With the Keystone Kops chase number as subject, Milton Rosenstock approached Jerome Robbins to ask who had been chosen to write the ballet music. Robbins replied that Jesse Meeker was going to be the dance rehearsal pianist and arrange the dance music, but no composer had been chosen.

One composer had volunteered to do the job—Jule Styne. But Robbins, while agreeing that Jule had "big talent," pointed out that he'd never composed serious dance music.

Rosenstock then said, "Listen, this guy pisses music. He knows as much about structure as I do. Maybe more. You can help him." The conductor continued to campaign for Jule, but also advised Robbins, "You've got to ease in with him. He's scared of you. He thinks you're God."

A little later, Jule said excitedly to Milton, "I'm going to write the ballet music."

Robbins remembers, "I asked Jule for themes, this kind of music; that kind. I said things like, 'Give me chase music here, give me fill-in music there . . .' Then the dance arranger took it and made it into the ballet, with my needs in mind. As I recall, I gave Jule the theme to the picnic ballet, so that was a collaborative effort."

Jule remembers something else about that "picnic" number. *We'd written "Papa, Won't You Dance with Me?," a polka that had "hit" written all over it. You need stage room for a polka, and it was being devised for the big picnic scene. But I saw that it wasn't being staged. Jerry was doing the cops-and-robbers thing over and over again. So I walked up to him and asked, "When are you going to stage 'Papa'?"*

Robbins replied, "I'm not going to stage that number."

Jule asked, "What do you mean, you won't stage it?"

Robbins answered, "Anyone can do it. It's a polka."

Jule asked, "Does that also apply for the soft-shoe number, 'I Still Get Jealous'?"

"Yes," said Robbins. "Anyone can do those two."

Jule promptly moved his target. "Mr. Abbott, when does 'Papa' get staged? Jerry doesn't want to do it. Neither will he stage the soft-shoe."

Mr. Abbott had already been complaining about Robbins spending so much time on the Kops ballet. Now, with arms folded, he called Robbins over. In clipped tone he said, "Jerry, Jule tells me you won't stage those two numbers. All right, we'll get someone else. His name is Sammy White." That was that, George Abbott style.

Robbins then walked out of the theater each time that Sammy White staged the numbers.

The rehearsals, with such as Abbott and Robbins around, continued rough and tense. During the first few days Phil Silvers, in particular, was having the jitters. They manifested in his throat. He squeaked and blew lines. He had the confidence of a rabbit and was plainly frightened of Mr. Abbott.

Phil's good friend Sammy Cahn soon went to Mr. Abbott to say, "If you want to see a miracle performed, just walk up to Phil and tell him, 'I'm very pleased with what you're doing.' "

Abbott pulled himself up to his full Protestant height and replied icily to Cahn, "I never tell an actor anything I don't believe."

Sammy tried to control his temper. "You know something: You can be wrong, and I know how wrong you can be."

At that moment, Jule was standing a few feet behind Sammy.

Abbott glared at Cahn. "I don't know what you're talking about."

"I'll tell you what I'm talking about," said Cahn. "Open with the closing. Open with the closing."

Mr. Abbott repeated in icy tones, "I don't know what you're talking about."

Sammy turned to Jule for support but saw that his partner had vanished. He wasn't visible anywhere. In fact it appeared that he wasn't even in the theater. Sammy said to Mr. Abbott, "I'll get back to you. Just remember what I said—Open with the closing."

Sammy then went searching for Jule and found him outside the theater looking at the traffic. Sammy yelled, "Why the hell are you out here? I had Abbott by the balls. I really had him."

Jule shifted around on his feet. "He didn't say it."

Sammy was stunned. "He didn't say it?"

Jule shook his head.

Sammy remembered watching *Glad to See You* as it turned over like a bloated whale after they'd shifted the last scene to the front, supposedly on Abbott's advice. Sammy sat down on the curb and looked up. "Jule, why did you tell me that?"

Styne laughed weakly. "You wouldn't have done it if it had been my suggestion."

Sammy sat there a long time and then admitted, "I guess not."

But Abbott later discussed *Glad to See You* with Jule, though he'd never witnessed the show. "When something is dying, you must go every night. It takes pain and patience. You learn from death."

High Button Shoes tried out at the Forrest Theatre in Philadelphia and though the critics were lukewarm to the book, they were captivated by Miss Fabray and ecstatic over Robbins's Keystone Kops ballet. Jerome Robbins was clearly the creative hero of the show, from the production standpoint. The ballet is now a Broadway classic.

On opening night in Philly, Fabray was on her third encore after "Papa," staged by Sammy White following Robbins's refusal to become involved. Phil Silvers was on next, standing in the wings, yelling "Get her the hell off!" Then Fabray performed "I Still Get Jealous," the soft-shoe number, also choreographed by Sammy White. She received seven encores.

Next day, Robbins went to work on both numbers. Fabray then began receiving six encores with regularity. *In my opinion, Jerry Robbins always had the right to be wrong. When he was wrong, and proven so, he accepted it gracefully and then immediately went to work for the good of the show.*

High Button Shoes moved to Broadway, opening October 9, 1947, with much the same results. The critics, voting the general Philadelphia reaction, cared little for the libretto but put the Proser–Kipness production into the hit category, joining such neighbors as *Oklahoma!, Brigadoon, Finian's Rainbow* and *Call Me Mister.*

Barnes, in the *Herald Tribune:* "The ballet is a classic, and Jule Styne has written a glittering score."

Time magazine termed Robbins's ballet ". . . a masterpiece of controlled pandemonium." Duke Ellington attended an early performance of *Shoes,* sitting in the first row, and after the ballet, leaned over into the orchestra pit and yelled "Aaaaaaaah," directly at Milton Rosenstock.

"That ballet music by Jule is not merely good music, it is fine music," said Rosenstock.

Frank Sinatra attended the opening night party in the Cottage Room of the Hampshire House, warmly and openly congratulating "his team" of songsmiths. Sinatra assumed they would remain with him.

At any rate, the upstart fellows from Hollywood, the Tin Pan Alley boys, had themselves a big hit show. *High Button Shoes* played for 727 performances on Broadway, winning the Donaldson Award. It was the only new musical of the 1947–48 season to pass the five hundred mark and Nanette Fabray reached stardom by the end of the opening week.

Firmly hooked by the musical theater, Jule stayed on in New York for quite a while, enjoying all the success. *I learned more from George Abbott and Jerome Robbins on that show than I could have learned on ten shows with lesser talents. I couldn't keep away from the theater.*

Sammy Cahn, a bit unhappy that some of his lyrics had been criticized, returned to Hollywood. But even before Jule left New York about a week prior to Christmas, 1947, Jerome Robbins told Milton Rosenstock, "Jule's been bitten, God help him."

Jule did not go directly home. He went to Chicago to be at his mother's bedside. Anna, at the age of sixty-three, was dying. He talked with her in the hospital room. She knew he liked the races. In her mind, Jule was still riding the street cars. She said, "Take the Lawrence Avenue street car to the end of the line. There's the N & W station, and take the N & W to the track . . ."

"Yes, Mama."

Frank Sinatra sent four dozen roses to the hospital each day. They were signed, "To Annie. Get well. Love, Frank."

Anna Stein didn't know very much about Frank Sinatra. She knew he sang popular songs, but she still preferred the classical music Jule had played as a child.

Jule told her he had a big Broadway hit. She squeezed his hand and said, "That's very nice. I'm proud of you."

Anna died Christmas Day, 1947.

9

True or not, I think that one doesn't easily leave Frank Sinatra; sometimes, the privilege of departure seems to be reserved for Mr. Sinatra.

—JULE STYNE, 1977

After the funeral, Jule went back to Elm Drive and Ethel and Stanley and little Nortie. He was now a successful Broadway composer and knew that it would only be a matter of time until he would abandon the sound stages of Hollywood; abandon Sammy Cahn; leave his family.

Nothing had changed at home. Jule and Ethel were polite to each other most of the time but psychologically they were already divorced. In the conversations they did have, Jule talked more about New York than Hollywood; more about finding himself another musical than work in the studios.

Yet he teamed with Sammy to write one song for Sinatra's *Miracle of the Bells,* co-starring Fred MacMurray. The RKO film, based on Russell Janney's best seller, limped along on sentiment and little else. Frank's song, "Ever Homeward," was forgotten by the time the house lights came up. In some ways, this film began the five-year decline of Frank Sinatra.

The last Styne–Cahn work for Sinatra, during that period, was an RKO attempt entitled *It's Only Money,* co-starring Frank with bosomy

Jane Russell and Groucho Marx. So dreary was this story of bank tellers, adding machines and bookies that RKO shelved it in 1948, finally to release it in 1951 as *Double Dynamite,* taking advantage of Miss Russell's extraordinary chestworks in the double entendre title. "Kisses and Tears" and "It's Only Money" were the Styne–Cahn tunes for this movie. Next up for Sinatra was *The Kissing Bandit,* with songs by other than Styne–Cahn.

After *High Button Shoes,* Jule had gone to Frank to say, "The reason that I'm going to write for the theater is that I'm scared. I find myself writing every song for you. That's not good. You'll suffer, too." Jule remembers that Frank stared at him, perhaps taking it the wrong way, though Jule admittedly hadn't chosen his words very well.

Jule further cut the cord by saying, "I can't build my career around you." Jule later said that what he really meant was, There's important show music I have to write. Frank just nodded, as Jule recalls.

Sinatra had recorded two sides from *Shoes,* "Can't You Just See Yourself in Love with Me," and "You're My Girl." They were good songs, but Jule knew that Frank had gone out of his way to do them. Jule continued, suicidally: "I'm now a musical dramatist. I've found out what I want to do. I find that I understand drama and that I can write for Broadway."

Frank nodded again.

From that day on it seemed to Jule that the relationship had cooled. There was usually a smile and sometimes "Hi, Shtimp," but it was never quite the same.

Styne–Cahn then went to Warner Brothers, out in Burbank, on a three-picture deal, two of which starred blue-eyed singer Dennis Morgan. The songs are not worth mentioning, nor are the titles of the films.

At Columbia, Sammy had quickly established himself with Harry Cohn. Now, at Warner's, Jule developed a relationship of a different type with studio head Jack Warner, a man unlike Cohn in many ways but very much like him in the power that he wielded. Warner was impressed with the success of *High Button Shoes* and Jule frequently joined him in the executive dining room. To Jule's relief, they seldom talked about Hollywood; mostly about what was happening on Broadway. At one point, Jule believed that Warner was ready to offer a producership. Jule had already made up his mind to decline. Warner's power frightened him. He realized that he felt more comfortable with the demanding exactness of a George Abbott or a Jerome Robbins than with Warner's empirical control.

For years the Messrs. Warner had owned an Argentine farce entitled *Romance in High C,* a story about a married couple gathering extramarital evidence on each other while on a cruise ship in the South Seas. There'd never been much enthusiasm in the studio story department for the property. Several writers had been exposed to it and had declined.

Then veteran director Mike Curtiz found himself deeply in debt to the Internal Revenue Service. Jack Warner's solution, forwarded to IRS, was to set Mike up in a company and at the propitious moment, Warner would buy the company, letting capital gains pay off the back taxes. Meanwhile, scriptwriters (and brothers) Julius and Philip Epstein very much wanted out of their Burbank contract. Little of the material they'd been assigned had been to their liking. So, in exchange for contract cancellation, they agreed to do the screenplay for another vehicle no one liked, *Romance in High C.* At Warner's suggestion, Styne–Cahn were assigned to the orphan Curtiz project.

Casting was an immediate problem. Comedienne-singer Betty Hutton read the Epstein script and returned it. A few weeks later, in New York, Jule stopped by the Little Club to hear Doris Day sing. He'd known the wholesome but insecure Cincinnati girl since her appearances with the Les Brown band. Day was a good possibility for the film, now titled *Romance on the High Seas,* he thought. What Jule didn't know was that Jack Warner had already rejected her—as sexless.

Also unaware of Warner's opinion, Sammy Cahn engineered a meeting between Day and Mike Curtiz. She came to Burbank in no special dress, no fancy hairdo, just with that apple-pie goodness from Ohio. She had the blues over an unhappy marriage. Mentally and physically, the former Doris Kappelhoff was in no shape to impress Curtiz.

Yet, singing "Embraceable You" for Curtiz, barely moving her hips, Day sold herself without even trying. There was a sincerity in her eyes that was compelling. She sang from inside. Curtiz ordered a screen test and this time Day rendered "What Do You Do On a Rainy Night in Rio?," moving her hips a trifle more.

Marion Hutton, sister of Betty, and Janis Paige also tested for the part. Two days later, Curtiz screened the three tests. Hutton was not adequate; Paige was better. But Day reached out, as natural as rain in Rio. Obviously, the girl that Jack Warner didn't want and the cast-off picture were made for each other.

Jule had written a tango four years previously, and on almost every new film job he'd played it for Sammy Cahn. He often used the tango as a "warm-up" song before settling to whatever piece of music was needed. Creatively, it served both men.

The team now sought a proper song for a night-club sequence between Day and Jack Carson. A Cuban setting, according to the script. As usual, Jule played the tango, warming up.

"That thing again?" said Sammy.

Jule shrugged and kept stroking the keys.

Suddenly sparking, Sammy said, "Play it again, slowly."

Jule did so.

"Once more, slower."

Jule played it again.

Sammy offered, vaguely, "Magic!"

Jule kept on playing.

"It's magic, it's magic," said Sammy, and went to his typewriter to begin pecking out the lyrics.

Newcomer Doris Day, though billed fourth in the film, fell in love with "It's Magic" and sang the song as if the magic had truly worked its spell. In a way, it had.

Day, signed to a personal contract by Curtiz, dominated the otherwise mediocre farce, and she soon became the studio's No. 1 property.

Jule and Sammy finished the Burbank deal with *Romance on the High Seas,* separated and did not see or really speak to each other for almost three years. There was no anger, no words. The partnership simply did a screen dissolve and Sammy went on to begin writing with Jimmy Van Heusen and others. "Be My Love," for Mario Lanza, was a Cahn–Nicholas Brodszky creation. Many others followed, and Sammy Cahn has won more Academy Awards than any other Hollywood lyricist.

Book
IV

THE
NEW YORK
STORY

1

My late father, Jack, had been in Europe with Duke Ellington, and on the boat coming back ran into Oliver Smith, the set designer, who said, "Wouldn't it be a great idea if someone made a musical out of Anita Loos's Gentlemen Prefer Blondes?. . .

—BUDDY ROBBINS, 1977

Having broken with both Sammy Cahn and Frank Sinatra, feeling restless, a bit depressed and uncomfortable at home, Jule flew to New York in mid-1948 and stayed in the Essex House apartment of music publisher Jack Robbins for five or six weeks. The second or third day, Robbins, just back from Europe, brought up Oliver Smith's idea of making a musical of *Gentlemen Prefer Blondes.* He said he thought Jule should be involved in it. In the mood he was in, Jule would have responded to almost any offer.

The idea of converting *Gentlemen Prefer Blondes* to the musical stage wasn't new. Florenz Ziegfeld, Jr., had first approached Miss Loos in 1925, promising a glittering song-and-dance production. But she'd already contracted the story of flapper Lorelei Lee to Edgar Selwyn for play treatment. After a successful Broadway opening in 1926, Paramount Pictures bought the screen rights and gold-digging Lorelei next appeared from the flickers of projection booths in a silent version.

Over the years, stage director John C. Wilson had periodically nudged Miss Loos to adapt her novel, play and screenplay into a musical. She'd been busy on other projects, but at last it fell together.

With Joseph A. Fields (*My Sister Eileen, Wonderful Town, Junior Miss,* etc.) as a distant collaborator, she began work on the libretto. Fields lived in Beverly Hills, not far away from Jule, and was brought into the project to lend experience. Miss Loos had never written a libretto, though she was confident that she could. Fortunately, the story, first serialized in *Harper's Bazaar,* presented few complications. It placed flapper Lorelei and her friend, Dorothy Shaw, aboard the *Île de France,* bound for Paris. The romantic romps that followed as Lorelei sought sugar daddies provided a bountiful but far-fetched comic plot.

Aside from Loos, the staff had a considerable depth of experience. John Wilson would direct; Herman Levin and Oliver Smith, produce. They, in turn, signed Agnes de Mille to choreograph; Miles White for costumes. Smith would design the sets as well as co-produce. Loos agreed to Jule Styne as composer on the glowing recommendation of mutual friend Mike Todd, who recalled—and recounted—Chicago days and his lyrics to "The Moth and the Flame."

Lyricist Leo Robin lived two blocks away from Jule and they knew each other casually. They'd never worked together though each man knew and respected the other's talents. A small, shock-haired, alert pipe-smoking man, Robin had written the lyrics for such songs as "Beyond the Blue Horizon," "June in January," "Love Is Just Around the Corner," Bob Hope's "Thanks for the Memory" and "Louise," forever identified with the late Maurice Chevalier.

One morning, after returning from New York, Jule tapped on Robin's door, and within a few minutes was asking his kindly neighbor if he'd consider writing lyrics for *Gentlemen Prefer Blondes.* Robin wasn't very receptive to the idea. He was making quite enough money writing film songs and his two previous attempts at writing for the stage hadn't been successful, the last one a typical Boston massacre. Critics had shredded *Nice Going,* starring Mary Martin, music by Ralph Rainger. Thinking of time and effort wasted, Robin sucked on his pipe for quite a while.

Jule pointed out that Joe Fields, busy on the libretto, was conveniently nearby for consultation; that Anita Loos, John Wilson, Herman Levin, Oliver Smith and Agnes de Mille were all highly respected professionals; that the idea of doing *Blondes* as a musical had been around for years, vine-ripened to be certain, likely ready for market.

Robin finally said, "Okay, as soon as I see a script, I'll see what I can do with it. I don't promise anything. Maybe I can; maybe I can't.

Maybe I will; maybe I won't." One factor that appealed to Robin was that he could work in the California sun. New York was not an attraction. He disliked the noise and jumble, as well as the weather, winter or summer.

Collaboration was begun about a week later.

Co-producer Herman Levin, later to present *My Fair Lady,* had practiced law before succumbing to Broadway in 1946 with *Call Me Mister.* Next was *No Exit,* and the co-producer of that show was his current partner, Smith. A practical man, Levin had played poker to earn several hundred dollars a week while trying to package *Call Me Mister.* He refused to return to courts and briefs.

About two weeks after Jule and Leo started combining talents, Levin's phone rang. On the other end were Styne and Robin, enthusiastically calling from Jule's home. The musical felt good, and Leo was now excited about the prospects. They placed the phone on the piano and the first rendering of "Diamond's Are a Girl's Best Friend" went over the Bell system in a raspy duet.

Levin liked what he heard and said, "Okay, boys, keep on going." He felt that if the other songs halfway measured up to "Diamonds," he had a chance for a hit.

Levin admittedly had problems with "Stynese" at first. "One of the things that can drive you up the walls with Jule is his constant gushing. He never stops thinking about a show. Then I learned to listen to everything, even when it didn't seem to make much sense. Somewhere along the way would be a brilliant idea. Okay, one day he came rushing in yelling, 'Hey, I got something new for the end of the first act!' It *was* new. Brilliant. It stayed in the whole way. Up to that time we were in deep trouble with the first-act ending. So the Stynese does work, even if it is wearing."

Both Jule and Leo were writing for the character of Lorelei Lee, tailoring their material to what was already on paper. At the time there was no thought of an unknown named Carol Channing. Levin and Wilson had profiled Lorelei Lee, from the Loos–Field libretto, as "terribly sexy, exotic, a cheap kept-lady." They were hoping to find a full-fledged star for the part, not an untried unknown, no matter how "terribly sexy" she might be. And having no idea of the identity of that star, Styne and Robin wisely confined themselves to pure character.

Robin found Styne an easy collaborator. "His reactions were good, and his criticisms of the lyrics were usually right. He is more than just a song writer or composer. Basically, Jule is a fine showman. He knows the value of certain material at the right points and plays up those points musically. Another place where we matched perfectly was that I'd rather write a whole new lyric than try to repair one that isn't working. Jule's the same way. If his music doesn't work, he'll discard it and try something entirely new."

Again, there was no special pattern to the writing; Robin most often provided only a title. "A Little Girl from Little Rock" went from title to music to lyrics. "We really didn't have any trouble with any of the songs, even though we had no idea that Channing would play Lorelei. I'd never even seen her; maybe I'd never heard of her. But, finally, we have this big, funny-looking blonde singing she's a little girl. That's just pure luck, my friend. No genius from any of us there."

One morning, Leo said, "Why don't we do a thing with Coolidge? He was President about then, I think. Keeping cool with Coolidge?"

"I like that," Jule answered.

In the afternoon Jule delivered his "Coolidge" music to Maple Street, and by the end of the next day Leo had set the lyric. It was all low-key and informal.

In September, with about half the score completed, Leo and Jule packed bags and headed for New York. Jule set himself up in style in a $75-a-day suite at the Hampshire House, a move he was later to regret. He was spending heavily, charging off everything to "business." A piano was rented and rolled into the suite.

Two or three songs, plus dance music and the overture, needed to be completed, and both men wanted to be on hand for the auditions, those often heartbreaking apartment or hotel performances given to raise money. The seeking of backers for a Broadway musical has always been frustrating. There is a natural wariness of a new show, particularly since a musical is more expensive than a straight play—an open invitation to be critical. Theater "angels" usually have thick wallets, never harps. Levin had estimated the budget at around $200,000.

Both in California and in New York, Leo Robin often got his best ideas while walking. In this he resembled Frank Loesser, though Loesser usually did his pacing indoors. Night after night, Jule walked Central Park with Leo, wishing that he was in a club or café instead. Not much was said during these three- or four-hour strolls, which was also typical of Loesser. Jule fought to keep his mouth shut. Leo sucked his pipe and walked. Ever so slowly. *All I could hear were crickets, distant traffic and Leo's pipe. I thought I'd go crazy, but sooner or later, maybe by 2:00 A.M., he'd come up with an idea. It was always worth the wait, no matter how much my feet ached.*

Meanwhile, Levin had begun his backer auditions. Oddly enough, though *Blondes* had been successful both on stage and screen, the usual New York play-angels were not impressed. There seemed to be a feeling that too much dust had gathered on the Loos play. At one audition, with Jule at the piano lustily singing the songs and Leo in a corner, quietly observing, the most affluent show investor in New York sat like a granite statue in the front row, arms folded over his belly, face expressionless. By the end of the third song, the man wasn't even listening. He'd found much better entertainment in a chat with his lady of the evening. At the end of the sixth song, Jule glanced at the talkative, disinterested angel, slammed the piano shut and exited wordlessly. Audition over!

Shortly after, another effort was made in the Library Suite of the St. Regis, a richly paneled room on the second floor of the hotel. Among the wealthy people attending that affair on a miserable, rainy night was General Sarnoff, with his RCA millions. Not a dime was raised, and to cap a wasted evening someone stole Herman Levin's umbrella.

Finally, Billy Rose, who owned the Ziegfeld Theatre and wanted the show to play that house, suggested to Levin that he bring together Leland Hayward, Richard Rodgers, Oscar Hammerstein and Josh Logan, definitely an uphill quartet for Jule Styne to entertain. However, the super-critical foursome liked both the songs and the book, and each agreed to put up $5,000. It was "seed" money, and the story was planted the next day in the New York gossip columns. Without mentioning figures, it was let be known that Hayward–Rodgers–Hammerstein and Logan were investing in *Blondes.* By 5:00 P.M. of the following day, Levin had his $200,000 and rejected another $100,000.

Anita Loos remembers that she first saw Jule Styne in Herman Levin's office at the initial production meeting for *Blondes.* They instantly became good friends. Everything that Mike Todd had said about Jule seemed to be true. Miss Loos discovered that Jule indeed was a "most charming and amusing man," and couldn't wait to introduce him to Ruth Dubonnet, her friend from Paris romps of girlhood.

Ruth Dubonnet had been one of the great beauties of the twenties, certainly one of the best-dressed women along the boulevards and in the smart cafés. She knew all manner of dukes and duchesses and writers and artists. First married to painter Walter Goldbeck, her next husband was the Comte de Vallombrosa. She was currently in the process of divorcing her third husband, André Dubonnet, of the apéritif fortune. From 1926 on, Loos, Dubonnet and Marjorie Oelricks, later Mrs. Eddie Duchin, frolicked their way through Paris society. Ruth was still a beautiful woman in 1948, when Oliver Smith invited a select group to a ballet performance at the Metropolitan Opera.

Dubonnet remembers the evening: "Jule was constantly taking pills. He was with a girl that night, and needed an aspirin. I gave him two and on the second day he told me how divine I was, then came over and slipped me the keys to his suite. I was so amused. He said, 'I hope you'll use them.' I handed them back but it gave me an enormous laugh. He was rather cute in a Kewpie-doll way."

She was something very new to me. She was chic, and so worldly. She knew so many things I didn't know and wanted to learn. She was both beautiful and "in," gliding gracefully along the paths of the Herbert Bayard Swopes, the Alfred P. Sloans and the Sarnoffs, an entirely new, lush and different garden for the man from Bethnal Green and Chicago's West Side ghetto.

Ruth introduced him to many people, theatrical and otherwise. "Mr. Baruch, for instance. I took him everywhere as my beau. These people didn't approve at first but accepted him when they saw how talented he was. I corrected his grammar."

Yes, I fell in love with her.

"When I first knew him, we drove into the city from the Swopes' and I lent him five or ten thousand dollars. I didn't know at the time that it was to pay off a bookie."

Stars such as Dolores Gray and Gertrude Niesen were being auditioned for the part of Lorelei Lee but none seemed to be quite right. Then Jule saw Carol Channing in *Lend an Ear,* a bright revue that opened in 1948. Next night, he was back at the theater with Anita Loos. In period costume, Channing could certainly look the part, Jule believed; she had something else, an off-beat new flavor. Loos agreed and said, "I like the satire in her." One by one, all the principals of *Blondes* visited *Lend an Ear.* Not all praised her.

Milton Rosenstock said, to Jule, "For Chrissakes, she can't sing and she looks crazy. Those big eyes, that funny voice. She's weird."

Jule replied, "I can work with her, I promise you. She's worth the try."

Levin remembers, "We took a chance on Carol. By that time we'd auditioned a lot of girls who read and sang for us, but she brought something else to the role. That satirical attitude that Anita Loos liked was a big factor. Then we all realized that we wanted something more than a sexy gold-digger and Carol offered that." She was signed, and another girl from *Lend an Ear,* Yvonne Adair, joined the cast as Dorothy Shaw.

Rehearsals got under way in the late fall of 1949 and Milt Rosenstock immediately noticed a great change in Jule Styne. "I truly think he set his style on this one, not only musically but in his whole dealing with the people, onstage and backstage. He began to handle me in a different way. Before it was always questions. Now, it was, 'I want this. I want that . . .' Now, he came on like whammo. I didn't buck him except on one or two little things. He wanted his head free. I kept thinking, 'Go, man. You'll make mistakes. You'll find your own way.' "

Jule started work with Carol Channing in a chilly rehearsal hall on Sixty-eighth Street. He said, "Let's do a chorus, Carol . . ."

Or, "Let's do half a chorus, Carol, and let's do it three or four times, baby . . ."

He was finding ways to work with the big-eyed, funny-voiced blonde; give her confidence in song; polish a natural style that was unique. In a week or so, Jule laid out the musical routine for "A Little Girl from Little Rock."

Rosenstock watched it, and heard it. He said, "It'll stop the show."

Jule looked intently at the conductor. "What will it look like on stop?"

Milton shrugged.

Jule hit a phony accent on the piano and brought Channing back onstage, teeth flashing.

Milton said, "Great."

Jule sent her off, hit a second phony emphasis, and hurried her back onstage, waving and bowing. "Now, by God, it's double-stopped," he said. Proof was opening night.

Meanwhile, Leo Robin had returned to his beloved California and Jule called Maple Drive one day to say, "We need something for the 'zipper king,' a whole new song." Josephus Gage, zipper-maker, was yet another sugar daddy that Lorelei had acquired in Paris.

Leo remembered that the libretto had described Gage as a health nut. He also remembers sitting for a long while, undoubtedly chugging on that monstrous pipe, then phoned Jule. "Listen—I'm alive, I'm a-tingle, I'm a-glow . . ." After all, the guy was a health freak.

"You got something," Jule replied. "Throw me some more lines." Leo threw a few more over the Bell System.

In another hour, Jule was back on the phone to California to play the music to the new "zipper king" song for Leo. The polishes were also accomplished by long distance, a quick and handy methodology even though it destroyed the layman's conception of highly creative people at work. However, the dial-a-song routine was a matter of necessity.

Early in this same period, Agnes de Mille came to Jule for musical ideas to help her re-create a dance act of the twenties. "What was that music? What were the show-stoppers?" she asked.

Jule recalled one act in particular, the Stuart Morgan Dancers: *Three men and a girl. Two of the men would swing her, and then release her, to be caught by the third. She soared about thirty feet, like Peter Pan flying without wires. Sensational finale to their act, and the music had a circus feeling to it.*

Miss de Mille moved quickly, hiring a female acrobatic dancer and three powerful males, all with acrobatic training. Jule went to the first rehearsal of the number and immediately felt ill. The girl was safely caught at about ten feet but the effect didn't faintly resemble the Morgan feat. He rendered an opinion. "Agnes, you've only got five weeks. The Morgans rehearsed for years for that act. I think you should forget it."

But de Mille was confident that the team could work up to fifteen or twenty feet. At the first theater rehearsal at the Ziegfeld, the girl fell short of that mark. She went about twelve feet, straight through the arms of the catcher and headlong into a steel pipe. Despite a brain concussion, she agreed to continue. She needed the work.

Wishing he'd never thought of the fabulous Morgans, Jule turned his back each time the girl took her final flight. *I felt so sorry for that kid. I really thought she might be killed.*

Gentlemen Prefer Blondes tried out at the Forrest Theatre, in Philadelphia, in late November. On the tense day of the first preview, with final rehearsal onstage, everyone doing one number, orchestra warming up, Jule came running down the aisle, bundled in an overcoat, scarf wrapped and tied over his head, yelling, "I'm going off the high board and nobody's going to stop me . . ."

The tension dissolved momentarily.

Then Agnes de Mille brought on her facsimile of the Morgan dancers for their turn, and Rosenstock hit the circus theme. The girl was thrown about fifteen feet, shooting through the arms of the catcher like a well-aimed bullet. She ended up in a groggy pile against a flat.

Oliver Smith ran down the aisle, screaming, "Stop it, Agnes. Stop it! Goddammit, you'll kill her."

The act was deleted four hours before curtain time.

Philadelphia critics raved about *Gentlemen Prefer Blondes,* especially about wacky Carol Channing. Two weeks later, the show opened on Broadway, with record advance sales of $600,000. That morning of December 9, 1949, Jule received a call from Frank Sinatra requesting four tickets. The singer was in New York to do a show with opera star Dorothy Kirsten. Jule had already surrendered his house seats to friends but quickly assured Sinatra he'd find four somewhere. He paid a scalper $100 for the seats and then waited in vain for a thank-you call from Frank. The slight was all but forgotten as reviews were reread:

Brooks Atkinson, the New York *Times:* "Happy Days Are Here Again . . ."

John Chapman, New York *Daily News:* ". . . just perfect. Carol Channing superb."

Coleman, *Daily Mirror:* "Smash musical."

Herman Levin hosted the opening night party on the roof of the St. Regis Hotel. Carol Channing entered toothily with a field of roses in her arms, and Jule Styne was swung into the room by two gorgeous six-foot showgirls. The show was performed 740 times on Broadway.

2

I had a gut feeling that there would be disaster when we went to work for Howard Hughes. Yet I was compelled to do it.

—JULE STYNE, 1977

After the holidays, and continual partying with Ruth Dubonnet, Jule returned to Hollywood, taking up residence in the green grandeur of the Beverly Hills Hotel, but visiting the Elm Street address occasionally to see his sons, never discussing the upcoming dissolution. Work was now at RKO Studios.

On opening night of *Blondes,* Howard Hughes had been the special guest of Anita Loos and Jule was introduced to the eccentric millionaire-billionaire. They exchanged a few words and a nod. Film producer Alex Gottlieb, under contract to Hughes's RKO lot, also attended opening night. Two days later, Jule was unexpectedly called by Gottlieb and summoned west to write the songs for *Two Tickets to Broadway,* starring Janet Leigh and Tony Martin.

Jule once again tapped on the door of Leo Robin's house and Leo, elated with the success of *Blondes,* instantly agreed to team with Jule on anything, even a project for Mr. Hughes. His films, by and large, had usually turned sour. Frustration and confusion and fear permeated them. With Robin set, Jule then suggested to Gottlieb that Kay Thompson be brought over from MGM to vocal coach Janet Leigh.

Gottlieb then signed Marge and Gower Champion to teach Leigh how to dance.

So away they all went into the mountains and valleys of Hughesland, a bit drunk with money-power, knowing that the wizard was somewhere offstage. A three-and-a-half month rehearsal period, unheard of for a second-rate musical story, was laid out. Kay Thompson began giving Janet her vocal lessons; Marge and Gower Champion worked on her intricate dance routines; Styne and Robin were concocting words and music for four songs; Hugh Martin was making vocal arrangements for eighty voices. Budget, of course, was of no consequence, Mr. Hughes being the executive producer.

Gower Champion's stage set for Leigh's "big number" was rigged on the largest stage at RKO and was about four stories high, with a winding circular staircase. It was so mammoth that some of it projected outside the stage. Even Busby Berkeley would have been envious of this awesome Gog and Magog. Suddenly, after more than three months of labor on that one number, the staff received word that Mr. Hughes personally wanted to "see it."

My God, what excitement. All of us fell apart. The Champions began to polish it as if Janet had only done it once. In a day or two, Marge and Gower were ready, and in walks Gottlieb. He has news. He says, "Mr. Hughes has never been on this lot. So he wants to see the number Thursday at one o'clock at the Goldwyn Studios."

The production department was stunned. Carpenters and grips sat down, weak from the thought of it. Did Mr. Hughes know what it meant to dismantle a four-story set, truck it three miles, and rebuild it in forty-eight hours?

As usual, the professionals recovered quickly. Within a precious hour, carpenters and grips, some borrowed from nearby Paramount, were swarming over the monster set, taking it apart. Trucks were soon lined up outside the studio, and by working some hundred men around the clock, the set was re-established at Sam Goldwyn's corner by noon Thursday.

Promptly at one o'clock, Mr. Hughes made his entry, along with a covey of assistants. He observed the number and quickly reacted by firing Kay Thompson. A few minutes later the Champions were fired, without explanation. By 6:00 P.M., composer Jule Styne had quit, along with lyricist Leo Robin.

The completed picture was said to have ruined the career of Tony Martin.

• • •

The Styne–Sinatra relationship flared up again briefly in 1950, first in Hollywood, then in New York. Frank was foundering that year.

Jule moved his piano to Frank's apartment above the Sunset Strip. *He wasn't singing anywhere near his level. His records weren't selling. His movies were mostly dogs.* Double Dynamite, *with Jane Russell. Jeez. People were harmful. They were talking about him being a has-been. So I said, "Frank, when you sing the No. 1 song, you've got to top them all." We rehearsed and then he went on to New York. So did I, a few weeks later.*

Sinatra opened miserably in New York. *I went to catch him at the French Casino, kind of a dive. He didn't know I was in the audience. I almost cried when he lost his voice. He said to the audience, "Come again some other night," and walked off the stage. He looked like death. It was terrible and I called him the next day.*

Frank said, "I want you to have dinner with me. Alone!"

They dined at The Red Devil, an Italian restaurant on Forty-eighth Street, and few people even looked at the singer-film star. In 1944, horses and cops had to control the crowds. Now, in 1950, he was lucky to have a waiter ask for his autograph.

Sinatra said gloomily, "Remember, Jule, we came in front of this place. Thousands of kids. Horses and cops. Now, it's so quiet."

Jule said he thought it was because *those* kids had grown up; that Frank had no new smash song; no good movies.

3

She loves what she's doing when she's doing it for love.

—ANITA LOOS, 1977

Ruth Dubonnet was pure, apple-pie American, born in New York's Dutchess County, blooded out of Revolutionary War stock. She'd whirled in from serene Dutchess at eighteen to romp in New York's social fountains. The brunette had a classic, blue-blooded beauty. Anita Loos said, "She was a female Valentino, that kind of beauty."

Ruth entertained a lot, usually small dinner parties in the town house, and Jule often played for the distinguished guests. Or they dined at exclusive restaurants or in the homes of the famed and wealthy. Show auditions were sometimes held in her living room, with Jule at the grand piano.

The Dubonnet community at large, so new to Jule, was not bounded by the Manhattan rivers. She took Jule down to the Hunt Ball in Maryland to mingle with the aristocracy of the horse world, including the Aly Kahn. Before they attended the gala first-night party, pre-Hunt Ball, Ruth advised, "Don't talk about show business."

"What'll I talk about?"

"You'll join in the conversations. They talk about many things, and you're very bright. You can fake what you don't know."

Jule agreed to do just that. He sat quietly at a table, containing Stynese nicely, and one man's talk was about the two thousand heifers he'd bought that day. Another gentleman discussed his horse working out at "5/8ths 59" or some such figure. For a period they all, excepting Jule, soberly discussed the best variety of pasture grasses.

Well, I listened to that for about an hour, and my only contribution was an interest in how fast that man's horse could run. I finally excused myself, got up and went over to the piano, played a medley and wiped the whole party out, for which they seemed grateful. Pasture grasses are worldly, but so is music.

Next night, at the Hunt Ball, where diamonds were just accessories and not necessarily friends, grinning Jule, attired appropriately, waltzed Ruth by the bandstand. Meyer Davis almost dropped his baton. What was Jule Styne, his itinerant piano player of the thirties, doing with the fox-and-hounds set?

About this time, out in Hollywood, there was another party, a posh affair but second-rate compared to the Maryland Hunt Ball. Ethel Styne was there, as was Sammy Cahn. Ethel said to Sammy, "You know that woman Jule is going around with? She's eight years older than I am."

Sammy replied, "Ah, he's just playing around. Don't worry about it."

Obviously still in love with Jule, though having filed for divorce, Ethel said, "You don't understand. She's eight years older than I am. Do you know what that does to me?"

There was no question but that Ruth Dubonnet was very much in love with Jule Styne, and his sons frankly hoped he'd marry her. They thought she'd make the perfect wife for their "playboy-composer" father. Jule indeed liked Ruth very much, loved her perhaps, but could not make up his mind over the next six or seven years that he *truly* loved her. Some weeks, yes; some weeks, no. A rather protective woman at times, Dubonnet seemed content with his companionship, his amusing chatter and his talent at the keyboard.

Jule, on the other hand, said he sometimes felt "that I was a claiming horse, running in a stake race. Yet I felt a deep attachment to Ruth."

The Chicago road company of *Gentlemen Prefer Blondes* was opening, and Jule flew out to attend the first night, also to visit his father. Isadore was very much in evidence in the theater as *Blondes* opened. As he walked down the aisle with the usherette, he tapped the program page that listed the credits. "Do you know who this is?"

The usherette shook her head, she later told Jule.

"That's Jule Styne and I'm his father," Isadore said proudly.

Yet, at the party following the initial Chicago performance, with Jule playing his songs, the cast singing, Isadore, from a position directly behind the piano, said, in a loud and disparaging voice, "You should have heard him play when he was eight."

The disappointment of not having a concert pianist in the family seemed to linger on long after Anna's death.

4

The good gambling that Jule did was on Broadway shows because his talent was on the line. Sometimes he won: sometimes he lost.

—DOROTHY DICKER, 1977

Jule Styne was "hot" on Broadway now, approached almost weekly with ideas or fully developed librettos. *Blondes* was still playing before packed houses, both on *the street* and in road companies. *High Button Shoes* was a summer-stock regular. Jule had a suitable "showman's" office at Forty-second and Broadway, and was definitely a part of the New York theatrical scene, getting mentioned in the gossip columns and recognized by theater people in Sardi's.

Against that background, in late 1950, Hugh Martin, the talented vocal arranger for both *Shoes* and *Blondes,* as well as that RKO–Hughes–Janet Leigh debacle, brought in an idea. Actually, it was a complete score, minus a book. He said to Jule, "Please listen to it, with my singers."

Whether he'd like it or not, Jule knew that he was in for a treat. Martin wrote brilliant material. And the score *was* a treat, even if the idea behind it was so vague as to be nonexistent. *A girl in Paris.* That was the total idea. Yet the individual songs were wonderful, Jule thought. He said to Martin, "I'm mad about it, but you must have a book. Without a libretto, you just have these songs."

A day later, Martin returned with a stranger to the office near Times Square and said, "Meet Harry Rigby. He's going to co-produce with you. He'll raise the money."

Harry Rigby seemed to be a nice enough man; he appeared to be honest, quickly admitting that he was a complete novice in the theater, and that was okay. Money was to be his chore and theatrical qualifications often meant very little where the collection of production money was concerned. Jule said to the excited pair, "Okay, I'll go find a book for you."

A few days later, Jule flew to Hollywood on other business and while there remembered a story he'd once read, intended for a movie that was never produced. He reread the story, thought it was perfect for Martin's score and located the surprised writer. The plot was simple enough: A French girls' school caught in the middle of World War II. One week it was occupied by French troops; the next week it see-sawed over to German soldiers. To survive, the girls had to play both sides. Charming story, Jule thought; full of girls and laughs, excellent ingredients for any musical. Jule posted $5,000 for a sixty-day option, and called Hugh Martin in New York to say he'd found the book. Martin said that was terrific; he couldn't wait to read it. But returning to New York two weeks later, Jule discovered that Rigby and Martin had already purchased rights to Ferenc Molnár's *Good Fairy* from Universal-International Pictures. Quite suddenly, Harry Rigby had decided he wasn't a novice, after all.

I was stunned by this move and out of $5,000 already. But Rigby assured Styne that he'd repay the option money once the show opened. Then, again without discussion, Rigby and Martin signed Nanette Fabray to star in the *Good Fairy* conversion. Nanette was in her thirties and had played the mother in *Shoes.* Now she would portray an eighteen-year-old. Jule was gasping.

"Fellows," he said, "I think you've lost your minds. You're doing all this and don't even give me the courtesy of asking my opinion. The story's all wrong and Fabray's all wrong."

Next, Rigby and Martin, this time after long consultation with their angry co-producer, signed Preston Sturges to direct. That, at last, sounded interesting to Jule. Sturges was a genius in the movies. Although he'd never directed a musical, he couldn't be discounted.

A fourth partner, Alexander Cohen, who'd told Joe Kipness that *High Button Shoes* would flop, had now joined the company. *Make a Wish,* as *Good Fairy* had become, would be presented by Cohen, co-produced by Rigby and Styne. *I was truly beginning to wish I'd hated*

Martin's songs when he brought them to me. I could feel "Glad to See You" hanging around on the next corner, beating albatross wings. Instinct told me to run.

Money-raising time was at hand, so Rigby laid out a tour in Pennsylvania, around Philadelphia. He claimed he had rich friends down there and could easily raise $50,000 in a few nights. Jule responded that he thought they could stay in Philly for a year and not gain a dime. The prediction appeared to be sound because the first four nights of the tour did not loosen a single wallet. The next morning Jule suggested they take the train back to Manhattan. But Rigby insisted, "The big one is tonight."

"Okay, one more for me and that's it," said Jule.

For the "big night," Martin's singers, Jule and Rigby were traveling in three rented cars, and on this snowy eve the vehicles couldn't climb the last icy hill to the mansion. So they all slipped and slid on foot upwards for almost a quarter of a mile, already late by two hours for the suburban date. When the middle-aged wealthy hostess met them at the door, she yelled to everyone inside, "Hurrah, the troubadors are here!"

Oh, my dear God, thought Jule. *Troubadors!* Singers and guitars. Wandering minstrels to entertain the coupon clippers. Inside, it was quite apparent that everyone had been drinking champagne since 7:00 P.M. *They're going to be asked to invest money in a show and half of them are drunk.* The hostess managed to seat everyone in her large living room and Martin settled to the piano.

One tipsy man shouted, "Play 'Blue Skies.' "

Veteran of several dozen grueling auditions, Jule whispered, "Play it, Hugh. That guy may have a million."

Hugh got to the middle of the chorus and stopped. "I'll have nothing to do with this. Let's go home."

Jule told him to "hang in." They'd been out for five days; they'd traveled forty miles to this party. They had to make the effort now. Jule asked the hostess to please introduce them. Her speech, more or less: "Ladies and gentlemen, you are now going to hear music from a forthcoming Broadway show. Hugh Martin is here. Jule Styne is here, and this is my friend, Harry Rigby, who will produce the show."

There was no applause, just the tinkle of bubbly glasses. It was apparent that no one had ever heard of Hugh Martin or Jule Styne. In fact, it was likely that Harry Rigby had only one friend in the room —the begowned hostess. Jule stood up to begin telling the story of the

Good Fairy and a woman piped up, "I saw that movie, with Jean Arthur . . ."

Jesus, I knew we were in deep trouble. They were already interrupting, these silly, drunken rich people and I said to Hugh, "For Chrissakes, play the first song." So he did "Meet the Lady Known as Paris," and the poor singers, still half frozen, somehow did a good job. But there was no reaction at the end. No applause. One woman asked for more champagne; a man left the room, for the john, I suppose. I looked at Hugh. He had tears in his eyes. Rigby just looked helpless.

A second song from the score was played and drew no reaction. Jule waved for Martin to stop and stood up. He said, "Look, ladies and gentlemen, I'm glad you're having a wonderful time but we've traveled a long way to be here and play these songs for you. We're cold and hungry and no one has even offered us a cup of coffee . . ."

The hostess scurried toward the kitchen and Jule stepped to the piano, asking Hugh to move over, then told those gathered, "It's obvious you don't know who I am but maybe you'll know my music." He began with "I Don't Want to Walk Without You, Baby" and finished with a *Blondes* medley, topping it with "Diamonds Are a Girl's Best Friend."

There was big applause now and Jule said, "All right, the man sitting here next to me wrote a classic, 'The Trolley Song,' a Judy Garland favorite." Martin played some of his work. More applause.

Forty thousand dollars was raised that wintry night but only two songs from *Make a Wish* were heard by the Quaker State angels. Finally, a Philadelphia financier, Tom White, posted the balance of what was thought to be the opening budget, $150,000. White was an unexpected angel, not from the party on the hill.

The afternoon of the first preview in Philadelphia, during final run-throughs, Jule entered the Shubert Theatre in a rented top hat and black cape, looking like David Belasco, to do his usual "preview afternoon pep show." He yelled, "Don't worry about a thing. I'm taking over."

"This time the tension wasn't released," said Milton Rosenstock. "Not at all. We knew we had a cold turkey, far beyond repair."

The turkey had one bold innovation: Raoul Pène du Bois had designed a Venetian-blind curtain for the production, with the slats opening slowly, enabling the audience to see the set in a novel manner. The heavy curtains had taken forty-eight hours to erect.

Opening night, Rosenstock finished the overture and the theater went completely dark. Then the Venetian-blind curtain opened just a crack. "I could hear creaking noises, chains rattling, steel scraping. There were two electric motors on that thing and they began to smoke. Nanette Fabray made her entrance but I went through seven choruses before the damn slats were horizontal. Nothing worked right."

The show opened to solid kills and Jule brought S. J. Perelman down to rewrite the book. Perelman said, "You're in France but the only thing French about this play is the scenery. Close it down five weeks while I rewrite." If the show closed for two weeks, it would close forever. Anita Loos journeyed to Philadelphia, took a look, and returned to New York.

Then Alexander Cohen summoned Abe Burrows to doctor it, at a thousand dollars a day. Minimum guarantee, $35,000.

A day later, the rebel in Jule came out. At a meeting in the old Ritz-Carlton, across from the ill-fated Bellevue-Stratford, Jule said to Cohen, "I'm giving up my share. I want out. I want a letter saying I'm not responsible for any money owed by this show." Cohen signed the letter without knowing that *Make a Wish* was already drowned in debt.

Four weeks later, on April 18, 1951, the hopeful creation of Hugh Martin opened on Broadway at the Winter Garden and on the sixth day closed. Hugh Martin never recovered from *Make a Wish* professionally. Neither did the investors. The show was staged for $450,000.

The Steins in Chicago, 1920—Claire, Anna, Isadore, Maurice and Jule.

At age 8, Jule played with the Chicago and Detroit symphonies, but soon discovered that his hands were too small for him to be another Paderewski.

Arnold Johnson's Band, in Florida for a 1926 engagement, provided the first big career break for pianist Jule Styne, third from left, front row.

Self-styled "black sheep" of the Stein family, Maurice mastered the saxophone and eventually joined Guy Lombardo's Band.

Vocal coaching, not clarinet playing, was Jule's main job at 20th Century-Fox Studios in 1937.

New Styne–Cahn songs were often demonstrated for Frank Sinatra, and this backstage session at the Paramount Theatre, New York, in 1943, was typical of the impromptu sing-alongs. Sammy's in the middle.

The Styne—Cahn songs for Anchors Aweigh, *a 1946 MGM release, were solid hits, as was the movie. Left to right: Jule Styne, Sammy Cahn, Frank Sinatra, director George Sidney, Gene Kelly and Axel Stordahl, Sinatra's arranger and conductor.*

Elaborately staged and costumed, the New Year's Eve "shows" at Frank Sinatra's house could have "played Vegas." Performing January 31, 1949, are, left to right: Sammy Cahn, Jule Styne, Rags Ragland, Frank Sinatra, David Shelley, Paul Weston and Axel Stordahl.

Jule's first wife, Ethel, died in 1963.

Ruth Dubonnet and Jule sailed for Europe in late spring, 1957 with Jule finally visiting London for the first time since childhood.

Jule's girl friend of the Gypsy *days was Sandra Church. Sammy Davis Jr. joined the duo for dinner at the Stork Club, New York, 1959.*

PHOTOGRAPH BY BILL MARK

Adolph Green and Betty Comden, who brought Jule the ad on the back of the New York telephone directory, that inspired Bells Are Ringing *(1965), the first of their many collaborations with Jule Styne.*

Jule's long-time manager and confidante, Dorothy Dicker, watches a rehearsal of Bells Are Ringing *in Palm Beach, Florida.*

PHOTOGRAPH BY MORT KAYE STUDIOS, INC., PALM BEACH, FLORIDA

The offstage feud between Dolores Gray and Bert Lahr during Two on the Aisle *was often funnier than what occurred onstage.*

Jule's "landmark musical" Gypsy *afforded Ethel Merman her first full-length dramatic role in the theater. Phil Silvers, center, appeared in Jule's first Broadway hit,* High Button Shoes.

PHOTOGRAPH BY BILL MARK

Listening to a playback at a Funny Girl *recording session are actor Sydney Chaplin, Barbra Streisand and Jule.*

British-born international cover girl Margaret Brown married Jule in June 1963.

5

I used to tell myself that I never hurt anyone but me by gambling. That wasn't true, of course.

—JULE STYNE, 1977

Over the years, Ethel Styne had pleaded with her husband to stop gambling; Jule's sister, Claire, had pleaded with him; Ruth Dubonnet said, "He'd swear he wouldn't gamble, and then I'd catch him. It was downhill and I knew it." It was more than downhill when one bookie in Hollywood threatened to use a gun. Jule borrowed $10,000 and Claire Bregman, wearing a red rose, met the man in front of the Beverly Hills Hotel and paid him in cash. "I was frightened," she said, "but not as frightened as Jule, I suppose."

During this mid-winter of 1951, Jule went to a retired psychiatrist recommended by Manny Sachs, president of Columbia Records. He'd asked Sachs to recommend a doctor removed from the Hollywood circle, one certain not to "blab." An elderly gentleman, then in leisure at the venerable Huntington Hotel in Pasadena, Dr. Stewart said, "I'll give you three weeks of my time, then turn you over to someone in New York when you go back there."

On the second or third day, Stewart startled Jule by saying, "Let's go to the track today." The shrink was taking him back to the site of his constant downfall. Stewart said that he often went to the track to "ease boredom." He said he didn't bet very much.

I could feel him watching me constantly. Every second. We went five or six times and he saw that I knew every shady character; every bookie; every waitress; even some of the guards.

At the end of three weeks, sitting in Stewart's room at the Huntington Hotel, uncertain as to what the doctor had or hadn't learned, Jule awaited diagnosis. He remembers Stewart finally saying, "If you hadn't gambled, you'd be an old man in Chicago. You'd own some flats and maybe be teaching music. Going to New York was a gamble; going to Hollywood was a gamble. Now, I'm going to tell you something that will be devastating to your ego, which is very large. You bet at the hundred-dollar window because it makes you a bigger man, a bigger winner. After the race, if you can show people you've won a thousand dollars you think you're a bigger man. You haven't done it for need. You've done it to satisfy ego. You're insecure about your talent, and you feel betting makes you a bigger talent. That's sick."

Jule wasn't at all convinced that he was gambling to satisfy ego. Yet ego at the hundred-dollar window was certainly a part of it.

One day during this period of analysis, while Jule was sunning himself by poolside at the Beverly Hills, Ed Beloin and Hank Garson flopped down to say hello. Beloin was one of Jack Benny's writers and had a play tucked under his arm. Jule read it that night, a story about an American actress whose career was fading. She went to Rome, quickly becoming a star, something she'd never achieved in Hollywood. The nonmusical play read "funny."

Returning to New York, with no notion of what the summer might bring, Jule took *In Any Language* to George Abbott, who promptly fell in love with it. A production deal was set within a few weeks: Jule to produce and post $10,000; George Abbott to direct and supply $65,000. Mr. Abbott had a busy schedule ahead and estimated that he couldn't do the play until the following year. That was all right. *In Any Language* went on the future board.

In late winter, while *Make a Wish* was making a straightaway start down the drain, French impressario Arthur Lesser approached Ruth Dubonnet, whom he'd known for a long time, asking her to invest in a revue. He was thinking of a Bert Lahr–Lena Horne show and had obtained the interest of Betty Comden and Adolph Green. No composer had been signed.

Dubonnet said to Lesser, "Are you going to fool around with just anyone for music? I can deliver Jule Styne, and furthermore, I won't invest unless you use him." She was also investing in musicals long before she knew Jule.

Lesser went back to Comden–Green with the proposal that they collaborate with Styne. As aforementioned, they weren't at all enthusiastic about teaming with a Tin Pan Alley man, no matter that he'd scored *Shoes* and *Blondes.* They'd been writing with Lenny Bernstein and Morton Gould, neither of them remotely connected with Tin Pan Alley or gaudy Wurlitzers or Hit Parades. Nonetheless, Comden–Green wanted the job. They hadn't had a hit since *On the Town* in 1944.

Jule then met with Lesser, an impressive man in his mid-forties. He'd been doing shows in Paris with the famed Patachou; he'd been Maurice Chevalier's personal manager for a time. *He dropped names of friends—famous actors, directors, concert artists. He smothered me with all these famous people and then showed me sketches of the show costumes by Pierre Balmain. Yet Arthur didn't have a word on paper. Betty and Adolph hadn't written anything; had no ideas as yet. There was no director; no libretto. But Lesser was already displaying his Balmain sketches. I couldn't figure it.*

Ruth warned, "Be careful of him, Jule."

Remembering that show, Betty Comden said, "We were already laughing. It was the flimsiest of things. We were all thinking he had a central idea for the show. There was absolutely nothing."

Adolph Green added, "A large pocket of empty air."

On that empty air pocket began the first collaboration of Styne–Comden–Green.

Betty and Adolph soon wrote a sketch for Bert Lahr, to be backed by Jule's music: Leo the Lion was quitting MGM because he was still in black and white while all other film company trademarks were in color. Leo was also enraged that the Pathé rooster was making considerably more money than he was; even the half-naked guy who rang the gong for J. Arthur Rank flicks had a larger salary. The sketch opened with Bert exiting an MGM projection room in a lion suit.

Lahr read the lion dialogue and told Lesser, in the presence of Comden–Green, "I'll do it, but the most important thing is my face. You have to get me the same face I had at MGM for *The Wizard of Oz.*"

Lesser, a hand-talker, an arm-waver, promised in a thick Parisian accent that he would obtain "zee face."

"Then everyone will know it's me," reminded Lahr.

Lesser again sprayed Bert with French and received in return one of Lahr's special looks, the skeptic look. From that day on, Bert, a worrier, anyway, fretted about his *Oz* face. Meanwhile, Comden and Green wrote sketches for Bert as Queen Victoria; as a Wagnerian Siegfried, a baseball player and a park attendant. Styne–Comden–Green provided a total of seven songs for Lahr and new co-star, Dolores Gray. Lena Horne had bowed out as female lead, reportedly concerned about lack of material.

A revue, above all, must have good costumes and good scenery. Eventually Jule happened to glance through the costume list and was shocked. *Nine pages of the worst stuff in town. It appeared that Lesser was dressing his show with a Safeway shopping list. All stock stuff, off the racks. One lion suit. One baseball suit. One Queen's dress. I said to Betty and Adolph, "Just wait until Bert sees that moth-eaten lion suit."*

No week went by that Lahr didn't phone Lesser concerning his *Oz* face. The calls lasted nine months, from the first conference until *Two on the Aisle* went into rehearsal in June 1951. Bert asked but one simple question each time: "Do you have my head?" He reported that Lesser filled the air with Patachou, Balmain and Maurice Chevalier, along with volumes of other French, none of which Bert understood.

The usual wardrobe run-through was held two days before dress rehearsal, with everyone fitting up and entering stage on call.

"Miss Gray, your first scene, please."

The voice was that of Abe Burrows, who, with Nat Hiken, had written the libretto. Burrows was also making his debut as a stage director.

With Lahr standing nearby, visibly unhappy with *Two on the Aisle,* Arthur Lesser and the world at large, Miss Gray entered in a stunning gown. The Frenchman, not unexpectedly, had taken excellent care of her. She looked sensational, even though the gown was not Balmain. However, well before the run-through, it was evident that Lahr literally hated her, guts and gowns.

"Mr. Lahr, your first scene, please."

Bert came onstage resembling a barrel beset with gas pains. He had five costume changes in the first act, and wore each costume over the other. There wasn't time to change. He walked around deadpan, displaying his rental, and exited, peeling off as he went. Passing into the wings, Jule heard him mumble, "Look at the clothes that bitch is wearing."

"Miss Gray, your second scene, please."

Bert was again standing in the wings, staring at Gray as she glided out in another beautiful gown. Carrying an umbrella, she did a turn, passing close to Lahr, who stood upwind of her perfume. That crackling moment was the beginning of one of the mostly deadly star feuds of the modern theater. The hate was mutual.

Leo the Lion was a second-act sketch. When called out by Burrows to present his beast suit, Lahr shouted to Lesser, in the first row of seats, "I'm not doing this scene without my *Oz* face. And this crumby suit looks like you got it at a Halloween party."

After nine months of promises, Lesser still replied, "Eet is coming, I promisss. Zee *Wizard of Oz* wass a long time ago."

"I'm not doing the goddamned thing," Bert yelled and walked offstage.

Jule, Betty and Adolph ran after him, following along to his dressing room. They pacified him for a few minutes but that was to no avail when Lesser stuck his head into the doorway. "Get out, get out," Bert screamed, and the Frenchman ducked away.

Styne–Comden–Green–Burrows spent hours convincing Bert that Leo should stay in the show. Even so, the lion sketch barely made it to the first preview in New Haven. Bert finally agreed to do Leo but would only wear the bottom half of the costume, long tail dragging. For the upper body, Bert chose a colorful California sports shirt, and then added claw gloves. The effect was more grotesque than funny. Leo was dropped in New Haven.

Of course, no "Oz face" ever arrived from MGM. There were no Balmain costumes. A lady who did skirts and ruffles for the Roxy Theatre chorus line designed what few originals there were in Two on the Aisle. *Better scenery could be viewed in summer stock.*

Opening in New York on July 19, 1951, a wretchedly hot night, *Two on the Aisle* surprisingly received fair to good reviews, and played 267 performances at the Mark Hellinger. The battle of the stars continued, and Lahr displayed his final disgust with Miss Gray by refusing to go on the road with her. He claimed he could become physically ill at the mere sight of Dolores Gray.

But some rather good songs came from the score of the frenetic Lesser production. "Give a Little, Get a Little," and "Hold Me, Hold Me, Hold Me," were prominent and still receive regular radio plays. They again indicate the lasting quality of Jule Styne's popular music.

What if Atkinson doesn't like it?

—JULE STYNE, 1951

Despite the collapse of *Make a Wish* and the generally mediocre reviews of *Two on the Aisle,* Jule was still "hot" as the result of *Blondes.*

In gambling idiom, I was shooting a "hot hand." So I decided to produce a show rather than compose the music, and went searching for revivals that summer of '51. I went out to Westhampton, on Long Island, for a few days and saw that Pal Joey *was opening in East Hampton at the John Drew Theatre, with Bobby Fosse, the choreographer, playing the lead. I'd always loved the show, and saw it—a chintzy little production. But the show itself stood out. So I went to Richard Rodgers to obtain the rights. We'd met during the mounting of* Blondes. *So I had that going.*

Reconstructing what followed, Rodgers said, "It all sounds marvelous. But who do you get to play the lead."

"I'll find a Joey," said Jule.

Rodgers was skeptical. Gene Kelly had been the original Joey eleven years previously but was tied up by MGM. Kelly would be wrong, at this time, at any rate, Jule decided.

"That's hard to do, find a right Joey," Rodgers remembers telling Jule. "Without him, you have no show."

Jule insisted that a suitable Joey was around somewhere and Rodgers finally agreed to have his lawyer work out a deal, fully expecting Styne to fail. The original production had disappointed Rodgers. In fact, it had distressed Brooks Atkinson as well. "Can you draw sweet water from a sour well?" he asked, in his *Times* review. And if this revival didn't have Atkinson's blessing, it could be a costly well.

Jule believed that the best starting point was to sign a top director, and went to Elia Kazan, then in New York preparing a film. Without committing himself, Kazan promised to help. He, too, liked *Pal Joey;* he, too, thought it should be revived.

Casting was discussed with Kazan and Jule suggested Vivienne Segal, the original female star of the show. Jule had neatly trapped her out of *High Button Shoes,* in favor of Nanette Fabray, a conspiracy about which, thankfully, she'd never learned. Now was her time, in another show. "Gadge" Kazan agreed. "She's the only one who should play it. You know she'll register. You know the critics will welcome her back. She's older now and that's for the better."

Next, Jule visited Miss Segal, Vera in the play. He found that she was eager to revive her role. He told her he'd just talked to Bob Alton and had an affirmative from Alton to re-create his original dances. Segal then asked who would direct.

"Gadge Kazan, I hope."

"Now, who is Joey?" Segal asked. "Remember, he has to be a helluva dancer. There's no Act I finale, just dancing. And he's got to look the part."

"I'll find one," Jule insisted.

Segal was also skeptical.

Alton set, Segal set, Kazan a name to drop, Jule reported back to Richard Rodgers, who was amazed that any progress at all had been made in two weeks. As Jule left the office, Rodgers again asked the plague question, "Who is Joey?"

Styne answered, "I'll tell you soon."

He'd spent days thinking about it, and among the possibilities only one man seemed to meet all the requirements—dancer Harold Lang. Gene Kelly was a superb stylist but Lang, in Jule's opinion, was a better all-around dancer. He could do ballet, for instance. However, he could not act, and Joey had to be an actor as well. Lang was known to Broadway audiences, but was not a "name."

Jule then met with Lang, who was slim and dark—a Joey physically—to say, "This can be the chance of your lifetime. I know your shortcomings as an actor, but Gadge Kazan will work with you. Bob Alton will do your choreography. You can't ask for more."

Lang agreed.

Back in Rodgers office that same day, Jule announced that he had his Joey. "Only one man in town can dance and sing that role; there's only one man who looks like Joey."

"Who is it?" Rodgers challenged.

"Harold Lang."

A distinct "hmh" look came over Rodgers's face. He knew, of course, of Lang's work. "Let's have him in the theater. Let's have him move around, sing some songs; read a scene."

Jule took a long time to reply, he remembers, thinking it out. Lang would be shot down if he read a scene. "Okay, he can move around and sing some songs. But I don't want him to read a scene. He's not ready for it. But all you have to do is tell me he's okay providing he meets the director's approval."

Rodgers nodded, though still uncertain of the whole project.

Jule went directly to Kazan's apartment and discussed the problem. Kazan agreed to "read" Lang if it could be done that afternoon. Lang arrived twenty minutes later.

Jule said, "Harold, I know you haven't seen the script of *Pal Joey* but . . ."

Lang interrupted. "I know it backwards. I've read it twenty times in the last two days."

"Okay," said Kazan, "but I don't want you to act. Just read me a scene. You know how cynical Joey is, try to get some of that in."

Harold read a lengthy scene while Gadge listened and was then dismissed. Lang was in and out of the Kazan apartment in less than half an hour.

Jule waited for the verdict.

"What this boy needs is something I can't give him," said Kazan. "I don't have the time to teach him how to act but I have a fellow who coaches. He'll find out what Lang can do and what he can't do. He won't try to improve what he can't do. He'll take advantage of Lang's ability to move."

The drama coach was actually a director, David Alexander, and Kazan promised to come in after one week of work, take a look at a first-act run-through and render an opinion. Kazan remained as an "advisor" to *Pal Joey*.

• • •

Richard Rodgers and novelist John O'Hara, author of *Pal Joey*, were bitter enemies. They'd been at odds since the original production, when O'Hara felt that Rodgers and Larry Hart took all the glory. Music and lyrics often override the fact that the basic story was contributed by someone else, and it was true that O'Hara had been pretty much a forgotten man when the first production was staged in 1940.

Jule made a date with O'Hara, who was equally as temperamental as Rodgers, and they lunched at the "21" Club. O'Hara said flatly, "The only thing I don't want ever to do if this show goes on is talk to Dick Rodgers. I loathe the man."

About ten days later, after Gadge Kazan had seen a first-act run-through, approving it, Rodgers and O'Hara had a strange rendezvous. Rodgers sat on the far side of the theater and two aisles away was O'Hara. They did not acknowledge each other. There was complete silence as Jule sat in the middle row and told Alexander to begin Lang's audition.

At conclusion, both men nodded their separate okays of Harold Lang as the new Joey and then left the theater separately, not even looking at each other so far as Jule could see.

Jule quickly set out to raise money for *Joey*. His first hope was a wealthy Chicago attorney, George Pollack, a farm lawyer, old friend and confidant, previously an investor in *Glad to See You*. Over the phone, Pollack promised $75,000 against a needed budget of $125,000. Then Jule got vague promises of several thousand more from other friends. He knew that Ruth Dubonnet could gather a few angels and would also personally invest.

His task was now to persuade Dick Rodgers to contribute the final $50,000. And why not? Along with the Larry Hart estate, Rodgers would own six percent of the revival. Jule also reasoned that Rodgers would have faith in the new production; view it as a good gamble.

So, with company manager Mike Goldreyer, Jule visited the plush Rodgers office two days later and proposed an investment from Rodgers–Hammerstein Productions, a very wealthy company. The pair had made out handsomely with *Blondes*, quadrupling their outlay of $5,000 each.

"What's the budget?" Rodgers asked. Up to that point, he hadn't inquired. Jule noticed a cold business edge in his voice.

"Estimated at $125 thousand."

Rodgers said flatly, "When you raise $115 thousand, I'll put in the last ten."

Jule was speechless. It was Rodgers' own show; he'd get a new album; probably new single records of "Bewitched, Bothered and Bewildered" and "I Could Write a Book," plus the satisfaction of seeing his work done properly. *I didn't argue with him. I was too shocked to say anything. I simply thanked him and left the office with Goldreyer.*

When Jule returned to his office, there was a startling telegram from Chicago. George Pollack, having already signed the letter of promise for his investment, had died of a heart attack. The $75,000 would be tied up in probate for months. In less than an hour what had seemed to be a reasonably smooth mounting of a Broadway musical had folded.

Next day, feeling some panic, Jule went to the office of Lee Shubert, owner of the prime theaters in New York, long a towering figure of the stage. Jule felt he might gather some momentum again by nailing down a top theater.

Shubert shook his head. "You're doing a revival and Atkinson hated it the first time around."

Jule declared he had a winner; that what Atkinson didn't like about the show was being altered. "I want the Broadhurst." The Broadhurst, on Forty-fourth Street, was one of Shubert's prizes, located in the heart of the theater district. If *Pal Joey* went in, the house would be booked for the best season, fall–winter. If the show failed, providing no percentage, Shubert could lose considerable money. He shook his head again, Jule remembers. In fact, Shubert's head seemed to be on a pivot that morning. "Are you going out of town?" he asked.

"One week in New Haven so they can learn how to hang the scenery."

"What are you paying Bob Alton?" A strange question.

"Two percent of the gross."

"For the same dancing they had last time. Alton repeats everything." Jule felt that Shubert was digging for negatives.

Jule spent the next twenty minutes adding up all the positives, inflating Kazan's involvement; Rodgers' involvement; how O'Hara and Rodgers had raved over Harold Lang; how Vivienne Segal thought that "Lang was better than Gene Kelly." Shubert listened but seemed restless.

I was fighting for my life. So what if I lied a little?

Jule remembers that Shubert sat for a few silent moments and then said, "I don't know why I'm giving you the Broadhurst but I admire your courage. Tell Weinstock [the Broadhurst manager] I said, 'Okay,' and I hope to hell you're right."

Jule hurried back to his office, excited over securing the Shubert prize. Soon, he visited Rodgers to proudly announce he'd gotten the Broadhurst.

Rodgers said, "I can't believe it."

Jule couldn't resist saying, "Just think what I could do if I had the money. You're making me raise $115 thousand to get your ten."

Rodgers clearly remembers replying, "Jule, why don't you give up? You can't get the money. People aren't interested. Give back whatever money you've raised and forget it."

"I'm not giving up," Jule answered angrily.

"Good luck," said Rodgers, as Jule went out the door.

I was choking now. With rehearsals beginning in a week, I needed payroll money. Mike Goldreyer told me I had an immediate need for $22,000 in scenery; $3,000 in costumes, which were already half completed. Jule met the first week's payroll out of his own pocket.

With the collapse of the production now imminent, Ruth Dubonnet raised $30,000; then during the second week of rehearsal hopes brightened again. In walked a casual friend and occasional producer, Leonard Key. "I've got a guy with the money," said Key.

"From this moment on, you're co-producer," replied Jule. "You get twenty-five percent for raising the money."

At the first meeting with the money-man, Mike Levy, Jule realized he was talking to a loan arranger, not an angel. For putting up $90,000, Mike Levy wanted $10,000 off the top, and a guarantee from ASCAP against Jule's royalties; the loan to be paid back in full within three months of the opening.

ASCAP not only frowned on such transactions but had a definite policy against them. Jule found a way to maneuver under the policy. The papers were signed and word got out on *the street* that Jule Styne was personally backing his own production. Either he was a fool, or he knew something about *Pal Joey* that Richard Rodgers didn't know.

As October ended, *Joey* had the necessary backing, plus a cash reserve:

$5,000 — Emil and Gabe Katzka
$15,000 — Ruth Dubonnet and friends
$80,000 — Mike Levy's loan
$15,000 — Anthony Farrell, friend and producer
$10,000 — Richard Rodgers

Rodgers said admiringly, "Through sheer persistence, and nothing else, Jule raised the money."

Jule had cast Lionel Stander to play the part of Ludlow Lowell simply because he was the best actor available for the role, which had previously been played by Jack Durant. But that elective brought reaction far away from Broadway. Though a fine actor, Stander was as much celebrated for being one of show-business's "unfriendlies," allegedly a Communist, and had taken the Fifth Amendment in congressional hearings. He was a pink-colored thorn on the pages of *Red Channels,* the anti-Communist watchdog magazine. Mere mention of Stander appeared to generate froth amongst those who rallied around Senator Joe McCarthy.

The Styne office, now uptown on Fifty-seventh Street, was bombarded with damning material on Stander; phone calls from around the country came in hourly, seemingly programmed, each applying pressure. During the third week of rehearsal, a picketing threat was made: If Stander remained in the cast, *Pal Joey* would have an unforgettable opening.

Jule called both Rodgers and O'Hara, admitting he was in deep trouble but also refusing to sack Stander. He pleaded with the enemies to meet with him, together, for the sake of the show; to present a united front. They agreed, and the meeting was held at the Broadhurst. Both men put aside bitter personal differences. O'Hara was outraged by the *Red Channel* efforts and Rodgers declared, "Lionel is right for the part. That's the only thing that matters. Keep him." Jule requested that they make a joint public statement, backing the actor for his talent, disregarding his political beliefs. O'Hara and Rodgers made individual statements the following day, and Stander remained in the cast. However, the threats continued.

Rodgers, now fully committed to the revival of *Pal Joey,* attended every rehearsal, taking notes; making suggestions. *The whole thing seemed to turn around on the Stander incident. I sensed determination from everyone. We were rising now out of ashes.*

New Haven, Connecticut, was white and cold the week before Christmas, 1951, when the production company entrained for the opening. An earlier heavy snowfall was on the ground and more flakes came down during the week. The opening was set for Christmas night, 1951.

Rodgers went up with the company, wanting to personally rehearse the orchestra. He paid no attention to *South Pacific,* running at the Majestic, that week. Jule had updated some of the orchestrations; the libretto had been changed to hopefully satisfy Mr. Atkinson. In the last scene of the original production, Vera Simpson (Vivienne Segal) became the heavy when she ordered Joey out of the house without a coat. According to O'Hara, Atkinson had found fault with the scene, in particular the shift of sympathy to Joey. Jule eliminated the coat scene, leaving Joey, always the heel, to remain a heel. *Why take the chance? It made sense, Atkinson's criticism. You're damn right, I wanted him on our side.*

Christmas morning, stage manager Neil Hartley and assistant stage manager John Barry Ryan, III, shoveled snow outside the Shubert Theater so that trucks could move up to the loading dock with set furniture.

About 10:00 A.M., Bob Alton decided that the taps of the chorus dancers in one scene weren't correct. He felt they created a sound that was harmful to the action. A little later, producer Styne put twenty-four pairs of shoes into a box, got a taxi and went off to locate a New Haven shoemaker who was willing to work on Christmas Day. By 3:00 P.M. new taps were on all the shoes, in time for the final run-through.

The curtain was at eight-thirty and we had a big Yale crowd. I was standing in the lobby like Warner Baxter in that movie Forty-second Street, *and said to Rodgers, "Gee, if we had the money, I'd like to do three weeks in Boston before opening in New York." Rodgers looked at me as if I were insane. He didn't answer.*

Pal Joey, with both Harold Lang and Vivienne Segal giving better performances than had Gene Kelly and Segal in the initial production, soared from the overture on. At intermission Anthony Farrell, who'd invested $15,000, walked up to Jule. "I'll give you eight to five for your big loan."

Farrell, too, had had a long-term romance with the stage resulting from a short-term human romance. Unable to find a theater willing to accept a drama written by his mistress-playwright of the moment, Farrell shopped around and discovered that Warner Brothers had the Mark Hellinger on the market. Told that the price of the Fifty-first Street theater was $3,000,000, he quickly wrote a personal check for that amount. The transaction took no more than ten minutes. After the purchase of the Hellinger, Farrell used his Albany family's ball-bearing fortune to back Broadway shows.

Jule answered, "I risked my whole ASCAP for that money. If we were bombing tonight, you wouldn't even look at me." This wasn't true; Tony Farrell, a "dear man" plagued with alcoholism, was an easy touch and made many contributions to the theater.

"Eight to five," insisted Farrell.

"I don't want eight to five. You get it even. What if Atkinson doesn't like it?"

"I don't give a damn," said Farrell. "This show is ten times better than the other one."

"Give me six to five," said Jule, setting a pattern to sell off the $90,000 Mike Levy loan in limited partnerships. This was accomplished in two weeks, Jule soon to realize that he'd set the wrong odds. *Pal Joey* paid off at four to one, a nice return on any tote board, and once more ample proof that Jule Styne was not a good businessman.

Richard Rodgers was beaming at intermission. His gravely ill wife, Dorothy, had been wheeled in on a stretcher and was there, misty-eyed in back of the theater, to see the full potential of her husband's work.

The New Haven opening was clearly rated a smash.

Mike Goldreyer had been complaining to Jule for at least a week that too much money was being spent; that the slim reserve they had would be drained off before they got to Broadway. Goldreyer had no idea that the limited partnerships were already being snapped up. Returning from New Haven on the N. Y. Central, excited over the opening, firmly believing they had a solid hit, a jubilant Jule wove down the aisle of the train car to stand beside Mike's seat. Jule said he'd just had a long talk with Bob Alton and they'd decided that for the final curtain at the Broadhurst every member of the chorus would walk on the stage with a greyhound.

"Mike, there's never been a finale like that," said Jule, putting him on. "Now, as soon as we get in, call that place that rents dogs and then go to the Astor and lease an entire floor to take care of them. You'll have to handle them personally. Twenty-four greyhounds! Wow, what a finale!"

"Yes, Jule," Goldreyer replied obediently. Mike had long been a foil, taking Jule's every request seriously.

A few minutes after the train pulled into Grand Central Station, Jule's second assistant, Sylvia Herscher, received a frantic call from Goldreyer. "Godalmighty, they've gone crazy," blurted Mike.

"What's the matter?" asked Sylvia.

"You've got to talk some sense to Jule and Bob Alton. They want me to rent twenty-four greyhounds and put them up at the Astor."

Sylvia laughed. "Haven't you learned by now?"

Clearly, Jule's mood was good; the problems of the show were safely behind him.

Pal Joey opened at the Broadhurst on January 3, 1952, emerging as the first hit of the season, a sellout from opening night. Incredibly, the revival had the longest run of any Rodgers and Hart show, staying at the Lee Shubert house for 542 performances, becoming the second musical revival in theater history to pass the magic five hundred mark. The show still holds the Broadway record for the longest-running revival, even surpassing the perennial *The Red Mill.*

Mr. Atkinson changed his mind about *Pal Joey.* He wrote that the revival "renews confidence in the professionalism of the theater."

The Critic's Circle named *Pal Joey* "best musical of the year," contrary to their own rules of awarding prizes only to new productions. The Columbia Records' cast album, with Lang and Segal, was a best seller. "Bewitched, Bothered and Bewildered" was born again, going to the top of the charts, providing more coin for Mr. Rodgers and the Hart estate. Columbia's musical mastermind, Goddard Lieberson, nominated this version of *Pal Joey* as one of the ten best musicals ever performed.

Jule could not have had a "fuller house" for his first venture as a theatrical producer. He soon moved his own "house" from Fifty-seventh Street to Fifty-first, setting up shop in a converted dressing room of the Mark Hellinger. His friend and backer Tony Farrell thought Jule might like to be closer to the smell of the theater; hear it breathe.

7

The relationship with a long-time spouse never really ends with divorce. It smolders for years, now and then catching fire in anger; dying out again for one reason or another. There are moments of memory and sadness.

—JULE STYNE, 1977

It was now time to think about *In Any Language,* the Ed Beloin–Hank Garson play to be staged by George Abbott, hopefully in the fall. This pattern of two or three simultaneous projects, all in various stages, was always to continue, with varying results. At times, the projects suffered.

One of the projects taking place during this period again involved Anita Loos. "He called me and said he wanted me to write a libretto for a musical starring Marlene Dietrich. It was something that came flying out of that fertile mind. So I got an idea for it, and told him about it. 'Go ahead, that's great. Do a treatment.' And we signed a contract. So I got about halfway through it, and he called again to say, 'Listen, forget about Dietrich. Split that character of Marlene's into three people. It's now going to be the King Sisters.' Well, that was quite a change, Marlene Dietrich to the King Sisters. I laughed and got back to work. I was just about through with the King Sisters when he called again to say, 'Forget the King Sisters. Put it back into one character and build it for Sophie Tucker.'

"I really began to despair over the whole thing. I didn't know what to do with Jule's changes of mind. So I went to a fortuneteller and said,

'I have a contract with someone and he's driving me nuts.' I told her the story of Marlene Dietrich and the King Sisters and Sophie Tucker. She went into a trance and when she came out she said, 'Forget the whole thing, forget it ever happened.' But I was furious with myself. It was all right to say 'forget it,' but I had a contract with Jule. Then I went home and looked it up. It had expired six months previously. I think that if you went to Jule and said you had an idea to do a musical about Albert Einstein, he'd say, 'Wow, that's sensational!' "

The day before the opening of *In Any Language,* October 8, 1952, George Abbott approached Jule to say, "I'll give you forty thousand for your rights. You'll make thirty thousand before curtain."

Jule replied graciously, "Mr. Abbott, if you said you were unhappy and wanted to quit, and wanted your money back, I'd agree. I might also agree if you just wanted to give me my ten thousand back. But when George Abbott offers me forty thousand for ten, he must believe he has a big, big hit. So I decline your kind offer."

Mr. Abbott replied, "Thank you for your confidence, Jule."

The play opened the next night and the reviews were not only bad but actually dismissed it. One paper alloted exactly seven sentences. An open-shut situation within the week, Mr. Abbott being $65,000 poorer; Mr. Styne only $10,000.

On October 28th, 1952, Ethel Styne told a Los Angeles Superior Court judge, "When he went to New York on his trips, I asked to go but he wouldn't take me along. He was critical of everything I did." Mrs. Styne also told the judge that she had become a living example of Jule's song, "I'll Walk Alone."

The divorce was granted. An out-of-court settlement awarded Ethel the 611 Elm Drive house, $1,500 monthly, and fifteen to thirty percent of everything he earned yearly over $100,000.

The grounds for the divorce was desertion, Ethel's lawyer choosing not to file on incompatibility. For Jule, it was a costly choice of legal terminology. Almost immediately, the Internal Revenue Service made a ruling that Jule's deductions of living expenses in New York, charged off as business over the past three years, were invalid. All the while, they maintained, he'd been a resident of California, with a legal domicile there. The IRS laid claim to upwards of a hundred thousand dollars. Over a thirteen-year period this initial debt to the government, including interest, ballooned to $650,000.

Of course, there were other costly side effects of the dissolution. From time to time, Jule wondered about the affection of his sons;

whether or not they loved him; missed him. During the period in which Ethel was going to court for her divorce, young Norton Styne was preparing for his bar mitzvah, a celebration that never occurred. There was an elaborate copy of the Holy Scriptures in the house, a gift of Grandmother and Grandfather Stein, and it was customary in some Jewish families for the father to present his son with an inscribed copy of the book on the occasion of bar mitzvah. One day the boy, thinking about the upcoming event, sat down and wrote in the book: "To Nortie, from Dad, with love." Jule did not learn of the pretense until years later.

I was shocked with what had happened to David Selznick.

—JULE STYNE, 1977

Even before Ethel went to court, and before *In Any Language* passed almost unnoticed into theatrical history, Jule had another project going. *Pal Joey* was still bringing in solid cash, and Bob Alton was interested in doing another show as quickly as possible. Alton's own stock was high as the result of the *Joey* reviews. Jule agreed, in September, that they should strike again, and decided on converting *Nothing Sacred,* a David Selznick hit movie, starring the late Carole Lombard, to the musical stage. He'd thought about it, off and on, for years. Based on a *New Yorker* short story, the screenplay for the comedy had been written by Ben Hecht and Charles MacArthur.

Jule had met Hecht during his Hollywood period and now contacted him to write the libretto, this time under the title *Hazel Flagg.* "Make your screenplay work for the stage." But Ben Hecht was ailing and in constant pain. He was almost broke and agreed to do the book for two percent of the gross, against an advance of $2,500. In earlier years, Hecht could make double that in one week.

Next contacted was David Selznick, whose fortunes had also faded. The famed producer of *Gone with the Wind* and other hits was now residing in New York. But his company still owned the rights to *Nothing Sacred.* Selznick sent his lawyer round and a verbal deal for the property was worked out within several hours. Then the lawyer said, "Now, Mr. Selznick would like an advance."

Jule countered, "I'll give him the usual deal. One percent of the gross or ten percent of the net."

"Mr. Selznick wants ten thousand now."

Jule immediately phoned Selznick to say that it was unheard of in the theater to pay $10,000 against one percent of the gross; that the property might not jell; the ten thousand could be lost in a dozen ways. Then he sweetened it: "The day I go into rehearsal, I'll give you ten."

Selznick asked to speak to his lawyer. They chatted a moment and then the lawyer hung up. "Mr. Selznick wants his ten now." Jule declined and the lawyer departed.

Within a few minutes, Jule began having second thoughts. *Pal Joey* was making money. Why not use the profits?

Bob Alton was already at work; Ben Hecht had about a quarter of the libretto finished. The project was under way. Why not?

The check was written that afternoon, made out to Selznick personally, not to his company. The lawyer said they didn't want a voucher statement, nothing on paper about the purpose of the check. A separate letter of agreement would be drafted later. Jule had an ominous feeling. Why nothing on paper? Why no voucher statement? He sat for a while, then uneasily signed the check.

Three weeks went by, and then the cancelled check was returned. His assistant said, "Jule, look at this! Selznick endorsed it but it's stamped Gristede's. Do you think he cashed a check that big there?"

Jule phoned Gristede's, the New York market chain, worked his way to the treasurer, identified himself and said he'd never heard of a grocery store cashing a check that large over the counter.

The market official sighed and asked for confidence. "Mr. Selznick owes us sixteen thousand dollars."

Jule hung up, feeling both embarrassed and sorry for David Selznick. *But these were all signposts, omens. In seven-foot letters. I should have quit that day.*

As soon as Hecht finished the libretto, Jule began writing the music, with Bob Hilliard as lyricist. David Alexander signed on as director, and the presentation credit went to Jule and Tony Farrell, his landlord in the Hellinger.

In late 1952, they signed Thomas Mitchell to play the male lead. He had agreed to do *Hazel Flagg* only if Helen Gallagher played the

Carole Lombard role—that of a brattish girl who wants to get away from New York and claims she's dying, allowing the city to open hearts and wallets.

Second female lead went to Sheree North after Jule flew to California to audition her at a strip joint. She was Alton's choice. Benay Venuta rounded out the principal cast.

Isn't it funny, I kept having that "Gristede's" feeling as the days went on. Mitchell was a fine actor but not right for the part, and I knew it. Gallagher was sensational when someone else carried the main load. She had great style and danced beautifully but again, wrong for the part. Lombard could touch your heart. Gallagher couldn't.

At the end of the first rehearsal in the Mark Hellinger, Jule stood up. "Ladies and gentlemen, I apologize. I haven't done my work properly. I'm going home and rewrite four numbers. I'll see you in a week."

Hazel Flagg opened February 11, 1953, to either chill, lukewarm or fair reviews. No one cheered show or cast, though Sheree North swamped Miss Gallagher for individual attention. Jule's music was too loud and cynical for Mr. Atkinson. Others agreed, more or less. "The music is loud and syncopated but banal," wrote John Chapman in the *News.* But out of the score came two excellent Styne–Hilliard songs, "How Do You Speak to an Angel?" and "Ev'ry Street's a Boulevard in Old New York."

The show closed quickly, but then Tony Farrell reopened it, starring Sheree North. *Another mistake. Once you have a dud, nothing can help. If you have a hit, they'll break the doors down. I learned that you should only pour money into a hit to make it a bigger hit.*

Hazel Flagg closed again, and only Gristede's benefited from the production.

Later in the same year doctors discovered that Ethel Styne had cancer of the uterus, and gave her no more than six months to live. Jule said to their oldest son, Stanley, who had been working in New York, learning the music publishing business and serving as an assistant stage manager on Jule's shows, "You have to go back and live with your mother and Nortie."

Jule wrote to Ethel, addressing her as Mrs. Jule Styne, telling her how sorry he was; suggesting she take a trip to Europe. She'd never been there.

Displaying the letter, Ethel said to her sister, Lillian, "Look, he still calls me 'Mrs. Jule Styne.' Oh, my."

9

Frank was always full of surprises. Master of the unexpected.

—JULE STYNE, 1977

James Jones's best-selling novel, *From Here to Eternity,* was being mounted for production at Columbia Pictures in early 1953, and Sinatra sought the part of Angelo Maggio, which Harry Cohn had already staked out for Eli Wallach. Whatever Cohn's choice, Sinatra believed that he was the best Maggio around.

In Africa at the time, sidelining the set where Sinatra's wife Ava Gardner worked with Clark Gable in *Mogambo,* he discussed the role with Gable. Some of Gable's success had been due to a natural humility, and "The King" advised Sinatra to swallow his pride, screen-test for Maggio and take it at any price. The part was to be fourth in billing.

Sinatra returned to Hollywood, tested for director Fred Zinnemann, flew back to Africa, and spent a few restless weeks awaiting word. Finally, Zinnemann, Cohn and co-producer Buddy Adler cabled good news. Sinatra signed for the role of Maggio. Salary: $8,000.

After completing *Eternity,* with Zinnemann ecstatic over Frank's straight dramatic acting and predicting an Academy Award, Sinatra returned to New York and called Jule.

He wanted me to listen to a new album. Songs for Young Lovers.

Included in it was my old song, "Sunday." For the first time in several years, he seemed optimistic. Between Eternity *and the new album, he thought he'd turn around and go back to the top. He seemed sure of himself again. This was the Sinatra of old, the one I loved.*

Eternity, released in September, did turn Frank Sinatra around. *The New Yorker, Newsweek, Time* magazine, usually murderer's row for the singer, sniping at him unmercifully, praised him unanimously. The album *Songs for Young Lovers* was a simultaneous hit.

It must have been in early October when he called me down to Atlantic City. He was at the 500 Club. So I went down, and we sat on the beach that sunny fall afternoon. Suddenly, people began to come like locusts. They were after Angelo Maggio, if not Sinatra. He yelled, "Follow me," and we ran.

Back in the hotel, Frank laughed. "Remember what we were talking about that night at the Red Devil? Now, I'm a star again."

"That's what you've always been about," Jule recalls replying.

The romance of Styne–Cahn–Sinatra was definitely on again in 1953 and 1954, although Frank's romance with Ava Gardner was apparently in an off condition. Both parties were protecting their privacy, but it was known that the marriage was in trouble. Close friends of Sinatra went so far as to say that their man was still very much in love with her. Gardner stayed mostly in Europe.

Having signed a twenty-week contract with Fox to do *Pink Tights,* co-starring Marilyn Monroe, Sinatra had insisted to producer Sol Siegel that Styne–Cahn do the film's songs. Both men were delighted to re-team with Frank, and were looking forward to working with Monroe as well.

The first time that Jule met Monroe was on Stage 4, at Fox, where she was being still-photographed by Milton Green, during the filming of *Gentlemen Prefer Blondes.*

I looked at her and had a feeling of doom. She was beautiful, but there was something in her eyes that spelled disaster. We became friendly, and I began to recognize that awful insecurity that some people talked about. Later on, in New York, at a big party in the apartment of director Sidney Lumet and Mrs. Lumet—Gloria Vanderbilt—I could feel that insecurity, physically feel it. Everyone was there. Comden and Greene, Sammy Davis, Lena Horne, Moss Hart, Kitty Carlisle, Phyllis Newman, George Axelrod, Walter Matthau, Martin Gabel, Arlene Francis, and others. Everyone who could entertain did entertain. I was at the piano and after about an hour of this block-busting private show, Marilyn came over and whispered, "Ask me to sing." So I did, and everyone yelled, "Yeh, Marilyn!" She came over and sat down on the piano bench beside me and sang "Bye, Bye, Baby." She was digging her fingernails into my upper arm with almost every word. Inside, she was like a drawn bowstring.

Sammy and Jule quickly completed the songs for *Pink Tights* and Jule began rehearsing Monroe, who was then doing a clumsy, garish film entitled *There's no Business Like Show Business,* co-starring Ethel Merman, Donald O'Connor and Mitzi Gaynor. *Tights* would start almost as soon as the other film finished. *I'd wait for her in her dressing room. I wasn't allowed to turn and look at her until her wig was off, and a bandanna thing replaced it. One day I asked her how she was. She stood in back of me and held my face. She said, "I'm tired, I'm so very tired." She'd made* Blondes *the previous year. Almost constant filming for ten months. They were wrecking her and she didn't want to do* Tights. *And, of course, Frank was commuting to Europe almost every weekend to save his marriage. Not a good way to start any picture.*

Balking, threatening to walk off, Monroe couldn't have cared less when Fox brought in Sheree North as Marilyn's possible replacement for the *Pink Tights* part. *What the stupid Fox front office couldn't seem to understand was that Marilyn Monroe did not want to do any film at that time. She was exhausted.*

Monroe finally checked off the lot and went to Japan with Joe DiMaggio. Meanwhile, Sinatra remained on salary for twenty weeks, as did Styne–Cahn and others. *Pink Tights* was postponed while the front office scratched heads, unable to pair Sinatra with Sheree North.

Jule, living at the Beverly Hills Hotel, came in late one afternoon and asked for the key to Room 314. The desk clerk informed him, "You don't live here anymore."

"Where do I live?" asked Jule, rather puzzled.

"Mr. Sinatra came here and moved you out. You'll be living with him."

That was typical Sinatra, Jule thought. *Surprise, surprise.* A pleasant one, however. Jule said to the bell captain, "Which one of the boys packed my bags? I want to tip him."

"Mr. Sinatra packed your bags and carried them out himself." That was also typical Sinatra, in a case of this sort.

Jule caught a cab to Frank's apartment at Wilshire and Beverly Glen and was greeted at the door by the butler. "Mr. Sinatra is taking a rest. Perhaps you'd like to rest, too. You're going to dinner with him tonight at Mr. Goetz's home. It's black tie."

Jule went up to his room. Every pair of socks had been put away by Sinatra. Every shirt was lying neatly in a drawer. Suits were hung up. When Sinatra packed, either for himself or anyone else, it was always a work of art. Jule had seen him do it in the past. He'd even provided a sun reflector so that Jule could tan himself on the little porch just outside the room.

I stood there wondering what this was all about. I couldn't understand Frank's motives. I knew he was going through hell with Ava and perhaps he just wanted company. I was flattered, of course.

In the early evening, Frank said, "Look, I hope you'll be happy here. Thank you for coming."

Jule replied, "For God's sake, don't thank me. Between us, maybe we can put it all back together."

Black ties were donned for the William Goetz party. Goetz was a veteran film producer. Very wealthy, Bill and Edie Goetz had an added touch of class—original Picassos in their powder rooms. Their sit-down dinners sometimes included sixty or so guests.

As Jule and Frank got into the car, Frank said, "You're not staying with me tonight."

Jule was astounded. "You've just moved me in."

"I know, but I've got a date, and the girl knows you."

Jule said, "Isn't that funny? Why didn't you leave me at the hotel? All my clothes are in your apartment."

Frank said, "You'll stay tonight at the Beverly Hills and then move back in with me tomorrow."

Jule ran back to the apartment, quickly packed a small bag with a toothbrush, shaving kit and pajamas. With his breathless passenger in the car again, Sinatra drove off to the Goetz home for the gold-plate dinner.

With at least fifteen female guests in attendance, Jule, sitting diagonally across from Sinatra, launched into a guessing game. Which lady? Discreetly, he pointed to one woman after another while the smiling Francis Albert shook his head.

Eventually Jule thought, to hell with it. This was again fun and games. Who cared who Sinatra was about to take to bed? *But, suddenly, he was gone, and I looked around to check all the females. None seemed to be missing. Then, I thought, Oh, my God, he took my bag. I ran out to the door and was handed a note by the Goetz butler. "See you in the morning."*

Party over, Jule took a cab to the Beverly Hills Hotel and the night clerk passed over the key to Room 314. "I don't live there anymore," said Jule.

"Yes, you do," said the night clerk. "Mr. Sinatra checked you in." Then a bellhop walked over with the small black bag.

Up in the room, Jule panicked. He'd left his pills in Sinatra's apartment and his ulcers were pulsating. The Goetz food, like the powder rooms, had been overly rich. Just before midnight, he called Sammy Cahn for assistance.

"Where are you?" asked Cahn.

"I'm at the Beverly Hills Hotel."

"I thought you were living with Frank."

"I was. But now I'm not. I'm calling from the Beverly Hills, Sammy, and I don't have my pills."

"What happened?" asked Cahn, wondering if his old friend was drunk.

"Tonight I can't stay there. He has a broad."

Sammy said, "Wait until I put my glasses on."

"To laugh, you have to put glasses on?"

Sammy was hysterical.

"Sammy, I'll tell you my problem. Do you have any Donnatol Extentabs?"

"I don't take them any longer."

Jule said, "If I don't take them, I won't sleep. My stomach's killing me."

Sammy told him to go to a Beverly Hills pharmacy and "ask for Jimmy and he'll give you two. Tell him who you are, and mention my name."

Jule got re-dressed in his tuxedo, took a cab to the pharmacy and asked for Jimmy. Jimmy had gone home, he was told. The pharmacist on duty did not know Sammy Cahn and refused to issue the pills without a doctor's prescription.

Jule called Sammy again from a phone booth. Sammy said, "Fuck that guy. Go back to Frank's apartment. You've got a back-door key, don't you? Use the back door and get your pills. Leave the cab down the street. Take your shoes off and go quietly. If Frank sees you, just say, 'I forgot my pills and I'm dying.' "

Jule did as instructed, entered through the back door, heard classical music playing and tip-toed up for his pills. As he was leaving, he saw the girl in the living room. The girl did not see Jule. Nor did Sinatra.

The balance of the night was spent in Room 314 and then at 9:30 the next morning Jule trooped sheepishly through the hotel lobby in his tuxedo, breakfast-goers eyeing him curiously.

During this same period, producer Leland Hayward signed a "showcase" deal with NBC-TV, and soon planned an hour of *Anything Goes,* the Cole Porter Broadway musical originally starring Ethel Merman. Hayward wanted Merman to repeat her role in a studio to advertise Colgate toothpaste. Serving as executive producer, Hayward offered the producer's job to Jule.

Former talent agent Hayward had presented *A Bell for Adano* as his initial Broadway production, to be followed by *State of the Union, Mr. Roberts, South Pacific* and others. He'd produced Merman's *Call Me Madam.* Jule and Hayward had first met during the nervous money-raising auditions for *Gentlemen Prefer Blondes,* and Hayward had later been impressed by Jule's handling of *Pal Joey.* But this NBC-Colgate venture was not to approximate any of his past shows. With only fifty minutes of playing time in which to cram at least ten songs, the libretto would occupy no more than twelve or fifteen minutes. It appeared to be a thankless if not hopeless undertaking, but Jule was anxious to try working for television.

He went back to Sinatra's apartment that evening to find his host busy in the kitchen, cooking spaghetti. Jule said to Frank, "Leland Hayward has asked me to do something for him."

Frank answered, "Do what he wants you to do. If Hayward asked me to do something for him, I would."

"How about if Jule Styne asked you?"

"That's a foregone conclusion."

Jule said, "You and Ethel Merman in *Anything Goes,* for NBC."

"Hey," said Frank.

Jule then busied himself as a first-time TV producer. He went to Bert Lahr, who hadn't spoken to Merman for about fifteen years. They'd co-starred in *DuBarry Was a Lady.* Jule said to Lahr, "I don't know what it was all about, but I know you and Ethel haven't spoken to each other for fifteen years."

Lahr replied, "I have nothing against her."

Jule said, "She's made for you. She's absolutely dying to do this thing with you."

Bert said, "You'll have to interpolate 'Friendship.' I'll do it if that song is in it."

Then Jule went to Merman. He said, "Ethel, I know you and Bert Lahr haven't spoken in fifteen years but he's mad to do this show with you. He's absolutely dying to do it with you."

"I don't have anything against Bert," she said. "But we must do 'Friendship.' "

"I wouldn't dream of leaving that number out," said Jule, and departed, his principal cast set except for a sexy girl. He got Sheree North, late of *Hazel Flagg.*

Anything Goes was live TV, a harum-scarum thing before the advent of tape. Costume changes alone were nightmarish. However, Sinatra, Merman and Lahr were all veteran performers and there was little complaint from them.

In dress rehearsal, Hayward approached producer Styne. "The timer tells me that you're three minutes too long."

Jule replied, "I hope the timer is right. Okay, I'll cut three minutes."

Some hours later *Anything Goes* was down to the last song, Sinatra singing the title tune in finale, when the booth frantically signaled to Jule that he was "two minutes short." He ran toward conductor Buddy Bregman, making a circle over his head, holding up two fingers. He gave the same signal to Frank, who began to laugh, and improvised, "In olden days . . . you see, ladies and gentlemen, we're two minutes short . . ."

Old-timers Merman and Lahr smoothly picked it up, ad-libbing, too. "How could we possibly be two minutes short?" The audience howled as the trio toyed with the lyrics.

Jule stayed on in the Sinatra apartment, fun and games continuing.

10

We didn't get lucky with "Three Coins in the Fountain," we just knew what we were doing.

—SAMMY CAHN, 1977

In the early winter of 1954, with *Pink Tights* canceled, Fox producer Sol Siegel, having moved upward from Republic Studios long ago, called Sammy and Jule into his office to admit that he'd made a "godawful" picture, *We Believe in Love.* Even the director, Jean Negulesco, had thrown up after seeing a rough-cut with Zanuck. Siegel said that the film needed a lot of help and that he wanted the team to write a theme song. He also pointed out that they'd been collecting salary during the past eighteen weeks for essentially doing nothing, though they'd completed the *Pink Tights* songs.

We Believe in Love, based on John Secondari's *Three Coins in the Fountain,* was then screened for Styne–Cahn and proved indeed to be "godawful," despite personal doctoring by Zanuck. Yet the photography of Rome's fountains was superb; the girls were also pretty.

Jule's first suggestion to Siegel was, "Why don't you call it *Three Coins in the Fountain?*"

"Can you write a song for that title?" asked the producer.

Sammy said, "It's a helluva lot easier than *We Believe in Love.*" Sammy was already rhyming in his head, and claims it took no more than twenty minutes to write the lyrics. Jule drew on his classical background to provide a "Mascagni feeling."

Next morning they met at Fox, matched words and music, polished and before noon played it for Siegel and Zanuck. Both men were pleased. Zanuck then called New York to inform Spyro Skouras about the song and change of title. Skouras was not pleased. He said the new title had "no commercial value." It was always a mistake to drop "love" from any title, he maintained. Within an hour, he was supported by the advertising and publicity staff, usual head-nodders.

Zanuck then phoned Styne–Cahn to say that he believed the only way to make the New York front office accept the title was to have it recorded by a major star.

Styne volunteered, "Why don't I try to get Frank to do it?"

This pleased Zanuck once again. Skouras and the advertising executives would debate a long time before rejecting a Sinatra theme.

Jule flew to New York on Friday, hoping to meet Sinatra either in Manhattan or at the airport, on the stopover en route home from Europe. Calls in New York indicated that Frank would be coming through Sunday night on TWA's Ambassador flight. Jule booked a seat on the same flight, boarded the plane and waited.

Just before the door closed, Sinatra came down the aisle to say to Styne, "Hey, what are you doing here?"

Jule said he'd come in on business. He settled beside Frank in the seat conveniently left vacant by the airline. About an hour out, after exchanging gossip bits, Jule said to Sinatra, "Get some sleep, Frank. Zanuck wants you to do a record for him in the morning." Very carefully, *Zanuck.* Not Siegel or Styne.

Sinatra responded that he was exhausted from the Atlantic flight; had no intention of recording for anyone, including DFZ.

Jule said, "It's set up for eight o'clock. You've been collecting salary for twenty weeks like we have, and they've got a picture that needs a lot of help. Zanuck said he'll give you anything you want."

Sinatra thought about it, and finally said, "Okay. But I don't want money. I'll do it for Sammy and you. I saw a painting in a gallery, and I want it. A Vlaminck. I think it's ten thousand." That was about forty thousand cheaper than Sinatra's usual rate for rendering a movie theme song.

"You'll get it," Jule promised, as if he owned Fox.

Frank asked to hear the song and Jule sang it above the roar of the Constellation engines but Frank was asleep before the final bars.

Sinatra and Styne arrived on the lot about 8:30 A.M. that Monday, and went to the recording stage, where a sixty-piece orchestra performed "Three Coins in the Fountain."

"It's very pretty," said Sinatra. He went over behind a flat, clearing his throat. He asked for juice and coffee, worried about his voice.

Jule said, "Frank, let's make one. Lay a track down. Then you can put the earphones on. Let's get something down . . ."

In the middle of the practice take, miraculous timing, in walked Spyro Skouras with the New York front office entourage. Frank knew how to soften them up. "Hey, the Greek!," he waved. "Hey, Charlie."

The orchestra began to play. With Sinatra ten feet away, Skouras had to admire the song. "It's wonderfulll . . ."

Then Sinatra sang it, and Skouras yelled, "Bravo!"

Zanuck and Siegel were home free. Ironically, the song became an immediate hit for The Four Aces group, not Sinatra, and went on to aid the film in grossing $9 million, not the anticipated $1.2 million. *But the difference was Frank Sinatra. Without him it wouldn't have gotten off the ground.*

Angelo Maggio paid off for Sinatra that spring, too. *From Here to Eternity* took eight Academy Awards, one of which was best supporting actor. Winner: Frank Sinatra.

Departing Fox, Jule gave himself some time off, played golf and saw friends; went out nightly. Among his stops was the Mocambo night club, on the Sunset Strip, where Sammy Davis Jr. was headlined. Jule had seen Sammy, still a youth, work with the Will Mastin Trio. Davis was now grown-up and just beginning to move his individual career.

No black man had starred in a Broadway book show for a long time, and Jule thought that Sammy Davis was not only ideal for a breakthrough but could, indeed, carry a musical. He had a few talks with Sammy who liked the idea, providing it could be a book show, not a revue.

"The sooner the better," Sammy finally said.

Jule pointed out that it would take six months to do the libretto and write the score.

"You'll do the score?"

"No, I'm tied up in TV but I'll get the best possible librettist and best possible composer and lyricist. I promise that." Jule also said he'd actively function as producer.

The William Morris Agency, representing Davis, immediately balked. Davis could make much more money in Las Vegas; in clubs anywhere. The show might fold; Broadway might not be ready for a black star. The agency had a dozen money-oriented reasons why Broadway was a bad risk for Sammy Davis Jr. However, the William Morris ten-percenters quickly found opposition, oddly enough, from Sammy's parents, particularly his mother. Mr. and Mrs. Davis, anxious to see their son starring on the legitimate stage, applied enough pressure to overcome all the Morris objections. A deal was made, though it was likely the show wouldn't be produced for a year or so.

In early summer, Jule was at CBS-TV, Hollywood, functioning as producer of *A Shower of Stars*, the first color extravaganza, a program alternating with *Playhouse 90.* Among his showering stars were Ethel Merman and Red Skelton.

Jule was a rather frantic TV producer. Staffers on *Shower of Stars* didn't like him very much. He was too demanding, they said; too impatient. Some found his "Stynese" to be plain incoherency.

One staffer who liked him, and realized that the garbling was mainly a case of mind-being-quicker-than-tongue, was a small, attractive blond New Yorker, Dorothy Dicker, secretary to Nat Perrin, executive producer of *Stars.* Dorothy, who was in her early twenties, discovered that she could decode "Stynese"; in turn, Jule learned that Miss Dicker could take dictation from him, a remarkable feat. They became close friends in a completely nonromantic way. Dorothy thought that what Jule really needed was someone to organize him, to keep track of those ideas that popped out like spring buds.

It's true. Dorothy was a model of efficiency and organization, which I'm not. She was protective and when she needed to be, tough. I told her that if she ever came back to New York, she should give me a call. That's the way we left it.

After several *Shower of Stars,* Jule went back to a more familiar type of staging, producing *Panama Hattie* for NBC-TV. Starring Merman, Art Carney and Jack Leonard, the musical was telescoped into an hour, repeating the *Anything Goes* formula, airing in late 1954. The flavor of the stage production came through but little else, given the short allotted time. Though he found the new medium exciting, the frustrations of the clock and the inability to be truly creative left Jule with little desire to continue on as a television producer.

Meanwhile, Jule had received a note from Sinatra: "I'd appreciate it if you'd move." There was no further explanation. Jule was both puzzled and a bit hurt, but packed up and transferred himself back to the Beverly Hills Hotel, Room 314.

It took a while for him to figure out why Sinatra was angry. Throughout the previous months, Jule couldn't resist talking about his life with Frank. After all, there was no choicer gossip in Hollywood than that involving Francis Albert Sinatra. Dinner partners or cocktail holders were always hungry for it, and Sinatra was almost paranoid about guarding his personal life. Some very private details began to float around and the source was obviously Jule Styne. "The note to please leave was very much deserved," Jule admitted.

By midsummer, *Peter Pan,* starring Mary Martin and Cyril Ritchard, was on the road prior to the New York opening and reportedly at loose ends. Playing at the Curran, in San Francisco, the show, with music by Mark "Moose" Charlap and lyrics by Carolyn Leigh, had received bad notices and was limping along. Producer Leland Hayward and director Jerome Robbins had already made a guess: They had a musical that wasn't musical enough; neither was it theatrical, in terms of Martin and Ritchard. Locating Comden and Green in Hollywood, where they were completing a film script, Hayward and Robbins also contacted Jule.

Peter Pan was definitely in peril. There was no over-all theme song. Ritchard did not have a character song. There was no "together" song for Captain Hook and Peter Pan. Jule said to Hayward and Robbins, "You've got two big stars and they never sing together. That's appalling. They have to have a duet." Then the plot songs were discussed.

In about a week, Comden–Green–Styne, who were living at the Fairmont Hotel, came up with eight new songs. First, they assembled an over-all theme, "Neverland," and then provided Ritchard with "Captain Hook's Waltz."

Comden–Green found the duet in "Are You Animal? Are You Vegetable?" Just what was Peter Pan? Captain Hook would like to know. The song went into the score.

Jule, of course, had coached Martin at Paramount in *Maid of California* years before, and remembered her voice range. "Mary, I want to hear that coloratura voice. A woman's voice, distinctly female." He then wrote a series of soprano cadenzas. "O, Mysterious Lady" was the result.

The show traveled on to Los Angeles and New York, and though the New York reviews were restrained, *Peter Pan* played fifty weeks on Broadway, due mainly to the presence of Martin and Ritchard. The later TV version, with the same cast, was judged more effective, drawing the largest TV audience to that time.

11

Jule was crazy about Jayne Mansfield
but he didn't have to cope with her. I did.

—SYLVIA HERSCHER, 1977

In traditional winner style, Jule and Sammy ran to the Academy Awards stage in the spring of 1955 to accept their Oscars for "Three Coins in the Fountain," best song from any film produced in 1954. Jule had previously been nominated for "I Don't Want to Walk Without You, Baby," "I'll Walk Alone," "It's Magic" and "It Seems to Me I've Heard that Song Before." He believed that several of the other songs were superior to "Three Coins" but appreciatively clutched his golden statuette, bestowed by Bing Crosby, and let Sammy make the acceptance speech.

A few weeks later, Jule bought a copy of the new *Rodgers and Hart Songbook,* a collection of all their hits, and mulled it over, then went excitedly to playwright George Axelrod, certain there was a smash musical contained therein, the very best of Rodgers and Hart. Axelrod's hilarious *The Seven-Year Itch,* starring Tom Ewell, had dominated the comedy season in 1952.

Envisioning himself as producer of Rodgers and Hart, Jule said, "George, I want you to do an original story, embracing this whole thing."

Axelrod replied that he wanted to think about it but the idea sounded good. Several days later, he lunched with Jule to outline the story of a black pianist who made the Hollywood party circuit, playing for people like Bill and Edie Goetz. He would play music by Rodgers and Hart, naturally.

The phone soon rang in Sammy Cahn's Beverly Hills home. "Listen," said Jule, "I'm about to do the biggest musical I've ever done."

Sammy said, "I'm braced."

Jule said, "Do you know *The Rodgers and Hart Songbook?*"

"Yes," said Sammy.

"I'm going to make a musical out of it," said Jule.

"You've sure got a score."

"It'll be sensational," said Jule.

"The Rodgers and Hart Songbook?" said Sammy. "You're going to make a musical out of it? Jule, why don't you write your own musical?" Sammy was also thinking that Mr. Rodgers should make his own songbook, if he so desired.

"You don't understand, Sammy. Who do you think will write this for me?"

"I'm braced," said Sammy.

"George Axelrod."

Sammy said, "Jule, please. If you've got Axelrod, put your music to his words. You can't make hits out of Rodgers and Hart songs. They're hits already."

"You don't understand at all," said Jule, and hung up with a bang.

Sammy understood very well. This was his old friend and ex-partner flying high on another creative balloon trip, possibly positioning himself for shoot down. Or perhaps riches.

Another week passed while Axelrod roughed out a story entitled "Tinseltown," tailored for black pianist Bobby Short, who sang Rodgers and Hart material in his regular night-club performances. Axelrod then chose Evelyn Keyes for the female lead; Johnny Desmond as the male lead. Styne and Axelrod were proceeding as if they'd open in the fall.

Within a month, they set an audition for Richard Rodgers who was in somewhat the same frame of mind as on the day Jule barged in to resurrect *Pal Joey.* Rodgers listened to Short, Keyes and Desmond perform such songs as "Funny Valentine," "My Heart Stood Still" and "The Lady Is a Tramp."

As the last notes faded, Rodgers said bluntly to Jule and George

Axelrod, "These are not my kind of singers and I don't approve of their interpretation of my music."

End of *Rodgers and Hart Songbook* production.

Jule and Axelrod left the Rodgers office with as much dignity as possible but anger set in on the down elevator and Axelrod said, "Goddammit, I'll write you an original play."

He fulfilled the promise by submitting a rough play script two weeks later, entitled *Will Success Spoil Rock Hunter?* Jule read it and promptly forgot about the *Rodgers and Hart Songbook* defeat. The play was a partial portrait of Axelrod himself, and even in rough read well. "I'll direct," said Axelrod.

The new Jule Styne production was launched that week with a scheduled opening date in the fall. There was one gaping hole—a sexy blonde to play the part of Rita Marlowe. Jule had no problem raising money. Axelrod was in demand; anything that he wrote drew the attention of play-backers.

"That blonde," Axelrod said, "she has to be the right girl. She has to be an animal. I'm not condoning her. I'm just making a comment on her. Just a pretty girl won't do. She's selling sex and that's what the audience will buy." Clad only in a towel, the blonde opened the play decorating the top of a massage table.

Three months went by, and Jule forwarded the final script of *Will Success Spoil Rock Hunter?* to Sammy Cahn. Sammy read it, liked it very much but recalled the conversation about producing a musical from *The Rodgers and Hart Songbook.* There wasn't a note of music in this script; there wasn't one line that had anything to do with songs of any kind. "You see," said Sammy, "Jule creates crazy situations which bring about marvelous things."

Axelrod interviewed blondes for several weeks in late summer and not one had the Marilyn Monroe ingredients that he wanted. However, down in Philadelphia, co-starring in a B-picture entitled *Burglar,* was a sexy blonde, a former bit player named Jayne Mansfield. She'd been a hundred *Misses* in Hollywood—Miss Nylon, Miss Hundred Percent Pure; Miss Orchid; Miss Perfect Body. She was the darling of the cheesecake photographers and the Los Angeles Press Club.

In the same town, agent Bill Shiffrin read the Axelrod script and called his New York representative, Marty Baum, describing the role. Baum eventually said, "Unless they have Monroe, we've got the girl for that part. She's the most uninhibited dame I've ever met."

Baum then arranged for Jayne Mansfield to come up from Philly and read for the part. She walked onstage in a red leotard, swinging her hips, smiling widely, lips glistening. Jule remembers his reaction on her entrance. *Sold on first sight. An absolute click.* She began to read and after less than a page Jule jumped up. He said, "Don't read anymore. You'll spoil the illusion. You look the part. You are the part. You're perfect. You're hired, if Mr. Axelrod agrees."

Axelrod saw her at 4:00 P.M. that afternoon and said, "Sign her." Mansfield joined the cast of Orson Bean, Tina Louise and a comparative newcomer, Walter Matthau.

Sylvia Herscher, associate producer and manager of the show as well as the Styne office, Rose Goldstein having departed, was assigned to shepherdess Mansfield through the disciplines of the theater. "My God, I couldn't stand her. She was always late to rehearsals. It got so bad that I finally had to call a meeting with her. She was supposed to wear a body stocking on the stage, but didn't like it and often showed up stark naked. She ran around backstage nude, and the wardrobe mistress had to wash her feet before she went on."

At a meeting with Jule and Axelrod, Herscher came up with a control idea—a publicity campaign about a newcomer in theater who was so well disciplined that she completely enchanted the cast and stagehands. Was Jayne Mansfield born with this sense of discipline? Did she realize how easy she made it for everyone? Jayne began to read the planted stories, began to believe them and improved somewhat.

"Jayne was living over at the Gorham Hotel, with her daughter, four cats and a dog. I held my breath every night until she showed up at the Belasco," said Herscher.

Playing on Broadway at the time were such distinguished productions as *Cat on a Hot Tin Roof, The Diary of Anne Frank, Inherit the Wind* and *My Fair Lady.* No matter the heavy competition, *Rock Hunter* played to full houses every performance and largely responsible was warm, sexy, dirty-footed and undisciplined Jayne Mansfield.

The play ran to 452 closing curtains and the marquee went dark only because 20th Century-Fox demanded Mansfield for the cameras, having bought film rights to the Axelrod–Styne production.

Jule profited handsomely on the Axelrod parlay from *The Rodgers and Hart Songbook.*

12

I think Dorothy Dicker always had a crush on me, ever since CBS in Hollywood. And I was in love with her but a different kind of love, like living with someone without living with them. I felt married to Dorothy eventually. I revealed things to her that I'd never tell anyone else. No matter where I am, I talk to her at least twice a day.

—JULE STYNE, 1977

For months, throughout the summer and fall, Jule had been struggling with the Sammy Davis Jr. show. No good book-writer wanted to touch it. Each writer made excuses, such as the impossibility of using the Will Mastin Trio within the framework of the show. It was apparent that none wanted to handle the "black" theme. One writer, shocking Jule, said he could easily come up with a story that involved a black man raping a white woman. Broadway was loaded with closet bigots, much to Jule's surprise.

Since the first discussion of the show long ago at the Mocambo, Sammy had lost an eye in an auto accident but had recovered and was now looking forward to opening in *Mr. Wonderful*, a show still without a script. Then two TV writers, Joe Stein and Will Glicksman, who'd never written a libretto, presented an outline to the Styne office: A talented black entertainer from New Jersey is afraid to cross the river and enter the white-dominated show scene in New York; a white agent discovers him on the Jersey side and launches his career along with that of his father and uncle. *An uphill story, and I knew it was razor-thin and full of faults, but it was the best thing I'd read thus far.*

Wanting a new sound for the musical, Jule began auditioning young composors and lyricists. A total of fourteen teams were heard and then newcomer Jerry Bock and his partner, Larry Holofcener, played and sang a dozen of their works. Jule signed them. He thought Bock, in particular, had great potential, and in a few months both book and score were completed.

Jule was disappointed when Bock and Holofcener presented their first group of songs. Each one had problems. *They simply didn't have the experience. Bock had great talent but they turned in the theme song, "Mr. Wonderful," at 108 bars. I said, "Fellows, this isn't an opera. You can't sustain 108 bars." Then Jerry wrote a song for the beginning of the show that had a definite Gershwin influence. I told him to keep his top line but take out the Gershwin chords. Then I began to see what was wrong. Holofcener was hurting Bock simply because of inexperience in writing for the theater. So I brought in George Weiss, a meat-and-potatoes man. Sammy wanted to do an Astaire number, and in three days Bock and Weiss completed it: a hit, "Too Close for Comfort," pure Astaire. Of course, Bock went on to write* Fiddler on the Roof *and* Fiorello! *so he did have that great potential.*

The creative problems were matched by financial ones. Backing for the estimated $250,000 budget was difficult to obtain for many of the same reasons that writers had fled from the idea. Davis wasn't known on Broadway, and the black issue came up again and again. No less than two hundred angels finally capitalized the show, some investing no more than $500.

Sammy arrived in New York on December 8, 1955, for rehearsals. The arrival coincided with his thirtieth birthday.

Jule asked, "What would you like to do tonight?"

Sammy said, "I'd like to go to the "21" Club, but they might not let me in."

Jule, feeling embarrassed that he should have to check ahead, phoned Jack and Pete Kreindler, owners of the exclusive "21," and said that he wanted to bring Sammy Davis Jr. as his guest for a birthday celebration. *I didn't want anything negative to happen. The Kreindlers made certain that Sammy was treated casually, yet royally. An everynight occurrence was how it felt, thank God.*

A few weeks later, the show went into a three-month rehearsal schedule, with comedian Jack Carter signed for the role of the talent agent; Pat Marshall to be his wife in the play.

The little blond secretary from CBS in Hollywood had returned to New York and was looking for work. Jule well remembered Dorothy Dicker and her incredible ability to decipher "Stynese" in dictation. He promptly added her to the office on a temporary basis—If *Mr. Wonderful* was a success, she could stay on. But Dorothy had the feeling that she would stay on anyway. There were other musicals projected beyond the Davis show.

Sylvia Herscher was still general manager of Jule Styne Productions and handled Jule's somewhat complicated personal affairs as well as business matters. It wasn't too long until Dorothy became very curious about some of the people who went in and out of the office. They didn't seem to be show people. In fact, Herscher had once asked Jule, very facetiously, "Are we casting *Guys and Dolls?*"

To Dorothy's knowledge, she'd never seen a bookie before taking up daytime residence above the Mark Hellinger. She was seeing them now.

Dicker was also very curious about some of the lengthy closed-door sessions between Sylvia Herscher and her boss. She gathered, finally, that they were about finances and then connected that subject to racing forms and bookies. All along she'd thought that working for Jule would be a daily treat of lovely music coming from the small piano in the inner office. Not quite. Dorothy settled in as secretary and "gofer" and theatrical office apprentice.

Mr. Wonderful tried out in Philadelphia in early March 1956, and the reviews were unanimously bad. Not one critic liked the show, though they all praised the individual talent of Sammy Davis Jr. and took note of Jerry Bock's sounds.

The morning after opening a meeting was called in Jule's suite at the Bellevue-Stratford. Sammy walked in wearing a Brooks Brothers suit and horn-rimmed glasses, every bit the star. Sammy Sr. was also present, as was director Jack Donahue, Jack Carter and Will Mastin.

Mastin, who was Sammy's uncle, stood up. There was a line in the play, spoken by Jack Carter, in which he said he taught Sammy Jr. everything he knew. Mastin said, "I don't want Carter saying that '*I* taught Sammy everything he knows.' How do you think my friends react to that line?"

Jule thought, Oh, my God, he's bringing reality into this. We're already in deep trouble and he's hawking lines.

Mastin went on. "And we want more to say in this show. We're performers."

• • •

Mastin and Sammy Sr. admittedly had little more than nonspeaking minor support roles. When Sammy Jr. sang "The Birth of the Blues," Mastin and Sammy's father kept time by touching their cuff links. *As written in the script, they were ornamental more than functional. They were lost in more ways than one. On exit the opening night, they'd said hello to the drummer. They didn't understand a book show, I suddenly realized. To them, this was just a different approach to their night-club act, where it was okay to greet the lead trumpet; have a dialogue with the audience.*

As Mastin and Sammy Sr. angrily left the room, the William Morris agent leaned over to Jule. "Unless you listen to what he says, he'll pull Sammy."

Aside from a gesture, Jule knew there was no way to meet Mastin's demands.

Davis stayed on to talk. He apologized and said, "Don't worry. I'll talk to them."

Jule replied, he recalls, "No, I understand how they feel. They're older people and they've never done a book show. Let me talk to Mastin. You stay out of it for the moment."

Jule then went to Mastin's room to explain. "In the show, Sammy isn't playing himself. He's playing Freddie Welch. So you'll have to tell your friends that we don't have Sammy Davis Jr. onstage. We have a character. You aren't playing Will Mastin, are you?"

The entertainer thought for a while. "I bet you think I'm dumb."

"Not at all. It only shows how much you love Sammy and how much you want to protect him."

Crisis over.

Mr. Wonderful opened March 26 in New York to eight bad notices. Again, Sammy's talent wasn't knocked but everything else about the show was thumbed down. The notices said, *Close the show!* Jule went home and wept that night. *Was my judgment so bad? Was I so wrong?* Ego shattered, he refused to attend the cast party at Danny's Hideaway.

Despite the bad reviews, the show was drawing enough at the box office to survive. It stood as proof that a black performer, comparatively unknown, could attract an audience. The show confounded a number of the creative nay-sayers.

And Dorothy Dicker, whose job was supposed to hinge on the fortunes or failures of *Mr. Wonderful,* had already become permanent. Jule took great delight in saying, "Dorothy, take a letter," knowing that "Stynese" would be tidily unscrambled.

• • •

In November, Jule's score for the TV presentation of *Ruggles of Red Gap,* starring Sir Michael Redgrave and Peter Lawford, was aired. Reviews were mixed. However, the year was not exactly a loser. *Bells Are Ringing* also made its debut that month. So the critical and financial chimes were tolling joyously for Styne–Comden–Green and Miss Judy Holliday as 1956 slipped into 1957, with *Bells* destined to play 924 performances.

And in the final days of 1956, producer David Merrick called to say he'd just bought the rights to *Gypsy,* the autobiography of Gypsy Rose Lee, the stripper who never really stripped. "How about you doing it with Comden and Green?"

Jule read the book and found it fascinating. There were moments for big onstage numbers and yet it almost seemed to be more adaptable as a straight play. Whatever it should become, *Gypsy* had the potential of being very different from the usual musical—a straight play with an overlay of music and dance.

Betty and Adolph were soon phoned by Merrick; they read the book and called back to say they'd like to try it.·

Styne–Comden–Green began work on *Gypsy* in early 1957, but Adolph and Betty soon encountered difficulties with the story of Louise Hovick (Gypsy Rose Lee). They could not find a suitable approach to the adaptation, particularly the character of Rose, mother of Gypsy, and her sister, Baby June, whose stage name later on was June Havoc.

Jule was shaken by their doubts. He said, "Okay, if you don't like it, let's tell Merrick we don't do it." But Comden–Green weren't prepared to abandon the property as yet. Then, in the spring, they received an offer from Warner Brothers to do the screenplay for *Auntie Mame,* and accepted, promising Merrick they'd work on *Gypsy* on the Coast.

Jule felt they were easing away from it. *Obviously, they'd cooled on it. So did I, at that time. I'd worked with them long enough to know that if they really felt strongly about something they'd move along with it. The character of Rose remained the problem.*

About the same time that Comden–Green went West, Jule flew to the Midwest. Ruth Dubonnet accompanied her fiancé on the sad journey. Isadore Stein was dying in a Chicago hospital. He was in a coma, and there wasn't much to be done. During one of the days at the hospital, Ruth and Claire asked Jule to swear on his father's deathbed that he would stop gambling. Jule flatly refused. "I won't do that. Don't ask me to do that," he told them.

Isadore died the same night that *Mr. Wonderful* pulled down a final curtain in New York. The play, bucking a racial tide all the way, had somehow lasted for a year.

In the late spring of 1957, Jule embarked on the S. S. *France* with Ruth Dubonnet and Anita Loos to at last "see" Europe. The London company of *Bells Are Ringing* was shortly to open. Milan, Florence, Rome and Paris were also on the agenda.

"He was the most sensational traveling companion," said Dubonnet. "He hadn't been to any of these places, and was most interested in the museums. It was a marvelous trip. I introduced him to everyone of social importance in Paris and we laughed our way to Rome."

Jule arranged for an audience with Pope Pius XII at the Vatican, and the pope asked Jule, "How could you ever write 'Three Coins in the Fountain'? You're not Italian."

Styne admitted, "Mascagni helped me."

On his return to New York, Jule hoped to find a rough draft of *Gypsy* from Comden–Green. None awaited, and now Jule suspected they were caught up entirely in *Auntie Mame* and no longer had any interest in the Merrick plans for *Gypsy.* Merrick himself phoned Jule several times to ask what he'd heard on progress. Finally, in late August, Merrick phoned again to say that Betty and Adolph had decided against *Gypsy.*

Jule had already begun preparation of another musical, *Say, Darling.*

Jule had by now moved into the garden apartment of Ruth Dubonnet's elegant townhouse on East Sixty-third Street. They often talked about marriage and both believed that the event would take place within months. Meanwhile, they were cozy. She enjoyed hearing the sound of his upright as he worked. Sometimes she carted lunch downstairs; sometimes the butler carried it down. The grand piano in her spacious living room was used both for the entertainment of guests and for "angel" auditions.

13

Although it has been costly a few times,
and usually loaded with frustration, I'll never stop
taking chances with new, young talent.

—JULE STYNE, 1977

The theater has so many potentials for disaster. You have a smash and then fall to the bottom with a lousy show, come back midway with something else, skid down again and come back with a hit. The whole thing is checkered, always a gamble. Say, Darling *was next, and do you know what did me in on that? A union. Not even a theatrical union. The theater has so many hazards.*

Richard Bissell had written a novel about show business, reflections on the harrowing but often funny complications that had occurred in an earlier Bissell work, *Pajama Game,* which had reached Broadway as a musical in 1954.

Jule read *Say, Darling,* laughed over it, and sought out the novelist. Bissell enlisted his wife, Marian, to co-author the libretto, and to them Jule added Abe Burrows. Five months of writing on the book began in late summer, 1957. Comden–Green were called in for lyrics and Jule got the score under way simultaneously.

Looking back at that story of the making of a musical, I think mostly about Robert Morse. The day he came in to audition for the part of Ted Snow, the eager young producer, I was in the rehearsal hall and *watched him. Abe Burrows, who was also directing, turned him down flat. Bobby looked ratty and seedy, and was. The man was absolutely broke; didn't even have sufficient food money. But I felt he was so right for the part that I stopped him on the way out and said, "Come with me." I took him over to Brooks Brothers, bought him a new suit, a shirt, tie and overcoat, and had him return the next day. Burrows hired him on the spot and be damned if Abe didn't say he'd never seen Morse before. Anyhow, he was sensational in the part, and I put his name over the title; raised his salary from $350 a week to $750. Another thing I remember about that show was a male dancer named Elliott Gould. First job in the theater for Gould.*

Opening April 3rd at the ANTA Theatre, *Say, Darling* was not attractive to Brooks Atkinson. He wrote in *The Times* that Bissell should "stick to tow-boating," subject of a previous work. However, Walter Kerr, of the New York *Herald Tribune,* took an opposite view: "Smart and sassy and wonderfully funny! Jule Styne's horrendous parodies of jukebox hits rent the air . . ."

The show ran for a year, turned a profit, and then became one of the many casualties of the New York newspaper strike. Without advertisements, box-office receipts plummeted.

Talent usually "hooked" Jule, for better or worse, and a recent Princeton graduate, Robert "Bo" Goldman, had begun to hang around the office, trying to wedge his way into the theater, meanwhile submitting TV scripts to the networks. None were accepted and Bo, recently married, was at poverty level. His bride was baking cookies to help the Goldman treasury along.

Jule took an interest in Robert Goldman not only because of evident talent but also because Bo was a severe critic, writing ten pages of what was right and what was wrong with *Say, Darling* and other shows. Finally, Bo and a young composer friend, Glen Paxton, did their own musical, dropping it on Jule's desk. Though it wasn't of Broadway caliber, there was a definite freshness and flair to it.

So I signed them and then came up with an idea for them, Pride and Prejudice, *of all things. I'm not sure why I started them out on a classic but I'd always thought there was a musical in it. Tough show to do, so I needed a very experienced book-writer to keep them on the path. Abe Burrows? He was from the* Guys and Dolls *school, of course; a funny man, a gag man. But why should Abe be typed? Why type anyone?*

Burrows was both surprised and flattered, and loved the notion. Everyone always came to him for comedy, and now he had a chance to do Jane Austen, requiring imagination and style as well as wit. "For casting, we should go British," said Burrows, a new Burrows. "Julie Andrews and Rex Harrison!"

Jule repeated, "Julie Andrews and Rex Harrison?" That was rarefied enough, a re-teaming of the *My Fair Lady* principals.

Abe began to write the script for First Impressions, *hewing to the movie version of* Pride and Prejudice, *but inserting a joke here and there, while Bo Goldman and Glen Paxton got busy on lyrics and score. But suddenly I discovered that Bo was really writing poems, not lyrics. Yet Abe liked the stuff. I thought he was in a trance. It all became precious, and precious is sure death in the theater.*

With *First Impressions* well under way, Jule heard, in early summer, 1958, that *Gypsy* was taking life again, with Ethel Merman in the lead role. Leland Hayward would produce it with David Merrick; Jerome Robbins had been signed to direct; playwright Arthur Laurents would do the libretto. Robbins and Laurents had very successfully handled those chores for *West Side Story.* A first-class team for *Gypsy,* Jule thought.

Jule, of course, had known and worked with Leland Hayward for a long time but David Merrick was a comparatively new resident of the Broadway stage. Yet his list of credits as a producer were already formidable. Beginning with *Fanny,* in 1954, and followed by *The Matchmaker* in 1955, Merrick was now the No. 1 producer, in quality as well as quantity. His output for 1957 had been *Look Back in Anger, Romanoff and Juliet, Jamaica.* This year he would open curtains on *The Entertainer, The World of Suzie Wong, La Plume de ma Tante, Epitaph for George Dillon.* At least three productions, including *Gypsy,* were planned for 1959. Broadway had not experienced a producer like David Merrick for many years.

No composer had as yet been signed by Merrick and Hayward. It was known that Cole Porter had been asked to do the music but had declined because of poor health. Irving Berlin had also rejected the job, supposedly because he "didn't like the story." *All sorts of composers were auditioning for it, I heard. I felt left out. I said to myself, "Why are they auditioning composers when Arthur Laurents's friend, Steve Sondheim, is there? He's both a composer and lyric writer."*

Carolyn Leigh and Moose Charlap had submitted some songs but they weren't what Robbins and Laurents wanted. In fact, no one at that time really knew what was wanted for *Gypsy,* including Robbins and Laurents.

Stephen Sondheim, a protégé of Oscar Hammerstein, was the candidate of the moment for both music and lyrics. Though relatively inexperienced, he was already recognized as a new and towering talent, and was strongly backed by Laurents. He had written incidental music for *Girls of Summer* in 1956; had lyricized *West Side Story.* Sondheim was at the beginning of a brilliant career. However, Jule, in mid-career, believed that his own talents were equal to any *Gypsy* demands.

I was tempted to pick up the phone and call Merrick to say, "Hey, what about me? Remember, you offered me the job first." No one can write better for Ethel Merman than I can. But I kept silent, hoping that Merrick would call me, anyway.

As the summer heat began to envelop New York City, Jule Styne was certainly the most prolific composer in the musical comedy theater. Measured by the popularity of his shows, he was already one of the most successful composers of all time. Even before *Gypsy,* the total performances of his eight credited scores were approaching the entire performances of George Gershwin's twenty-three musicals. He could not be blamed for considering himself a worthy candidate for the projected Merman show.

Merrick did call Jule soon afterward to say, "Steve Sondheim wants to do the music and lyrics but Ethel wants you to do the music. I want you to do the music and Leland wants you to do the music. But Steve insists that he do both. We're trying to work something out."

Jule answered, "He collaborated on *West Side Story* with Lenny Bernstein. Why can't he collaborate with me?"

Merrick said, "Steve's very sensitive."

Jule replied, "So am I."

Merrick said, "Don't take on anything else. Give us a week."

Merrick and Hayward might have been sure about Jule Styne, as was Ethel Merman and Jerry Robbins, but Arthur Laurents didn't share their enthusiasm.

In fact, Laurents was at first very reluctant to undertake *Gypsy.* "I read the book and thought it was amusing and fun but I wasn't all that enthused."

Co-producer Leland Hayward kept after Laurents for weeks, lunching him at fancy places, attempting to convince the playwright that he should join the Merman show.

Laurents recalls that, finally, the mother, Rose, struck him as the most interesting character. "I've always thought that anything you write in fiction must have universal appeal. Mothers and children. There you are. In this case, the mother was interesting because she was a gorgon, and when I directed Angela Lansbury and the cast in London I told them what I thought was never made clear in *Gypsy:* the desire for recognition. Everyone has this need—every single character in *Gypsy* wanted recognition, and the only one who didn't get it was the one who most needed it: the mother."

After Laurents agreed to do the libretto, he was immediately faced with three problems: "Number one was that the girl was going to have to become a strip queen, but that couldn't be the climax because the story was really about the mother. Then I got the idea for 'Rose's Turn,' in which that overwhelming need for recognition came out, after which the whole piece fell into place. Then there was Ethel Merman. I'd never met her. I took her to Sardi's. She had a Horse's Neck. I said to her, 'This woman could be considered a monster, and I want to know how far you're willing to go.' She replied that she'd do anything I wanted her to do. She wanted to be an actress in this show! The third problem was the score. I'd worked with Steve Sondheim. I'd actually brought Steve to *West Side Story,* and I wanted him to do this show too. Then I heard that Merman's agent had put the kibosh on. Merman, too. So we had no composer."

Then Jerome Robbins suggested Jule Styne, a proposal that did not generate much enthusiasm in Arthur Laurents. "I'd never met him. But to my mind, musicals were beginning to take a different turn in the fifties. I knew Jule wrote great 'tunes' but this was a dramatic piece and I didn't know that he was capable of turning out a dramatic score. But Jerry was a great booster of his and said he'd get Jule to come and play for me. I replied, 'Oh, it's Jule Styne. You can't ask him to audition for me."

Robbins said flatly that Styne would, indeed, willingly audition.

Laurents was still surprised when Jule agreed to perform, without the slightest resentment. "It's not a question of humility nor lack of pride on Jule's part. He just doesn't stand on protocol. So we went to Jerry's apartment on Seventy-fourth Street and Jule played some of his hits. He also played some things that had been cut from *Bells Are Ringing.* The music had more guts than I thought possible. Listening to it, I realized that this man had a far greater range than I had thought. I also believe that when you work with better people, you become better. So I then readily accepted Jule as the composer."

About this time, Laurents discovered that Messrs. Hayward and Merrick had not obtained a release form from June Havoc, Gypsy's sister, for her part in the story, the character of Baby June. Laurents asked them, "How can we do this show without her release?" His contract specifically called for Havoc's clearance of Baby June.

"Oh, we'll do it," said Hayward and Merrick.

Then Hayward said to Laurents, "Come on up to Stratford, and we'll see June Havoc. She was playing Titania in *Midsummer Night's Dream* in the Connecticut town. They arrived late, went backstage, and then on to June's home. She kept on her full make-up, including sequins and headdress, during the disconcerting hour that followed. Her eyesight must have been more than 20/20 because she said, "You were late, but of course, you didn't come to see my performance, only to get my name on that piece of paper."

One moment she was charming, saying that *Gypsy* was a wonderful, delightful book. The next, she turned on Laurents. "It's a vulgar book. You're supposed to be a playwright. Why do you want to make a play of this?"

He replied, "I find it touching."

"I'm touching," said June Havoc. "Not her. She's cheap. She eats out of tin cans."

The release form was not signed that night but Laurents went ahead with the character of Baby June anyway.

14

Before I wrote anything for Merman, I bought every album she'd ever made and played them again and again. Gee, I must have played them for a week.

—JULE STYNE, 1977

Jule had first worked with Ethel Merman at 20th Century-Fox in the late thirties, as her vocal coach, and more recently as producer of *Anything Goes* and *Panama Hattie.* He knew her voice and range. The relationship had always been easy and fun. Merman said, "The thing I knew about Jule was that his music was singable and commercial. Up to *Gypsy,* I'd only worked with George Gershwin, Cole Porter and Irving Berlin. And I felt that Jule was perfect for this show. So I insisted on him."

Merrick and Hayward then met with Stephen Sondheim and he finally agreed to collaborate, only to do the lyrics. "Yes, I had misgivings," said Sondheim. "And for two reasons. First, it had been agreed that I'd write both the music and lyrics. The deal, with Leland, Merrick, Laurents and Robbins was firm, I thought. But Ethel had recently been in *Happy Hunting,* which was not a success—the songwriters were unknown at the time, and perhaps she didn't want to take that chance again. I'd done the lyrics for *West Side* and I guess my credentials were okay for her in that field. Yet I wanted to write music, not only lyrics, and I felt I'd been delayed long enough, so was about to bow out of the project. Before I did, I went to my mentor, Oscar Hammerstein, and discussed it with him. He persuaded me that the experience of writing a show for a star would be invaluable. Also, it was now September and rehearsals were already set for January. So it would be six months out of my life at most. I also very much wanted to work with Arthur Laurents and Jerome Robbins again. So I said yes.

"My second misgiving had to do with the fact that Jule's shows had been in a rather traditional mold—what used to be called 'musical comedy,' songs and block comedy scenes. I didn't know how he'd adapt to another way of thinking, whether he'd be willing to keep his eyes and ears on character and story rather than hit songs . . ."

When Sondheim had finished reading the *Gypsy* book, he'd said to Laurents, "This is really a play. I don't know why you need music."

Laurents had replied, "You're dead wrong. It's much larger than life. It wouldn't work as a straight play." Laurents felt that the music would enable him to enlarge his characters, sketch them in quickly and broadly.

Steve had first met Jule, very casually, at a party in Leonard Bernstein's apartment. A second meeting had occurred when Sondheim's score to a musical, *Saturday Night,* was played for Jule and Joe Kipness as prospective producers. Sondheim eventually shelved the score.

Sondheim remembers, "My first impression of Jule, anywhere, was at the piano. He played mostly Styne but not exclusively—Jule and Arthur Schwartz are anomalies among established composers in that they're very generous about playing other people's songs. I was impressed by the enthusiasm with which Jule attacked the keyboard, and by his nervous good humor."

The day Sondheim finally paid a visit to discuss the work ahead, Jule was trodding about the garden apartment in Dubonnet's townhouse, very nervous. *I thought he might hit me over the head, knowing that he wanted to do the whole show. He was young, ambitious and a huge talent. But he was also very gentle, and we got along fine.*

Sondheim remembers that Jule handed him thirteen "trunk" songs, ones culled from various unproduced shows or movies, or that had been cut from previous excursions and were gathering dust in the composer's so-called trunk. "I thought we should write everything fresh, for the particular moods and situations of the show. I think Jule was a bit disappointed (out of impatience, not ego) but we did wind up using one of the trunk songs, namely 'The Cow Song.' "

Jule played a few things. One had a percussive accompaniment, a dum-da, dum-dum, a stripper walk type of thing, and there was a tune for it. "Not the tune, but that percussive thing would be wonderful for something, and not the stripper walk," said Sondheim. At that moment Jule understood that Sondheim really *did* know music.

Sondheim then said he was going over to see Arthur Laurents and find out where he was with the libretto. "When I get his ideas, we'll go to work. But let's write a different way, perhaps not the way you've ever done it. Let's work evenly with Arthur. I'll stay close to him and he'll tell me what he wants lyrically. We should let him decide for us. Then when he gives me an idea, I'll know what song is in Scene One. By the time we've written that, he'll catch up with us and we'll go on to Scene Two."

It *was* a different way of writing for Jule. Laurents got his first scene set, and Steve brought it back, saying that Arthur would like them to musicalize the first two pages of dialogue, not lyrics. They did "Some People," which was Merman's opening number.

Laurents told Sondheim, "We'll need a song where she tells the old man [her father], 'I'm leaving this goddamn place. I'm getting out. I need eighty-eight dollars. I had a dream last night . . ."

So Steve said to Jule, "You know that percussive thing, give me a long strain for 'Some People,' something slow . . ."

Sondheim came back the next day and Jule played the "long, slow strain," with the percussive accompaniment, and it became the patter for the "Some People" sequence. Laurents to Sondheim to Styne.

Sondheim often wrote a simple quatrain after a visit to Laurents, and then Jule set his music.

The show felt good, even while Steve and I were creating it. I knew I was creating work that I'd never done before. Marvelous lyrics came to me from Steve. When you write with him, you actually feel good as a composer. He places value on the music, what kind of word fits each note. When you soar musically, he knows he must say something as important as the notes. He never asks for extra notes. And he doesn't put the full value on the rhyme, like most lyricists. The thought is the main thing with Steve. In most cases, I wrote the music first, and then he wrote the lyrics. Steve said that the music must set the character as well as the words.

For a number to end Act I, Scene 6, Jule played Steve a theme he'd written years before for a film that was never produced. Sondheim soon fashioned words to "Little Lamb." The trunk material which was at first rejected by Sondheim was now beginning to rear a musical head.

The first few songs were presented to Jerry Robbins on tape.

Robbins was wildly enthusiastic about them but it was evident that he didn't like "Little Lamb." Jerry seldom rejected anything out-of-hand, but sooner or later he'd make his thoughts known.

Sometimes, Styne–Sondheim tried a song on Laurents who was quite the opposite of Robbins in this regard, quick to voice an opinion. "I don't like it."

"Why not?" either Steve or Jule would ask. Laurents would then explain in detail.

Sondheim remembers, "The only thing annoying about Jule's working habits is how fertile he is. He teems with ideas. I work very slowly and laboriously. This was both stimulating and frustrating. Jule doesn't allow you to get discouraged. I prefer to get discouraged, but it was a good change for me. If he's hurt when you don't like something he doesn't show it. He just comes up with another tune. Jule would rather write a brand-new song than rewrite one that has good things but isn't quite there."

One by one, the songs were completed. "Small World," in Act I, Scene 4, sung by Mother Rose (Merman) to Herbie (Jack Klugman), was an example of Sondheim's full brilliance:

> Funny, you're a stranger who's come here,
>   Come from another town.
> Funny, I'm a stranger myself here—
> Small world, isn't it?
> Funny, you're a man who goes traveling
>   Rather than settling down.
> Funny, 'cause I'd love to go traveling—
> Small world, isn't it?

Jule said, "No rhyming. Oh, my God, that's great."

Then Sondheim shifted pace and rhymed indeed. But the words really didn't seem rhymed:

> We have so much in common,
>   It's a phenomenon.
> We could pool our resources
> By joining forces
> From now on.
>
> Lucky, you're a man who likes children—
>   That's an important sign.
> Lucky, I'm a woman with children—

Small world, isn't it?
Funny, isn't it?
Small, and funny, and fine.

One line caused Jule to gasp. *I'm a woman with children.* He told Sondheim, "Jesus Christ, Sinatra can never sing that song. No man can."

"So?" said Sondheim.

Jule Styne couldn't change that quickly. He usually thought of who could sing the song, even while the notes were coming together. He could not shake Tin Pan Alley that easily, always conscious of the feminine-masculine import in the lyrics.

To end Act I, Styne–Sondheim completed "Everything's Coming Up Roses" for Merman. Despite Sondheim's objections to trunk songs, Jule had sneaked them in. "The Cow Song" was definitely not the only trunk tune. The "Roses" melody was originally intended for *High Button Shoes,* entitled "Betwixt and Between," lyrics by Sammy Cahn. It served well for "Roses," though Sondheim altered a musical line for the new title. Robbins had remembered the deleted song and suggested its use.

Another Styne trunk item was "You'll Never Get Away from Me," sung by Merman and Klugman in Act I. It had been written for *Pink Tights* and Marilyn Monroe, and had rested in Jule's trunk for five years, with one exception. Jule had used it, in another guise, in *Ruggles of Red Gap,* entitled "I'm in Pursuit of Happiness," lyrics by Leo Robin.

Steve was both shocked and angry to learn of it long after *Gypsy* had opened. "If I'd known it had been used in *Ruggles* I wouldn't have set the lyrics." Yet the song worked, and beautifully, Jule pointed out defensively.

Okay, I have a mountain of trunk songs and I use them when they're right. Just because a song doesn't work for a particular show doesn't mean it can't work for any other show. Didn't Gershwin do that with "The Man I Love"? That song was in five other shows before it found the right home.

Soon enough, Steve and Jule played and sang some of the Act I songs for Merman, performing in Ruth Dubonnet's townhouse, with Oscar Hammerstein an interested listener. Ethel cried sadly when she heard "Some People" and then had happy tears for "Everything's Coming Up Roses." The entire Styne–Sondheim score for *Gypsy* was written in about five weeks.

After eight songs had been completed, Jule called Sondheim to ask if he'd mind performing the work done thus far for Cole Porter. Merman had told Jule that Cole, bedridden, both legs amputated, was at his very lowest point. She thought that hearing the work might stimulate him to write again. Unlike Jule, Sondheim hated to "perform," even in a living room, and only did it when necessary. But he'd met Porter on one other occasion and quickly agreed.

Sondheim, Jule and Merman arrived at Porter's apartment several nights later for dinner. Porter was carried in, and they dined. Then, after dessert, the composer was made comfortable in a large chair and Steve sang the entire score, as Jule thumped away on a bad piano. Porter murmured audibly in appreciation when Steve hit the "egos-amigos" release in "Together."

My piano was facing the other way and I was glad because I didn't want Cole to see the tears streaming down my face. There was a special magic to our performance, I think. We had to battle emotion and we gave more. Cole had written some of Merman's biggest hits. Now, he didn't have the strength to applaud so he tapped an ashtray with a spoon to let us know he appreciated the score. It's a sound I'll never forget.

At this point, with Act I completed, Jerome Robbins and Arthur Laurents had different concepts of *Gypsy.* Strangely enough, neither man knew the other man's thoughts. Aside from his collaboration with Sondheim and Styne, Laurents had worked pretty much alone to date. Jerry believed the story was to be played against a panorama of vaudeville in the United States, and Hayward, working closely with Robbins, had already hired animal acts and jugglers. They were stunned when they saw the script and realized it was a "small story musical."

When both acts were completed, Robbins read the full libretto and said, "We have to have a burlesque scene in this." After all, it was about Gypsy Rose Lee.

Laurents replied, "I think it will slow the story. The audience will be interested in the people—the mother and the children, and to some extent, Herbie. Not one of them has any place in that burlesque scene you're talking about."

Nonetheless, Laurents sat down again, toward year's end, to write a stripper scene. Robbins then went to Jule to say he was counting on Jule's knowledge of burlesque to set the right stripper sound.

15

When Jule becomes wildly excited about a show,
that's all he thinks about and talks about.
Any other show becomes an orphan.

—BUSTER DAVIS, 1977

Julie Andrews was not signed for the role of Elizabeth Bennett in *First Impressions,* which was now ready for presentation in Philadelphia. Polly Bergen was Abe Burrows's final choice for the Elizabeth of this musicalized *Pride and Prejudice.* Then Abe selected Farley Granger, who was not exactly Rex Harrison, either, for Fitzwilliam Darcy. Hermione Gingold was cast as Mrs. Bennett.

With *Gypsy* mounting, Jule thought very little about *First Impressions,* though he believed that Polly Bergen and Farley Granger were suitable for the roles. Sylvia Herscher and George Gilbert were handling the show while Dorothy Dicker ran the office. Jule visited rehearsals now and then but more to play the wildly exciting music from *Gypsy* for the cast than to advise about remedies for impending catastrophe.

First Impressions was hopeless from the first curtain and previewed to across-the-board kills. Abe Burrows made changes on the hour and Jule stayed on for a few days to advise. There were dances in the second act that seemed to slow it down. They were deleted, at Jule's insistence.

Two nights later, arranger Buster Davis was in the back of the theater with Jule while the show was in progress. They were near the orange-drink stand and overheard a conversation between the two young sellers. One seller said, "There isn't enough dancing in it . . ."

Jule could hardly contain himself until the final curtain went down. He then ran backstage to shout at a startled Abe Burrows, "What this show needs is more dancing."

Buster Davis wasn't satisfied. He returned to the orange-drink stand to say, "During the second act, you claimed there wasn't enough dancing in this show. What makes you say that?"

The seller who had spoken earlier answered, "I wasn't even talking about this show. I was talking about the one across the street."

Davis said, "It's truly remarkable, this mercurial changing of Jule's mind. He can suddenly argue against the very thing he said the night before, with just as much enthusiasm and just as many reasons. It isn't necessarily wrong in the theater, but it is confusing."

First Impressions opened in New York on March 19, 1959, and Mr. Atkinson termed it a "mongrel musical." Having had a mongrel by its slippery short tail for months, Polly Bergen, Abe Burrows and Sylvia Herscher all ended up in Mt. Sinai Hospital, suffering from exhaustion and other things. They wrote notes to each other. Sylvia did not return to the walk-up office in the Mark Hellinger except to tidy up affairs. Dorothy Dicker moved into the managerial spot. By now, the pert blonde knew quite a lot about the ups and down of the theater; something about bookies, too.

Jule survived *First Impressions* nicely, though he lost $150,000 on the venture. He didn't seem to mind. He was dashing all over Manhattan happily playing "Everything's Coming Up Roses."

Around this period, he sent all the songs from *Gypsy* to Frank Sinatra, certain that Frank would go for two or three. No answer. The silence had lasted almost five years.

16

I wasn't at all surprised when Jule fell in love with Sandra Church. She was young and beautiful, and it was about time for him to have another romance.

—DOROTHY DICKER, 1977

Jule had come in late to the final audition of Jack Klugman as Herbie, being held at the Amsterdam Theatre at Forty-second Street and Seventh Avenue. Klugman had been auditioning for three tiring weeks, and had been sent to a vocal coach by Robbins with hopes that something could be done about his singing. "Small World," at times in duet with Merman, would tax a professional singer, and Klugman was frightened of the song; of any song he'd be required to sing.

Robbins, Merman, Sondheim and Hayward were present at the Amsterdam that morning, slightly jittery. They were convinced that Jule wouldn't approve of Klugman for the role of Herbie. They thought Klugman was perfect for the part with the exception of his singing voice. Robbins said, "We've heard everyone but this is the man we'd like." Jerry had seen Klugman, then at the beginning of his career, in a segment of *Playhouse 90.*

A singer's audition for Jule was often an ordeal—for the singer. Jule usually asked them to go higher and higher, simply to determine their range. But his presence alone, backed by a half century of experience, was an obstacle. Singers had been known to sweat and freeze when he stood with an ear cocked.

Very nervous, Klugman played the scene for Jule and did an excellent reading; Robbins then said, "Jule, there's only one problem. This man can't sing."

Jule grinned. "So what."

They all relaxed, except Jack Klugman. He'd warned them that if Merman belted "Small World," he'd walk out. She sang so softly, so un-Mermanly, that her voice cracked. Then Klugman did his solo, and exited in disgust.

As the actor left the theater, Jule said to Robbins, "He's got a lousy voice but he sounds real. That's all that counts, isn't it?"

Klugman was informed at home that he had the role.

The show then went into rehearsal on the tiny stage of the Amsterdam with Ethel Merman rightfully complaining to Jerry Robbins that she had no number that allowed her to stay on stage and acknowledge the applause. She exited promptly after each of her songs. "I want to be able to say 'thank you.' I have to have one number to finish on stage."

Sondheim and Styne were hard at work on that number, "Rose's Turn," the Arthur Laurents key to all the building blocks of the *Gypsy* story, the summary of what Mama Rose was all about. Laurents had laid it out months earlier, but a few attempts by Jule and Steve hadn't yet produced the music and lyrics.

Jule had the burden of setting the music first. *I wanted to give Ethel something big, and went over it carefully with Laurents. In my mind, I wanted to review her life musically, a rough thing to do. At that moment, Rose was saying, in effect, the children don't need me anymore but, by God, they better understand what I've contributed. It was her turn to tell everyone that they were what she'd made them. It's rather easy to say in words but to say it musically is more difficult.*

What complicated the writing of "Rose's Turn," which was originally designed as a ballet number, was that it followed a hint of strip number by Gypsy Rose Lee (Sandra Church), a taste of her new life on the Minsky circuit. Whatever followed had to be powerful enough to wipe out the strip scene.

Further, there was an agreement that Merman could not hear any new number until Robbins had heard it and approved. The first version they played for the director brought a swift "nope."

"What does 'nope' mean?" Jule asked.

"The material has to be bigger, It isn't now. She has to sing for at least five minutes, solid. I'm not going to do it with staging or tricks. Now, give me that five-minute number . . ."

Laurents also rejected this first version, which was incomplete. Sondheim remembers that Robbins and Laurents thought it was "too square."

Jule sat down at the piano and began to improvise a theme. Robbins listened, shrugged, and walked away. *God, here we were struggling, and he shrugs, and walks away . . .*

One day, Jule and Steve entered the Amsterdam to announce that they'd finally found "Rose's Turn." Robbins listened again and at last gave his approval. That same night, at about 11 o'clock, Robbins stopped the rehearsal so that Ethel could hear her new song. Jule playing, Steve singing the Merman role, "Rose's Turn" was welcomed into the show. Steve sang in the darkened theater:

(*Shouting right out to everyone now*) HERE SHE IS, BOYS! HERE SHE IS, WORLD! HERE'S ROSE!! (*She sings*)
CURTAIN UP!!!
LIGHT THE LIGHTS!!!
(*Speaking*)
Play it, boys.
(*Singing*)
You either got it,
or you ain't—
And, boys, I got it!
You like it?

ORCHESTRA Yeah!

ROSE
Well, I got it!
Some people got it
And make it pay,
Some people can't even
Give it away.
This people's got it
And this people's spreadin' it around.
You either have it
Or you've had it.
(*Speaking*)
Hello, everybody! My name's Rose. What's yours? (*Bumps*)
How d'ya like them egg rolls, Mr. Goldstone?

(*Singing*)
Hold your hats,
And hallelujah,
Momma's gonna show it to ya!
(*Speaking*)
Ready or not, here comes Momma!
(*Singing*)
Momma's talkin' loud,
Momma's doin' fine,
Momma's gettin' hot,
Momma's goin' strong,
Momma's movin' on,
Momma's all alone,
Momma doesn't care,
Momma's lettin' loose,
Momma's got the stuff,
Momma's lettin' go—
(*Stopping dead as the words hit her*)
Momma—
Momma's—
(*Shaking off the mood*)
Momma's got the stuff,
Momma's got to move,
Momma's got to go—
(*Stopping dead again, trying to recover*)
Momma—
Momma's—
Momma's gotta let go!
(*Stops; after a moment she begins to pace*)
Why did I do it?
What did it get me?
Scrapbooks full of me in the background.
Give 'em love and what does it get you?
What does it get you?
One quick look as each of 'em leaves you.
All your life and what does it get you?
Thanks a lot—and out with the garbage.
They take bows and you're battin' zero.
I had a dream—
I dreamed it for you,
June,
It wasn't for me, Herbie.
And if it wasn't for me
Then where would you be,

Miss Gypsy Rose Lee!
Well, someone tell me, when is it my turn?
Don't I get a dream for myself?
Startin' now it's gonna be my turn!
Gangway, world,
 Get offa my runway!
Startin' now I bat a thousand.
This time, boys, I'm takin' the bows and
Everything's coming up Rose—
Everything's coming up Roses—
Everything's coming up Roses
This time for me!
For me—
For me—
For me—
For me—
FOR ME!

As Steve finished the last word, Jule looked over and saw that Milton Rosenstock was weeping, and then Merman, weeping too, rushed to stage center, yelling, "It's a goddamned aria!" It was longer than Robbins's required five minutes.

After that, each performance of "Rose's Turn" drained her, and always on the last "FOR ME!" she looked at Rosenstock as if pain had left her body.

The problem with June Havoc continued. She still hadn't signed the release and kept wanting changes made in the play's script. Laurents made as many as feasible, then took the hard line. Obviously, June Havoc wanted Baby June to be adorable. Laurents finally refused to make a change, one which, in his words, would have "established Rose as a triple monster," and David Merrick's lawyers advised Merrick not to sign the Laurents contract until the playwright complied. At that point Harold Freedman, Laurents's agent, threatened an injunction to stop rehearsals of a show the producers didn't own. Merrick solved the matter by saying, "I'm a lawyer. I know the libel laws. We'll change her name to Baby Claire." Laurents readily agreed to make that change.

Three-quarters the way into rehearsal, the period during any show when nerves begin to fray, words become terse, it was evident that the play was considerably overlong. Laurents had twenty minutes of marked cuts in his script, one of which Jule had suggested. "If you cut that out [in the second act] and telescope this, you can get rid of a big hunk." The cut was made.

Eventually Robbins said to Laurents, "Steve tells me you have twenty minutes of marked cuts."

"That's perfectly true," said Laurents.

"When are you going to take them?" Robbins asked.

"When you cut twenty minutes from those kiddie numbers."

Jerry replied, "Okay, you take your cuts and I'll take mine."

Then there was trouble with the ballet music. Robbins had hired Betty Walberg and rehearsal pianist Johnny Kander to score the dance toward the end of the first act. The composers didn't deliver what Robbins wanted, though Kander went on to write *Cabaret, Zorba* and *Chicago.* At the same time, Jule and Jerry were feuding over "Little Lamb." Robbins believed the song was too sentimental and would hurt the show.

A few nights later Jule came into the theater about ten o'clock—Robbins rarely regarded the hour. Jule was a little drunk, another unusual circumstance. Seldom did he have more than one or two drinks before dinner. He sat down in the first row.

Robbins came over to ask, "Jule, who were the great dance teams in the night clubs of the late twenties?"

Styne answered, "Veloz and Yolanda," and then arose, proceeding to demonstrate their particular style of dancing.

Jerry suddenly got excited and I went over to the piano and began improvising. At the end, I looked at him with intent to say, "Baby, I know how to do this."

Betty Walberg and Johnny Kander then took the improvisation and adapted it to the dance. The ad-libbed music that Jule wrote that night on a half-high is still in *Gypsy.*

As if he didn't have enough involvements, Jule Styne fell in love once again during the *Gypsy* rehearsals, this time with Sandra Church, the beautiful young brunette who had been cast as Gypsy Rose Lee. She was thirty years his junior but Jule had never paid much attention to age, and had definitely not subscribed to any September song. Obviously, the new affair of heart was complicated by the very old affair with Ruth Dubonnet.

Within a week or so after rehearsals had started, Jule was completely taken with Sandra Church and seriously thinking of marriage again. He had, of course, thought of marrying Ruth this past year but had reexamined that circumstance. *I fell madly, but madly, in love with Sandra.*

The beautiful young lady was impressed with all the attention and professed affection from the composer. The romance added to the excitement of *Gypsy*'s approaching debut, as staff, cast and hopes moved on to Philadelphia.

In time, Sandra asked Jule, "Why do you want to marry me?"

Jule replied, "You're young, you're beautiful and I'm in love with you."

She introduced him to her mother, sundry uncles and aunts and friends. She wasn't certain she wanted to become Mrs. Jule Styne but it was something to think about.

17

Once, Ethel told Irving Berlin, "Call me Birdseye.
The show is frozen." No new songs could go in.
She's tough and knows what she wants and she's usually right.

—JULE STYNE, 1977

Jule had finished the show's overture, and the music was rehearsed in Philadelphia's Masonic Temple, where Rosenstock was putting the orchestra through his last rehearsal. "It was awful," Rosenstock remembers. He looked over at Jule, whose face was red with embarrassment.

Rosenstock said, "Don't get excited. Let's try it again." The second time through was no better than the first. There was a piano at the other end of the studio and they dragged it over.

Rosenstock asked, "How do we end it?"

"End it, my ass," Jule replied, "Let's start from the top." Part by part, they began fixing it, but then Jule yelled, "Nothing's happening in the strip number . . ."

Of the three trumpets in the orchestra, the second was strongest, Rosenstock remembers. "He wasn't the best horn, but his chops were good. He could blow loud. Now Jule hadn't said a word about that trumpet, but he knew. He was sitting there at the piano, honking away, when he suddenly yelled, 'We got to make it alive.' Then he ran over to the second trumpet and said, 'You play this—a rup-rup-tuppppata-ta-tup.' And Jule wrote in the exact notes."

They ran it again. "It sounds fine," said Rosenstock.

Jule was uncertain.

The next afternoon, in the theater, Robbins said, "Now, let's hear the overture." The high command of Laurents, Robbins, Hayward, Merrick and Sondheim were there.

Rosenstock took the orchestra through it, and at conclusion, there was dead silence. Rosenstock turned from the podium to see all of them staring at Jule. Robbins's thumb was pointed down. Jule went up to them, conferred for a few minutes, and then moved down to the orchestra pit.

"What's wrong?" Milton asked.

"They don't want it."

"They're crazy," said Rosenstock. "What *do* they want?"

"Play a chorus of this, play a chorus of that. The same old shit. Christ, I knew it."

Jule walked away.

Down the aisle came Robbins, headed for Rosenstock. "He was giving me that cold fish look that kills people, a Robbins specialty like nothing else on earth."

Rosenstock said, "Jerry, you're wrong, you're dead wrong. After what we've gone through, you can at least let it play for one performance."

Jerry said, "Okay. We do the preview with it. If it doesn't go, we do the choruses."

Rosenstock said, "Okay with me."

"Not okay with me," yelled Jule. "We open with this goddamn overture. I'll not cut one minute of it."

A moment before the first curtain of the preview, Jule went to second trumpet Dick Perry to say, "When we come to that part with your high E-flat screams, I want you to stand up and blow the ceiling off."

Then Rosenstock raised his baton to begin the beleaguered *Gypsy* overture. He remembers, "When Dick got up and started riffing and blowing he didn't get past three bars until the audience began applauding. They were still bravoing when I hit the cue for Merman's entrance."

Preview audiences often defy a first night, and the first act of *Gypsy,* though it played well, seemed to arouse no great enthusiasm, though Merman was cheered as an individual performer. But the audience had apparently expected a striptease story and what was unfolding on the Shubert stage had little to do with taking it off.

At intermission, Rosenstock went backstage to hug Jule. "Don't worry about the overture. You heard it go."

Robbins walked up. "I still don't like it."

Jule shrugged.

Gypsy opened to mixed reviews. The best was in the *Philadelphia Bulletin:* "There is only one reaction to *Gypsy* and that is unconditional surrender. Jule Styne has written the most serious score of his career."

Over the next nights in Philadelphia, Jule visited Merman's dressing room after she finished Act I. The performance was so trying that she seemed exhausted with even just the first act behind her. She would be sitting bent over in her chair, her head in her hands. Usually, neither of them spoke. She'd await the buzzer for her onstage call, and then leave. But one night she said, "Hey, I want to tell you something. This is a hard show to do every night."

Along about now, June Havoc came to Philadelphia to see *Gypsy.* The actors had been having trouble with the name change of the character June to Claire, and the confusion sometimes resulted in Baby Clune or an approximation. Havoc was unhappy with that situation. In a name sense, she wasn't in the show at all. She signed the release and the true name went back into the script.

And over the next five weeks, prior to New York, Laurents and Robbins snipped away at the show. It was still a bit overlong. The second or third week, Robbins summarily cut "Little Lamb," Gypsy's number midway of the first act. The cut was made without consultation with Jule or Laurents.

Jule heard of the cut and requested that the number be returned to the score. Robbins refused, without giving a reason. Jule then walked up to the stage and said, with great dignity, "Mr. Robbins, I have notified my lawyers in New York that I'm withdrawing the entire score unless "Little Lamb" is put back in tonight."

Robbins surrendered.

Gypsy left Philadelphia in mid-May to begin New York previews prior to the May 21st opening. The show by now had been "frozen"; everything had been ironed out. Laurents, Styne and Sondheim were mostly satisfied, as was Ethel Merman. Jerry Robbins was always harder to please, always the perfectionist.

At about three o'clock on the afternoon of opening night, Jule walked into the Winter Garden during the orchestra warm-up. Several days previously, he'd asked Leland Hayward to make certain that platforms were placed in the pit, raising the orchestra to increase the sound. Jule saw that no platforms had been provided. The two previews had been played without them. He went up to Hayward. "Where are my platforms?"

"The music is loud enough," Hayward answered.

"What the hell do you know about music, Leland?" Jule asked, walking away from Hayward and up to the stage to confront Robbins. "Jerry, I know you're responsible for those orchestra platforms not being here. You're destroying me. I should throw you into the pit."

Robbins replied that the producers were the culprits and looked around for stagehands to provide the platforms, but they'd all gone home. Hayward departed the theater; then Robbins went home.

Jule was suddenly alone with George Gilbert, who said, "I'll get some bar stools. That'll raise 'em a foot or so." Gilbert trucked the stools in between three-thirty and six that evening. Then later, as the theater filled, Jule ran down to the pit and lifted the velour, draping it back over the top rail.

At intermission, Robbins said to Styne, "You could hear the music all right."

"Yes, baby," Jule replied, "they're sitting a foot and a half higher, on bar stools."

The New York opening-night audience was impressed, as were the critics. The new musical was generally acclaimed, with only a few objections registered anywhere. Merman was solidly approved, the critics unanimous in claiming it was the best performance of her career. The critics were also unanimous in praise of the Jule Styne score. Highly regarded London critic Kenneth Tynan said, "Jule Styne is the most persistently underrated of all popular composers . . ."

There was quite another performance at the cast party, which took place at the other Jules Stein's swank office. During the celebration, while Jule was playing a medley, Ruth Dubonnet had an unfortunate encounter with Sandra Church. Whatever was left of the romance between Jule and Ruth came to an end. Mrs. Dubonnet soon departed for Europe and Jule soon vacated the garden apartment, by request.

Yet he was indebted to Ruth in many ways. She'd come into his life at a time when he was emotionally and financially shattered. She'd sorted things out for him in an orderly fashion, enabling him to reach a new level of creativity.

Then Sandra said to Jule, "Look, I'm too young for you. I don't want any children in my life. You have your children. I don't need to marry you, and you don't need to marry me."

Undoubtedly the best score Jule Styne had ever written, *Gypsy* ran for a year and a half on Broadway, returning a profit of more than a million dollars. Jule was now into big money, between his share of the *Gypsy* receipts and the cast album royalties. Yet he saw little of it. He was far behind in his alimony payments to Ethel; his debt to the Internal Revenue Service was now some $400,000.

The financial future looked so bleak that Dorothy Dicker contacted every major casino in Las Vegas, cutting off Jule's credit, knowing that he was soon going west. Dorothy now managed both his personal and professional finances, a thankless task.

After one verbal donnybrook in Jule's office, Dicker shouted, "I've had it. I'm leaving!"

She went into her own office and began stripping her desk. A few minutes later, Jule edged in to say, "If you leave, I'm leaving, too."

Dicker broke up. A totally devoted lady, qualified to battle in and out of the office, Dorothy's crisp sense of humor helped her ride the carrousel.

When a United States senator insults you,
you swear you'll have nothing to do with him.
But when he becomes President of the United States . . .

—JULE STYNE, 1977

Just before *Gypsy* went on the road with Ethel Merman in late 1960, after first opening in Los Angeles, Jule called up a friend, Bobby Freedman, a dedicated playboy, to say, "I want to take a very pretty girl to the *Gypsy* opening."

Freedman replied, "Take my girl, Maggi Brown. She's at Fox, under contract to Ray Stark. Beautiful redhead. International model."

Jule phoned Maggi Brown from New York to say, "Look, mark this date down. I'll call you two or three days ahead." He then flew to Los Angeles, via Las Vegas, to oversee the orchestra handling at the old Biltmore Theatre.

Off and on, Jule had dated Rocky Cooper, widow of Gary Cooper, and she called him the second day he was in town, just to chat. Then a mutual friend said, "Why don't you take Rocky to the opening?"

Jule said, "Sure," forgetting all about beautiful model Maggi Brown.

• • •

No two musicals or plays of the more than twenty credited to Jule came about in the same way. A good number of them were accidental, falling together.

Jones Harris, son of actress Ruth Gordon, and the late director, Jed Harris, was a young rebel whom Jule found to be bright and amusing. He'd been introduced to Harris, who was then twenty-six, by Ruth Dubonnet. Harris spent quite a lot of time at P. J. Clarke's, the lively bar on Third Avenue, though he seldom drank. "He was a terrible rebel, almost incorrigible, and would go to a party and toss the most expensive piece of crystal out the window. Yet I liked him, and we went around together. He and Jackie Kennedy were close friends."

Jule had long ago read *Do Re Mi,* a novella by Harris's stepfather, Garson Kanin, and thought it might be a good idea for a musical. Twentieth Century-Fox had owned the property for a while. Finally he said to Jones, "Why don't you come in and produce something for Broadway? Your father was a great director; your mother is a great actress; your stepfather is a writer-director. You've been weaned on the theater."

Nothing happened for months, then Jones said, "Why don't we do that *Do Re Mi?* I'll get Garson to write and direct it."

Jule agreed, and Harris packaged the creative side, signing David Merrick as producer. Kanin wrote the libretto; Comden–Green joined the staff to do lyrics to Jule's music.

One afternoon Jule was walking out of Lindy's, the popular Broadway eatery, and came face to face with Phil Silvers. He hadn't seen Phil in several years.

Styne: "You interested in doing a show?"

Silvers: "Yeah."

Styne: "It's a story of how the Mafia comes out of retirement. Gar Kanin wrote the book. Betty and Adolph have done the lyrics . . ."

Silvers: "I'll do it."

Nancy Walker was signed to co-star.

As usual, Jule attempted to slip in a "hit" even before the show went into rehearsal. Just as soon as Comden–Green had set the lyrics to "Make Someone Happy," Jule proclaimed it to be definite "gold record" material. *It's a funny thing about songs and it doesn't apply to any of the other arts as much—you almost know when you've got a hit song. When you've got that right idea and the right words and the right sound, then you go all the way with the right singer.*

There was always quite a lot of jockeying in the record business for the cast album of any show that had hit potential, and RCA wanted the album of *Do Re Mi.* Jule said to Merrick, "We'll make a trade with them. Have them get a single out now, before the show opens, and then we'll talk about the cast album."

Merrick–Comden–Green sat there thinking. They didn't want to be too heavy-handed with all-powerful RCA. Jule said, "Never mind your thinking. I'll tell you who I want for 'Make Someone Happy'—Perry Como."

On the stormy day that Hurricane Donna brushed New York, Styne–Comden–Green were in the studios of RCA-Victor, on East Twenty-fourth Street, to demonstrate the score of *Do Re Mi.* The taping button was pressed, and the trio began the new score, sufficiently impressing four RCA executives.

Perry Como didn't do a lot of records, but many of the recordings that he did undertake became hits. When he sang the right song, it became ageless, as he seemed to be. Jule had said to Merrick, "Let me dicker. They'll give us this single and we'll get Perry."

Jule went to Como's artist and recording representative. He was told, "Well, Perry's a funny guy that way. If he likes something, that's it. If he doesn't like it, that's it, too. Nobody can move him. I can't."

"Make Someone Happy" was a rangy thing. Jule sent the middle of the song way up, "Once you've found her, put your arms around her . . ." He knew Perry might have trouble at that spot vocally, but was willing to take the chance.

Next day, Como heard the demo record, and said, in effect, "That's it." And "Make Someone Happy," by Como, was No. 1 on the charts three months before *Do Re Mi* opened, quite successfully, at the St. James Theatre on December 26, 1960.

No show was without its demands for seats—favors for friends and business associates, sometimes extraordinary requests. Jule's house seats, always an annoyance rather than a reward, were parceled out with some care by Dorothy Dicker. Often the list of requests was two pages long.

During the first week of the run, Jule was getting dressed to go to the theater—he always attended the first or second act in the early weeks, simply to monitor the music. The phone rang in his apartment, and a voice said, "This is Salinger." The voice seemed to be filtered, as if coming from a boat or aircraft. It had an overlay of radio call.

Jule said, "Salinger who?"

The voice kept on, "I'm with the President and we're flying to

Washington tonight. He wants to see *Do Re Mi.*" Press secretary Pierre Salinger was taking a slight liberty. John F. Kennedy hadn't been sworn in as yet, having narrowly defeated Richard Nixon in November.

Jule immediately said to himself, Why should I do anything for Jack Kennedy? *I'd never been treated so rudely by any man. Or seldom so.*

The rudeness had occurred while Kennedy was still a senator. The Kennedys, staging a charity affair in New York in the late fifties, had wanted Sammy Davis Jr. to perform. Peter Lawford had tried and failed; others had tried. Finally, Jones Harris had been approached by Jackie Kennedy and Jones, in turn, had appealed to Jule. Davis agreed to do the show as a favor to his former producer.

The night of the party Jule was escorted to the Kennedy table by Jones Harris and was introduced to Jackie Kennedy as "the man who landed Sammy Davis for you."

Just then Senator Kennedy walked up and Jackie said, "John, this is Jule Styne, who arranged to get Sammy Davis for us."

Jule held out his hand but Kennedy walked on by, a smile on his face, his eyes fastened on a pretty girl who stood behind Jule. *It's happened to everyone, but you feel like such a fool, your mouth open and your hand sticking out..*

Nonetheless, Jule replied to Salinger, "I think every seat is gone, but I'll try." He rushed to the St. James and found that all seats were taken, including the house seats. The entire theater had been bought out by a New Jersey synagogue. But Merrick's manager, Jack Schlissel, suggested, "Why don't you find out who's sponsoring this and ask for their seats?"

About six, Secret Service agents began to arrive, and then about seven-thirty the sponsor arrived in full-length mink, plastic wedgies and a row of orchids almost to her knees.

Jule approached her, "Mrs. Jacobson, I'm Jule Styne and I composed the music for this show. I need a special favor from you." The Jacobsons, naturally, had prime seats: C 102 and 103, as near as Jule can remember.

He said, "The next President of the United States would like to have your seats for the show tonight. He's on his way to Washington. Now, I'll be happy to have two chairs placed near the orchestra for you, and give you eight tickets to any other performance."

Mrs. Jacobson answered, in a heavy Jewish accent, "If the President of the United States wants my tickets, let him ask me."

Jule thought, Oh, Christ, she wants him to beg her for them. He did not stop to think—she doesn't believe you. Jule replied, "He'll ask for them."

Salinger had said that Kennedy would be timed to arrive during the overture, when the house lights were down. A moment after eight-thirty, the limo pulled up in front of the St. James and Jule had fifty feet in which to explain the problem. Kennedy, overhearing, said, "I'll ask."

Mrs. Jacobson was waiting in the lobby. President-elect Kennedy strode up to her, took the tickets and said, "Thank you very much. You're most kind."

Mrs. Jacobson slid slowly to the carpet.

In the spring of 1961, Buddy Robbins walked into Jule's office with a collection of short stories by Edmund Love. "Here's a musical for you," said Robbins, always on the lookout for material that might enrich his employer, Chappell Music Company.

Jule read the ten stories about lost souls, and was inclined to believe that if they could be linked together and had one central character they showed possibility. David Merrick had the same feeling and bought the property. Comden–Green also took a liking to the Lowe collection.

So *Subways Are for Sleeping,* score by Styne, book and lyrics by Comden–Green, went into rehearsal in the fall under the direction of Michael Kidd, who also choreographed. Sydney Chaplin, late of *Bells Are Ringing,* starred, along with Carol Lawrence, but *Subways,* launched low-key in a matter of months, mostly slept for several hundred performances at cut royalties, despite fair reviews.

Out of it, however, came three hit songs—"Comes Once in a Lifetime," "Be a Santa" and "I'm Just Taking My Time," one of the richest ballads, musically, that Jule had ever written.

Also out of *Subways* came a major talent named Michael Bennett. He was in the chorus line of the show, his first. Jule watched him work and then went up to him. "You're too good for the chorus line," said Styne to Bennett. The same line of dialogue was used in Bennett's own *Chorus Line,* a smash musical of 1976.

Curiously enough, the Sinatra–Styne relationship came to life again during the *Subways* period and then collapsed just as quickly. Prior to rehearsals, Jule was in Hollywood in behalf of several ventures. One meeting was with Richard Zanuck, son of Darryl F. Having inherited some of his father's talents, young Zanuck was production boss. Jule suggested doing a musical version of *A Tree Grows in Brook-*

lyn and then gambled boldly, as prospective producer-composer, by saying, "It's for Sinatra and Monroe." Jule further pointed out that the *Pink Tights* score, paid for, and never used, would fit *Brooklyn.* Zanuck reacted with enthusiasm and said, "Get Sinatra and Monroe, and you've got a quarter-million bonus up front."

Jule went to Sinatra, briefly outlined the project, and said that "Monroe was crazy to work with him because he was the greatest." Frank replied, "Never mind Monroe. It's a great part for me."

Jule then approached Monroe. *I told her that Frank was crazy to work with her because she was the greatest.*

At the time, Sinatra and Monroe weren't exactly on speaking terms, but a date was set for the two stars to meet with Jule at the Sherry-Netherland Hotel in New York on the following Monday. *Marilyn seemed so excited about doing* A Tree Grows in Brooklyn, *just as excited as Frank.*

On Sunday, while Jule was breakfasting, radio music was interrupted by a news bulletin: Marilyn Monroe was dead.

19

I went down to the Bon Soir and was wiped out. I went down every night for a month and said to myself, "This has to be Fanny Brice." But Barbra Streisand couldn't be Fanny Brice. We'd already signed Anne Bancroft.

JULE STYNE, 1977

Mary Martin had read Isobel Lennart's screenplay of the life of Fanny Brice and wanted to do it, but not as a movie. She saw herself in it as a stage play, a musical, and sent a letter to film producer Ray Stark, Fanny's son-in-law. Stark had tried to launch the Fanny Brice story a number of times in Hollywood but had never obtained studio backing. Now, he thought it might be a good idea to try Broadway first. His wife, Frances, was anxious to have her mother's life story told on stage or screen.

Stark came to New York to establish an association with David Merrick, who could guide him through the intricacies and turmoil of mounting a musical. Stark then called Jule, at the suggestion of Merrick; next, he called Steve Sondheim. Merrick thought it might be a good idea to reteam the *Gypsy* combination.

A meeting was arranged in Merrick's office, with Mary Martin, and her favorite director, Vincent Donahue; Stark, Steve and Jule. Also present was Isobel Lennart.

Jule listened as Stark talked, as Mary Martin talked; as Donahue talked. *Suddenly, it was all uninspired. Something was wrong and the meeting just petered out. I can't tell you what was wrong.*

Leaving the office, Sondheim said to Jule, "I don't want to do the life of Fanny Brice with Mary Martin. She's not Jewish. You need someone ethnic for that part. Fanny was a hokey comedienne and Mary's terrific with characters, but this is East Side New York and she can't do it."

Jule partially agreed. "Okay, Steve, I don't think there's a show here yet but let's wait until they call." Jule very much wanted to work with Sondheim again.

A few days later, Mary Martin abandoned the idea.

Time passed, and then Jule was invited to another meeting in the Merrick office and on this occasion Jerome Robbins was present. In the interim, Robbins had given the script to Anne Bancroft, who liked it.

Jule thought she was a possible. *The only thing that held us up was whether or not she could sing the part. I didn't exactly know what kind of score I'd write but I planned to give her every consideration as one of the finest actresses around. So she came to my apartment and was very shy. She warmed up after a while and sang about ten songs. Her voice was pleasant enough, and I knew she could act. So the possibility of her being a musical personality did in fact exist.*

Jule was then asked by Stark, Robbins and Merrick to use Dorothy Fields as lyricist. Jule objected. *Frankly, I didn't want Fields, not that she isn't a great writer. But we had a female librettist, a female star, and I was truly afraid of balance. Sondheim had checked out, and they left me with Fields. Had Bancroft been the first choice, Steve might have stayed in.*

In the late winter of 1962 Jule informed Stark and Merrick that he was going to Florida for a month, sit in the sun and try to fashion some music for Bancroft. *One had to be careful in writing for her. Her range was limited and I had to find material she'd be able to handle.*

But already there was a second choice for "Fanny," though this choice hadn't gone beyond the mention stage. A month earlier, Jule had read a newspaper story on *I Can Get It for You Wholesale,* in which there was a rave about a Jewish girl named Barbra Streisand, who was playing second lead. He'd attended the show and was impressed by Miss Streisand. Merrick, producer of *Wholesale,* had also mentioned Streisand as a possibility if Bancroft didn't work out. The latter seemed remote.

Streisand had first drawn attention at the Bon Soir, a Greenwich Village night club, appearing there for eleven weeks in 1961, and then had picked up momentum in an off-Broadway revue, *An Evening with*

Harry Stoones. But she was still an unknown when she auditioned for *Wholesale* director Arthur Laurents, who persuaded David Merrick to sign her for the role of Miss Marmelstein. During rehearsals Laurents fought a nightly battle to keep her in the cast. She did not appeal to David Merrick. This state of things lasted until the opening night of *I Can Get It for You Wholesale,* at which time she drew the deserved raves.

Not thinking very much about Streisand, Jule flew to Palm Beach, sat in the sun and played golf for two weeks, then went to work—for the voice of Anne Bancroft. After turning out five songs, he took a morning off for golf, and then went shopping in the afternoon. On the street he spotted Bob Merrill, composer-lyricist whose credits included *New Girl in Town, Take Me Along* and *Carnival.* Each of the shows had had respectable runs and Merrill was a proven talent. Jule had already met the big, blond man briefly when he'd been brought to New York by George Abbott.

Jule said, "Come on in here. I'll buy you a cup of coffee. I want to talk to you." He told Merrill about Dorothy Fields and the Fanny Brice story.

Merrill said, "She's marvelous."

"No question she's marvelous, but for some strange reason, even after two minutes, I feel a chemistry with you. Don't ask me why. But will you write five songs on speculation?" Jule had never before asked a lyricist to work on spec, but it was probably the only way to get Merrill involved.

Several months previously, they'd lunched in New York and had discussed collaboration but not for *Funny Girl.* Merrill replied that he'd try.

Merrick was also disturbed over the female imbalance of the staff; he didn't think that Fields was right for the show.

Bob Merrill had a fascinating history as a songwriter. He'd gone to Hollywood when he was twenty-one to become an actor and ended up as a dialogue director for Columbia Pictures. While working on a Western near Tucson, Merrill was approached by an extra who asked, "Did you ever write songs?"

Merrill replied that he hadn't; what's more, he'd never thought about writing songs.

"I'm trying to get someone to write for me," said the girl, who was named Dorothy Shay. She added, "I sing these funny hillbilly songs but don't have enough of them for an album."

There was cloud cover during many days of the filming and Merrill, along with the rest of the company, sat idly waiting for the sun. "She kept after me, and there was nothing else to do, so I finally wrote a few for her."

"They're wonderful," she told Merrill.

Bob didn't believe her, and after the picture was finished, he forgot he'd ever written them; forgot about Dorothy Shay. Then, about six months later, Merrill received a call from a record company requesting verification of his authorship. After a few weeks he received a contract and then a check for $500. Shay's album, "The Park Avenue Hillbilly," came out and overnight Bob Merrill was a songwriter, doing novelty tunes at first.

Styne and Merrill went on back to where Jule was staying, and Jule played the five melodies he'd written for the new show. Merrill began making notes and Jule suddenly realized he was going by the numbers —4-2-1-5. Merrill quickly admitted he couldn't read music or play any instrument. But Sammy Cahn or Leo Robin hadn't been able to either, so that was no problem.

Merrill finally went home and called Jule that night to say he'd read the libretto and loved it. "Let me give you an idea, Jule. I notice that Isobel Lennart refers to a very special person a number of times. Fool around with that lyrically—a very special person."

Jule said he would.

In three days, Merrill came back with lyrics for all five songs, including "Don't Rain on My Parade," a very different piece, musically, with Fanny Brice patter in it; "Who Are You Now?"; "The Music That Makes Me Dance," and one that wound up in the trunk, "When I Talk About You."

Working with Bob Merrill was quite different from working with Sondheim. Bob was much faster. He did a dummy lyric, agreed on a title, and then locked himself up and worked alone. *They were all brilliant, those lyrics he'd done in three days.*

At his house, Merrill worked with an octave and a half of keyboard, actually a set of bells. He could carry the keyboard around in his hands, and often did. His numbering system was distinctly his own, but not too much different from those supplied with a child's dimestore xylophone. The system might not have worked for Sammy Cahn or Leo Robin but it served Merrill's purposes.

Most noontimes during the month they collaborated in Palm Beach, Jule had a running gin game going at the house in which he was staying, where he was a guest. The tab was kept on paper and no money was exchanged at the table. Merrill usually sat in the warm sun on the patio, paying little attention to the game.

One noon, Jule suddenly said, "I'm due at the dentist." He called over to Merrill. "Bob, do you play?"

"A little."

"Sit in for me."

The first hand was played and Merrill threw two cards. A tycoon said, "Gin." He played the second hand, threw two more cards, and the tycoon said, "Gin."

After four or five losing hands, Merrill turned to the man who was keeping score and asked, "What is this costing a point?"

"You're in six thousand."

Merrill felt himself in cold sweat, but couldn't get out of the game. He dropped his loss to about $5,000 by the time Jule returned. Merrill said, "You son of a bitch, you pushed me into this game. I'm out five thousand."

Jule said, "I'm terribly sorry," to his new friend and collaborator, and immediately arranged for the check to be signed over to a charity as a tax deduction.

Merrill refused to participate any further in Jule's gambling activities.

In the middle of the Palm Beach collaboration, Merrill asked, "By the way, who will play Fanny Brice?"

Jule hadn't volunteered the information. "Anne Bancroft."

"Oh, Christ," said Merrill, "she'll never like these songs. I know the lady. We wound up in a terrible fight at the Old Colony. She'll hate every word I write."

"The words are very good."

"You don't know Anne."

Jule promptly changed the subject. "You told me the other night to work on a 'very special person.' I think I've got a helluva melody for it."

Merrill remembers interrupting, "Jule, I tell you that Anne Bancroft can't sing any of these songs."

Jule said, "Forget Bancroft and listen now. 'Very Special Person' —here's how it goes: Da-da . . . da-da-da-da . . . then way up, da-da-dahhhhhhhhhhhhha—da-da-aa . . ." He played the entire song.

"Great," Merrill yelled. "But now it ain't gonna be 'special person.' Listen." Then he ad-libbed, while Jule played the melody again: "People, people who need people, are the luckiest people in the world . . ."

The song "wrote" in thirty minutes with Merrill scribbling the lyrics as Styne played the melody over and over.

Nights, they did the society whirl. Merrill said, "Palm Beach in the winter has to be the best place in the world to write a musical. You go to all the parties and try the songs. Sometimes we went to two or three a night, playing and singing what we'd written."

Most of the time, Jule dated Wendy Vanderbilt, who was then nineteen, and Merrill dated another young socialite, Baby Jane Holzer. Merrill recalls that "Jule looked on Wendy as sort of a mascot. But he can be a great companion to a woman, funny and irreverent. The four of us would go up and down Worth Avenue, eating French fries and shrimp, just having fun. All the good, basic writing of *Funny Girl* was done against that background—parties and fun."

There were moments that weren't fun. Although Merrill had discovered Jule's fondness for card games during the noontime gin rummy sessions, he had no knowledge of Jule's gambling problem until one terrifying morning when a "fat fellow" walked into the house to say to Jule, very softly, "Pay up or I'll break both your arms."

In the past, Jule had given large sums of money to strangers such as Fatty, only to learn that the visitors weren't with the mob at all. They were free-lance collectors. *I made some quick calls and found out that Fat didn't belong. He'd just heard that I owed money and decided to try his hand at getting some.* Not long afterward, Fatty was shot to death in Miami Beach.

Merrill said, "I was completely floored. Here was this laughing little man who made such beautiful music, my new partner, and he was up to his ass in barracudas. It was frightening."

Jule finally called Ray Stark, in Hollywood, to say, "I've written six songs with Bob Merrill; maybe it'll be seven by the time we see you. Dorothy Fields is out; Bob Merrill's in, or I don't do the show."

Stark still favored Dorothy Fields. He registered little enthusiasm for Merrill.

Jule insisted that Merrill was exactly the right lyricist for the new show and that the songs would prove it.

Stark agreed to listen to the songs, and set up a meeting in Hollywood, but made no promises about Dorothy Fields.

A few minutes later, Jule called Merrill. "We're leaving tomorrow night for Los Angeles."

Merrill said, "Baby, I don't fly."

Jule answered, "Baby, you do fly, because we've got a meeting with Ray Stark day after tomorrow."

"No way," said Merrill.

Bob Merrill took the train everywhere—Chicago, Washington, New York, California. If he couldn't ride the train, he took a bus or drove his own car. He flew only in "dire emergency." Jule finally convinced him that this was a dire emergency.

"That whole trip was a disaster for me," Merrill remembers. "I got drunk in the cocktail lounge waiting for the National plane to take off for Los Angeles; then we weren't up thirty minutes until we hit a violent storm. Lightning. I wanted to die." The lyricist arrived in Los Angeles a complete mess. Styne slept most of the way, Connie Bennett style.

The seventh song had been written before the pair left Palm Beach. Merrill had given Jule a title, "Sadie, Sadie, Married Lady," plus a few key lines. The melody was set within half a day, and Merrill's lyrics were completed two days later.

In early afternoon, Jule and Merrill played the songs for Stark and Jerome Robbins. The latter said happily, "Now, I've got a show."

At about three o'clock Miss Bancroft walked in. She saw Merrill standing by the piano. He said, "Not a muscle moved in her face. She simply stared at me, and I looked away from her and began singing the songs as Jule played, ending with 'People,' which is difficult because of its range."

Miss Bancroft sat deadpan during the thirty minute Styne–Merrill performance, and then arose. "I want no part of this," she said. "It's not for me."

Jule immediately thought of the girl he'd seen in *I Can Get It for You Wholesale,* the Miss Marmelstein whose last name was Streisand. Wisely, he did not mention her to either Robbins or Stark. That could come later. There was always a danger in advocating the lead roles; sometimes resentment.

Stark had the visitors to lunch the next day at his home, and Jule was seated beside a tall, beautiful redhead. He knew many of the beautiful ladies in Hollywood, but had never met this one. Yet her face was somehow familiar. It should have been. All over California were Esso billboards, including a large one on Sunset Boulevard, displaying a stunning girl in a sunbonnet. The stunning girl was now a few inches away.

"I'm Jule Styne. Who are you?"

"Maggi Brown." The voice was very British.

A moment later, Maggi Brown explained her presence at the luncheon. She was an actress under contract to Ray Stark and 20th

Century-Fox. She could have added—originally Margaret Ann Bissett Brown, English WASP, product of Birmingham, Radnorshire, Devonshire; daughter of art-teaching parents. Budding actress by way of jewelry designing and floristry. Former occupation, highly paid international model. "Maggi" was a stage name, one that she didn't particularly like.

"Can you act?" Jule asked.

"I don't know," the willowy, serene actress-model, replied. "I've done the Ernie Kovacs TV shows, but no films as yet."

Jule said, "Read me a page of script and I'll tell you whether you can act or not."

Maggi Brown turned away. Who was this pushy know-it-all? The name hadn't registered, nor did she connect it to the very short telephone conversation she had had with him the previous year. Had he hummed a few of his tunes, she would have recognized her luncheon partner. Her first attempt on a penny whistle, as a child, had been "Give Me Five Minutes More." Except for a stiff good-by, they did not speak to each other again during the afternoon.

Some two weeks later, Ray Stark invited Maggi to return to dinner at his home. She took a taxi. Jule brought Sandra Church to the same party, driving her automobile. Their romance was over, of course, but they remained good friends. Then Sandra left the party early, taking her car. She had a dawn call for make-up at Universal Studios, where she was co-starring with Marlon Brando in *The Ugly American.* Two of Stark's guests were now "without wheels."

After dinner, viewing a new film in the producer's home projection room, Jule found himself sitting by the beautiful redhead. Soon, she leaned over to whisper, "You are the rudest man I've ever met in my life."

Jule•was astonished. He didn't think he'd been that rude at the luncheon. He was kidding the lovely British actress.

Maggi Brown whispered on. "You had a date with me for the opening of *Gypsy* a year and a half ago. I bought a four-hundred dollar dress to go with you. You didn't even have the courtesy to call and break the date. I didn't know who you were two weeks ago. The name slipped by me. I know who you are now."

Jule felt his face turning crimson in the darkness. He whispered back, "There's nothing I can say. I was rude. You must forgive me."

They sat in uncomfortable silence and when the screening ended, Stark drove Maggi to her apartment. Jule rode along on his way to the Beverly Hills Hotel. As she got out of the car, he said, "Please have lunch with me tomorrow. Polo Lounge at twelve-thirty. I have to apologize to you."

Maggi arrived at the Polo Lounge, in the hotel, promptly at twelve-thirty, but fifteen minutes later Jule was called to Columbia by Stark. He said, "Finish your lunch and sign my name. I have to go but let's have dinner tonight."

Maggi laughed, "You're insane."

They saw a great deal of each other for the next two weeks. Jule took her to Hollywood Park, Las Vegas, Lake Tahoe—all gambling places, naturally. "He was the most alive person I'd ever met. His energy and enthusiasm were so contagious. Being with him was like being caught in a hurricane and enjoying every minute of it."

Toward the end of that two-week period, in May, Jule told his sister, Claire, "I think I'm going to marry Maggi Brown."

"Does she like you?"

"Yes, she does. I'm going to ask her to marry me."

Jule went back to New York and called Maggi two nights later, asking her if she'd like to become his bride. "Next week, or next year," he said.

Maggi opted for next week. "Aries commit first and then adapt later."

"You have to be here Sunday," said Jule. "We'll get married Monday night."

"You have a date."

Dorothy Dicker met Maggi Brown at the Plaza Hotel, took one look at the tall beauty, red hair accentuating the porcelain skin, and said to herself, "What does she want from him?" Maggi was twenty-six; Jule was fifty-six. If she was looking for money she had a surprise coming. With apprehension, Dorothy then made the wedding arrangements, firmly believing that Jule was headed into another kind of disaster. Her suspicions of the beautiful lady from England remained for a long time.

Margaret Ann Bissett Brown and Jule Styne were married the night of June 4th, 1962, in the office of Temple Emanuel, with Jerry Robbins as best man. Dorothy Dicker listened to the vows, and wondered what would happen. Among the things that did happen was a change of first name. "Maggi" became Margaret again. The stage name was no longer needed.

"When we got married, we were virtually two strangers," Margaret admits. "It was some time before I came down to earth and got to know my husband well enough to love him instead of his glamorous façade."

Jule had described his style of life to her as "Beverly Hills, Belmont, Saratoga, assorted weekends this summer; black-tie openings and parties in the fall; winter in Palm Beach." Life would be so exciting, so romantic, she thought.

"You better go shopping," he advised.

So Margaret did just that, at Saks Fifth Avenue, and the bill was around $5,000. Margaret could not understand, at the time, why Dorothy Dicker reacted so frantically. Knowing what was in the bank and what was owed, Dorothy said sternly to the bride, "Shop as seldom as possible," but refused to say why. Jule had instructed Dorothy not to tell Margaret about the perilous state of his financial affairs; not to dare mention the gambling.

Margaret said to Dorothy, "I think my husband has two wives," a rattling statement but near to the truth.

The Stynes soon flew to the West Coast to attend "A Salute to Jule Styne" at the Hollywood Bowl, Jule conducting the symphony orchestra; Tony Bennett and Shirley Jones starring in the summer concert. Jule wanted to play a Haydn concerto that night, backed by the full symphony, simply to prove that he wasn't all "pop." He played the Haydn beautifully in rehearsal, but got the jitters before the performance and canceled it. Though nervous herself, Margaret bathed in the applause and attention given to her new husband. They flew home a few days later.

Without a star, the Fanny Brice story was stalled, but Jule eagerly accepted the suggestion of David Merrick that he go see "Barbra Streisand once more." She was in a return engagement at the Bon Soir and as Jule watched and listened to her he thought, This has to be Fanny. He went backstage to talk to her manager, Marty Erlichman, and was encouraged. Margaret and Jule went to the Bon Soir twenty-eight times.

Meanwhile, Jule asked Margaret if he could borrow $50,000. She was staggered, assuming he was a wealthy man. She'd worked hard to save up the money, earned from modeling, but she withdrew it from her savings. The need seemed urgent. She'd overheard conversations about money. She'd also seen a scrap of paper in the apartment. Dates were on it, and next to them the figures $10,000; $5,000; $7,000. She had no idea what the figures meant. Dorothy knew.

As his bride settled in, Jule was deeper in debt than he'd ever been, both with tax agencies and the bookies. Dorothy would cash a check for $20,000 or $25,000, walk down the street, meet a bookie on a certain corner and pay him off. She'd established a good relationship with most of them, browbeating them if they pushed too hard.

Margaret recalls, "During the first year we fought a lot, but eventually I felt I could say what he'd told me, 'that I'd made him happy,' which made me happy, too. I think I expected a movie version of a composer—hours of emotional hair-tearing with a background of me, tea and sympathy. Not a bit of it. Jule writes in his head, of course, and is surprisingly peaceful around the house."

Margaret had always thought that her exterior was much better than her interior. She had traded on her looks, and one night the subject of beauty came up. Jule said, "I didn't notice whether you were pretty or not. I liked you. That's all." Margaret took it as a tremendous compliment.

In late summer, with *Funny Girl,* so titled by David Merrick, still without a leading lady, Jule and Bob Merrill turned to Dickens to produce music and lyrics for an NBC special, *Mr. Magoo's Christmas Carol,* an animated hour starring Jim Backus, Jack Cassidy and Morey Amsterdam. Scrooge and Bob Cratchit temporarily replaced Fanny Brice as music subjects.

While David Merrick was toying with the idea of Barbra Streisand to fill the star void, Ray Stark and Jerry Robbins had been on a Bancroft replacement hunt. They'd discussed the part with several singers, including Edie Gorme. She wouldn't do it unless husband Steve Lawrence could play Nicky Arnstein and Lawrence wouldn't make a good Nicky, they decided. Stark and Robbins had also flown to the Midwest to talk to Carol Burnett, who said, "I'd love to do it but what you need is a Jewish girl." They returned to New York empty-handed and Jule felt it was now time to nominate Streisand. He called Robbins instead of Stark. "You've got to go see Barbra Streisand. She's Fanny." He felt that Robbins might be more receptive than Stark.

The director of *Funny Girl* agreed to go. "But I'll see her by myself," said Robbins. "You're too enthusiastic." Robbins came away with the same enthusiasm.

Barbra auditioned for *Funny Girl* a few days later. *She looked awful. She wore black boots and a red Cossack-type coat. All of her clothes were out of thrift shops. I saw Fran Stark staring at her, obvious distaste on her face. Streisand looked to be anything but a star.*

She read a scene with the stage manager but the reading did not go well. Robbins had worked with her for almost an hour and was dismayed that she didn't remember what they'd rehearsed. He called up to the stage, "You're supposed to cry, Barbra."

The twenty-one-year-old girl looked straight back at him. "Mr. Robbins, I can't cry with these words."

There was a moment of stunned silence at the impertinence of this new actress. The usual penalty would be to politely ask her to leave the theater. Then Isobel Lennart stood up. She said, "I don't blame you, Miss Streisand. They're terrible words. And they're mine."

Jerry Robbins laughed. He knew he was dealing with an honest person. She couldn't read what wasn't there.

However, Fran Stark said to her husband, "She'll never play my mother." Very probably no actress would have satisfied Fran Stark. Her husband now obviously approved of the shabby-looking girl but couldn't very well say so in front of his wife. Nonetheless, Streisand was signed to play Fanny Brice.

Also summoned that day was Sydney Chaplin, who had just closed in *Subways Are for Sleeping.* Sydney was not an unknown quantity to Robbins or Styne and his audition for the part of Nicky Arnstein was almost rubber stamp.

It would appear that *Funny Girl* would go along smoothly now, the stars having been set and the score written, but then Robbins went to Stark, after getting into an argument with Isobel Lennart to say that he didn't think Isobel could dramatize the play. He acknowledged that she was a fine movie writer but he wasn't certain about her ability as a librettist. Stark refused to replace Lennart and Robbins exited, beginning a chain of squabbles and departures that eventually included the good-by of David Merrick.

During many periods over the next year and a half, *Funny Girl* wasn't funny at all.

20

The man is impossible, infuriating, inconsistent, irresponsible and illogical, but never, ever mean or evil. He is also exhilarating, irrepressible, irreplaceable and never, ever boring. He forgets birthdays and anniversaries but brings flowers for no occasion. He'd give me the moon quite happily and blame the IRS when the bill was overdue.

—MARGARET BROWN STYNE, 1977

The first year of the Jule Styne–Margaret Brown union was one of glamour, discovery and fights. Margaret quickly learned that her husband was extremely jealous. Her single girl habits of talking to men brought up accusations of flirting. Jule decided that his wife was very opinionated.

The Stynes, ensconced in a fashionable apartment sixteen floors above Fifth Avenue, with Central Park across the way, went about marital adjustment in a mostly normal fashion, with a few notable exceptions.

One exception still brings a smile to Margaret's face. "Jule is a hypochondriac of long and noble vintage, consequently very healthy, but one of his early weapons in an effort to change me was to collapse. I began to be suspicious about the fourth time. I heard sounds of furniture being overturned. I waited. Silence for a few minutes and then pencils fell loudly. I went into the room and saw Jule lying very dramatically under the piano bench surrounded by the spilled pencils. He looked the picture of health. I stepped over him and began dialing the phone. He raised his head to ask, 'Who are you calling?' I said,

'Your doctor.' He then announced that all he needed was some tea and got to his feet. That performance was never repeated again. Never was it dull that first year."

In late May 1963, with *Funny Girl* lacking a director, and on the shelf again, ABC-Paramount announced that it would invest more than $1 million in three Broadway musicals, to be presented by producer Lester Osterman and composer Jule Styne.

ABC said that the shows were an original, *A Girl to Remember,* starring Carol Burnett, with book and lyrics by Comden–Green, music by Styne; a musical adaptation of the film, *The Ghost Goes West,* and a Sam and Bella Spewack adaptation of *Mrs. A.,* the Richard Aldrich biography of his late wife, Gertrude Lawrence. They appeared to be impressive properties.

A Girl to Remember, to be staged by George Abbott, was scheduled to open at the Mark Hellinger Theatre, on November 23. At the same time, Jule was also polishing the score of Brecht's *Arturo Ui,* for David Merrick presentation, also in November.

"Good God," said Dorothy Dicker to Jule, "I hope you don't take on anything else right now." She eyed the schedule—three musicals in preparation, three more to be prepared—with misgiving. But she also knew why Jule was crowding his creative life so feverishly: money. Her father had just lent Jule $20,000.

While all this was going on, Barbra Streisand was no longer an "unknown." She'd appeared on a Bob Hope TV show to much acclaim; she'd appeared in Hollywood to more acclaim; she was now into big money in Las Vegas, a star no less, with top billing.

So the summer passed, somewhat frantically, and then in September Jule was notified that Ethel Styne was in critical condition in Cedars of Lebanon Hospital, in Los Angeles. Jule sent her flowers. "Ethel looked at the flowers with such love, and then sadly shook her head," her sister, Lillian, said. She died September 2, 1963.

The new director of *Funny Girl* was Bobby Fosse. *He came in with a whole new set of ideas, some brilliant, on how to make it work. By now, Bob Merrill and I were dizzy. Then, just as suddenly, Fosse quit. In early September, Stark had been checking on Fosse's capabilities. Bobby heard about it. It was just as well. Barbra wasn't sure she wanted Fosse.*

During that upheaval, Jule postponed the debut of Carol Burnett's *A Girl to Remember,* but the David Merrick production of *Arturo Ui,* with music by Styne, opened as scheduled on November 11, at the Lunt-Fontanne Theatre, starring Christopher Plummer. The play traced the rise of Hitler in Chicago gangland terms, and Jule was right at home. This score was ninety percent "barrelhouse" and has become a classic among buffs of that musical style. Unfortunately, reviews were poor and *Arturo Ui* closed after one week.

"What I find remarkable about all this," Merrill said, "was that right in the high heat of preparing *Funny Girl* Jule was opening these other shows, having written most of the music the previous year. How the hell he managed to keep them separated, I don't know."

Milton Rosenstock began working with Jule on the *Funny Girl* score a few days after *Arturo Ui* bowed in and out, developing orchestral approaches. The score had now been on Jule's piano for more than two years.

"Why are you keeping it there so long?" asked Milton.

Jule answered, "Because I don't want to forget that I wrote this score and that we're going to put it on."

About ten days later, November 26, Milton and Jule were watching the John F. Kennedy funeral, looking at the horses, hearing the drumbeats. Then they began talking about the show and got excited. Jule jumped up and went to the piano, sat down and began improvising.

Margaret stormed in. "How dare you, Jule? Playing when the President is dead!"

Jule stopped but it was one of the few times that he stopped polishing the score over a period of three years. He wrote a total of fifty-six separate pieces of music for *Funny Girl.*

After the departure of Bobby Fosse, the show was shut down again for several months. Finally, Merrick said to Stark, "What you need now is a director with a complete understanding of production. You need Gar Kanin." It was Merrick's last contribution to *Funny Girl,* and he had made many. Merrick soon removed himself from the embattled musical. Stark became sole producer.

Kanin heard the score but didn't rush to join the staff. The production had a stormy history; the star might be difficult. He was leaving Sardi's one early afternoon as Jule and Margaret arrived and was cornered by the composer for almost half an hour. Finally worn down by "Stynese," he called Stark and agreed to direct. So Kanin reported to the Fanny Brice story with still another list of changes. Streisand, however, though she was relieved that Fosse was gone, was even less enthusiastic about Kanin. In fact, she wanted Robbins back and said so.

Jule began to work with Barbra the same way he'd worked with

Channing for *Blondes.* He wanted Streisand to go into rehearsal completely prepared and she came to his apartment ten or fifteen times to run through the songs. Several new numbers had been written. *Although there was still a lot of friction at the direction end, everything seemed to be going well enough at the music end.*

Not always, however. Jule irritated Merrill a number of times when they collaborated in the apartment above Central Park. "Jule was writing with me, and I was concentrating deeply and suddenly he'd get up and leave in mid-bar. Say nothing. Just walk out. He'd make a phone call to his bookie or I'd find him in the kitchen making soup. Then we'd work for another ten minutes and he'd disappear. I'd look for him and Margaret would say, 'He's asleep.' So I finally bawled the shit out of him and made him work at my place. Nothing changed. He did the same things there. And I'd needle him about the gambling. I'd see him down the street in a phone booth. I'd see him with a scratch sheet. I'd ask, 'Where you been, Jule?' He'd answer he'd gone out to get some tea. The hell he did. He went out to place a bet. Clearly, he was a gambleholic. One day I remember he came out of this brownstone where he'd been playing poker. He was grinning ear to ear. But when he reached the curb, two men came up and said, 'We'll take that. Now, you only owe us $14 thousand.' "

Margaret said, "The first time I knew that he was a chronic gambler, a sick gambler, was at a party given by Fran and Ray Stark in our honor. Sammy Cahn sang a revealing parody. But when I asked Jule about it I got angry, evasive answers. During the next few years, I tried, as others had tried, to stop his gambling. The last way I tried was to be his bookmaker. The first day he won, and I paid him two hundred dollars. After that he'd give me his bets every night and I'd calculate the results the next day. Three months later Jule was betting on every race in the country and I was spending seven or eight hours a day bookkeeping. He owed me $2 million by then. One day he came home with an English racing form. Well, I'd never received a penny for his losses and I didn't want to beat him up the way the bookies had threatened. I began to feel like a bird in a rapidly rusting gilded cage . . ."

She was also a pregnant bird, but her luck was as bad as Jule's. The good tidings that she would give birth to their first child turned to sadness a few months later when she had a miscarriage and lost the baby.

21

I could not believe what was happening to us.
And couldn't understand why it was happening.
The best song in the whole show was in danger.

—BOB MERRILL, 1977

The new director of *Funny Girl,* Gar Kanin, called a staff meeting. The first thing he said was, "I want to discuss a song called 'People.' I don't think it's right for this play."

Jule and Merrill gasped simultaneously.

Kanin continued, "At that moment, Fanny's leaving. She's just met the fellow. Why should she become philosophical?"

Jule replied, "I think it's the best song in the show. It's certainly Barbra's best song." Yet he remembered that Jerry Robbins and Bobby Fosse hadn't liked it, either. They didn't feel it was right for the Brice character. To tell the truth, they had accommodated Styne–Merrill by leaving it in.

Now, we're hearing it for the third time. I looked over at Bob Merrill. Maybe "People" didn't *belong in* Funny Girl? *The show was the thing. We could write something else and shove "People" into the trunk.*

Merrill, normally a soft-spoken man, stood up. He seldom had much to say at any meeting but when he did it was often with pile-driver force. He'd been up most of the night before listening to Barbra make a single of "People," starting at 1:00 A.M. The "cut" was long, a few seconds over four minutes. Manager Marty Erlichman had said, "We're going to get a lot of pressure to make this shorter but not one note is going out." By her final take, at about 3:00 A.M., Merrill knew that she had a huge hit; that he and Jule had a big hit.

So now, standing six feet two, he said to Kanin, "I'll tell you about this song, Gar. It has to be in the show because it's the greatest thing she's ever done. She's just made a single of it that none of you have heard. It's going to be a solid hit. When you put the right light on her opening night and she sings this song she'll bring the house down. Let us try it for a few performances."

It was obvious that "People," a ballad, was in jeopardy again. If it did not stop the show on opening night, there was a distinct possibility that Kanin would chop it out.

Ballads are seldom show stoppers. The exceptions included Enzio Pinza's "Some Enchanted Evening," from *South Pacific.* Barbra would have to duplicate this feat.

Merrill remembers saying to Kanin, "I'll give you my word that we'll start writing a back-up song."

Rehearsals began in January, and during the second week, with the whole company on the stage of the Winter Garden, Gar Kanin said to Jule, "That new song you fellows are writing—I think it's very promising. How about giving the cast a treat and singing it for them?" Merrill remembers almost every word of the completely unrehearsed scene that day.

Jule answered, "Garson, we're not ready to sing the song for them. We haven't polished it as yet." A climax number for Streisand, "I Tried," had been completed several days previously. But neither Merrill nor Jule felt it was ready for performance.

Garson said, "Jule, darling, we're all family here, and we love the way you play and the way Bob sings. It's such a treat and a piece of history to hear the songs now. Do the song for us. It'll be wonderful."

Merrill began to feel electricity in the air.

Jule said, "Garson, sweetheart, the song isn't ready to be heard yet."

Kanin said, "My dear man, certainly Barbra wants to hear it; she's waiting right here to hear it."

Jule replied stiffly, "She'll hear it in time."

Kanin said, "Well, Jule, I don't understand. What could be on your mind? This isn't like you."

To the contrary, it was very much like Jule Styne. While he might play an unpolished song for the delivery man, or do an impromptu rendition at a party, he would rarely perform unfinished work before star and cast. Though the gesture might be appreciated, the risk was too great.

Merrill later said, "Songs are very fragile. A poor presentation, at the wrong place and wrong time, could mean the end of a potentially good song."

Either voluntarily, or on request, Jule had presented incomplete work for principals of several other shows and each time had suffered.

Additionally, Styne–Merrill felt a measure of professional embarrassment over Kanin's request. Their song was not ready; the star awaited. So Jule flatly refused to perform "I Tried" and thereafter also refused to support Kanin, seldom speaking to him.

That same week, Streisand was in trouble. Her singing wasn't up to her usual standard. Trying to listen to everyone, she seemed to be getting tighter and tighter. Finally, there was open conflict between Kanin and Streisand. He kept asking her to repeat things. As one rehearsal ended, it appeared that Barbra might be out of the show, at Kanin's insistence or her own.

One morning, Milton Rosenstock went to the Winter Garden and there was Streisand, alone on the stage. With rehearsal scheduled for eleven, Milton always arrived a half hour early and usually had the theater to himself for fifteen or twenty minutes. Barbra was sitting on a high stool in the glow of the work light. "She looked almost like a statue. Motionless."

Milton said, "Good morning."

She answered, barely audible, "Good morning."

"You all right?"

"Yes."

"What are you doing?"

"I'm waiting."

"Okay," said Rosenstock, shuffling music. He felt a dread, as if a dynamite fuse had been lighted in the theater.

The cast began to wander in, and she still sat there in the glow of the light as if to say, goddamit, you didn't expect me today, did you? Defiance was all over her face.

The run-through was supposed to start in the middle of the second act, where rehearsal had ended the previous day, but Kanin said, "Okay, let's take it from the top," looking directly at Streisand. Most of the time the cast was given prior notice for a complete run-through.

Rosenstock said, "This was now a direct challenge from Kanin to Streisand. Okay, baby, you're playing games with me. Now, let's see how well you can play, Miss Barbra . . ."

Rosenstock remembers an absolute hush in the theater for a few minutes. Then, as the music started, what Streisand did went purposefully against every instruction Kanin had given her. If she was supposed to stand still, she moved; if she was supposed to move, she stood still. "She was running all over the stage, doing crazy things. She was like a maniac, improvising. As I looked back toward the seats, I saw Garson sitting with his mouth open. Then Jule was on me in a minute, squeezing my shoulder until it hurt. His face was white. He literally snarled, 'Leave her alone, Milt, she's on fire. Just follow, follow . . .' "

Jule thought he knew what was wrong with her. Barbra had told him she was confused; that there were times on the stage when she didn't know what was required of her. Simply, this was rebellion.

She finally cracked up on "Don't Rain on My Parade," and began to sob, saying to Rosenstock, "I'm sorry, I'm so sorry . . ."

Stopping the music, Milt said, "That's okay."

As she walked off the stage, everyone applauded, and rehearsal for that day was canceled by Kanin.

A few days later, Barbra said to Rosenstock, "I got it now. It's a duet."

He asked, "What do you mean, a duet?"

"I'm not alone up there. I've got you. I've got the whole orchestra. I'm not up there alone."

"Jesus Christ, no, you're not alone," said Rosenstock.

Streisand did not like "I Tried," the song that Kanin had requested early in rehearsal. She heard it, and promptly said she wouldn't do it. Styne–Merrill, not certain of the material, retreated and did a reprise of "Rain on My Parade" for the finale, a Gar Kanin suggestion.

Whenever there was disagreement with the star over material, there was often a Laurel-and-Hardy touch to the Styne–Merrill collaboration.

Merrill remembers several such incidents. "We would go into a meeting with Barbra planning to say exactly one thing and nothing else. The thing we would *not* say is, 'Barbra, the reason you don't like this song is because you can't sing it.' We will not say that, okay, Jule?"

"Okay."

"Now, Jule, what we are going to say is this: 'Please, Barbra, just try it again tonight. We're working on it, and we'll improve it.' Okay, Jule?"

"Okay."

"That is the exact plan agreed upon in the hotel room and just before going out the door to see Barbra, Jule stops me to say, 'Okay, we got our strategy.'

"Yes, we're going to say to Barbra that we know the song isn't right but give it another performance. Just try once again.

"We go down the hall and just outside Barbra's door I say, 'Okay, Jule, we're all set.' Remember now.

"Jule nods, and in we go, and the moment he spots Barbra, literally running for her, he yells, 'Barbra, the reason you don't like that goddamn song is because you can't sing it!' "

By this time, Barbra had gained confidence. She told vocal arranger Buster Davis that his ending for "Sadie, Sadie" wasn't right. He argued and lost, reluctantly changed it, and he discovered that Miss Streisand was entirely correct.

The rehearsals continued, each day fused and ready for explosion. There was script trouble and music trouble. One bright spot during the rehearsal period, for Jule, anyway, was the discovery of a young pianist, the third rehearsal pianist, eighteen-year-old Marvin Hamlisch. "That kid is loaded with talent," he told Rosenstock.

Stark wanted to fire Hamlisch for economy reasons, but Jule insisted that he was needed. Then Jule persuaded the boy's parents to let him finish Juilliard, arranging party play dates to help finance the schooling. Finally, he recommended Marvin to producer Sam Spiegel for a scoring job. Hamlisch soon became the brightest and best of the new film composers and then scored *A Chorus Line* for Michael Bennett.

Funny Girl opened in Boston with second act and over-length problems. Thirty minutes had already been cut from the show, and at least five songs were shaky. Isobel Lennart put in long hours on repair. Boston critics hailed Streisand but found much fault with the book. The tryout moved on to Philadelphia, another thirty minutes having been deleted. The Philly critics echoed those of Boston—the show had hit potential if the libretto problems could be conquered.

Both Boston and Philadelphia critics were startled by the lack of standard "Fanny Brice" material. Not once was "My Man" or "Second-Hand Rose" or "I'm an Indian," all Brice songs, heard. Rather than saddle whoever would play Fanny with the Brice favorites, forcing comparison, Jule had taken the flavors of the familiar songs to create new ones. "The Music That Makes Me Dance" was born of "My Man"; "Sadie, Sadie" was first cousin to "Rose of Washington Square." The only songs that were pure Streisand were "People" and "Don't Rain on My Parade." Though they were not written specifically for her, Jule believes he was likely influenced by his first impression of Streisand as Miss Marmelstein. He agrees with Merrill that Anne Bancroft could not have handled "People."

Merrill and Styne stayed with *Funny Girl* throughout the shakedown period, Merrill constantly between amusement and amazement at the conduct of his partner. Though Jule had spent a lot of time in "café society," he leaned toward junk food, taking Merrill into the bowels of Philadelphia or Boston to eat at tiny, cheap Chinese joints. On the road they often polished at night, working until one or two in the morning; at which time Jule would usually wander the streets to find a coffee shop and gorge on ice cream and cake.

Then he would come back to the hotel room, put on the worst ancient TV movie and watch it until four or five. He'd be in the theater promptly at eight or nine in the morning, but by noon, he'd be asleep in the back of the house. Yet if the orchestra hit a wrong note he'd be up and flying down the aisle, screaming. "I swear to God he can hear wrong notes in his sleep," Merrill said.

The New York opening was postponed five times while extra weeks were played; the second act was still weak. A total of five songs had been cut since Boston. Streisand let it be known that she was more than ever uncertain of Garson Kanin. She wanted Jerome Robbins to return to his former post.

Ray Stark, having fought with Robbins over Isobel Lennart, was now thinking about the upcoming film version of *Funny Girl,* quite certain that he had an international box-office star in Streisand, and agreed to rehire Robbins as production supervisor, hoping also to retain Kanin. The latter declined to stay on with Robbins in command, and resigned. *Funny Girl* was back where it started and Streisand was happy at last.

Just as Robbins had made many early contributions, supplemented by those of Bobby Fosse and Gar Kanin, he now made immense last-minute contributions. One of Sydney Chaplin's songs, "You Are Woman," had not been registering. It was sung during a comedy scene with Fanny Brice in a red dining-room set. Robbins said immediately to Styne–Merrill, "It won't go over alone for Sydney. Can you write a countermelody to tell us what Fanny is thinking? Use that accompaniment but write comedy lyrics for it."

They quickly did sixteen bars and grabbed Robbins in the theater lobby. He listened to it, approved and rehearsed it the next day. The countermelody went into the next performance and registered for Chaplin–Streisand.

Funny Girl opened at the Winter Garden March 26, 1964, four years after its conception, to mostly excellent reviews, Streisand repeating her personal successes of Boston and Philadelphia. The show was to remain on Broadway for 1,348 performances.

Jule stayed on in New York the first few nights and then flew to Hollywood, arriving at Academy Award time. The Oscar affair was emceed by Sinatra that year. By now, "People" was the top record in Streisand's beginning career, literally "her song," winning three gold discs. Styne and Merrill won a gold circle for the cast album. Much to Jule's dismay, Sinatra refused to record "People."

Late one evening, Jule went along to a large party at Milton Berle's home and was soon playing "People" for fifty or so guests. He was singing it when Sinatra walked in. Frank moved to the piano, looked down at Jule and said, "You blew it."

I didn't know what he was talking about. Maybe I blew it because I didn't go to the award ceremonies.

Sinatra added, "You didn't know where to go on bar sixteen," and walked away.

Ruth Berle said, "Jule, didn't you read the piece in *Look* magazine?"

Jule hadn't read the article but quickly went upstairs to Ruth's bedroom and opened the magazine. Sinatra had written about songwriters and singers but hadn't mentioned his two current tunesmiths, Sammy Cahn and Jimmy Van Heusen. The only singer he'd mentioned was Tony Bennett and the only song, "People," which he dismissed. Sinatra had written that the song "fell apart in the release," meaning the middle.

I had to laugh. The day he criticizes "People," it is No. 1 on the charts.

Jule returned downstairs and walked over to Sinatra. He said, "Frank, why did you have to go out of your way and pick on 'People'? You have every right not to like me, but why pick on my songs? On Bob Merrill?"

Sinatra walked away and Jule didn't hear from him for another three years.

The Internal Revenue Service was quite happy that *Funny Girl* was a huge hit. They were now confiscating all of Jule's share of the box-office receipts—about $2,000 weekly. Then came the final blow: The IRS put a lien on Jule's ASCAP earnings. Every source of income was suddenly stopped.

22

During the "crunch," I always called it a "tunnel," for it had Dorothy's reassurances like a light at the other end; we were living on thin air. Lying was the hardest part—making excuses for not doing or going; not seeing or buying.

—MARGARET BROWN STYNE, 1977

While the cash registers rang merrily at the Winter Garden, Margaret, again pregnant, was confined to bed in hopes of avoiding natal complications. The problems swirled around her. Then, finally, Dorothy Dicker told her about the crisis in detail.

For quite a while, Margaret had suspected her husband was in deep trouble. "But I had no knowledge of just how deep it was. I was left gasping when I found out that the IRS was not only collecting all our income for back taxes but also charging penalties on them. And we'd be forced to incur more penalties and interest because we weren't paying any current taxes, either—neither federal, state or city. There was no hope of ever catching up. So we had two choices—bankruptcy or taking a big loan, paying off the IRS and living on practically nothing while all income went to returning the loan and trying to meet current taxes. Somehow Dorothy performed miracles. She held up that light at the end of the tunnel. We were fed and sheltered; we were living in that swanky neighborhood and were almost penniless."

The "crunch," as Dorothy termed it, or the "tunnel," as Margaret called it, had been creeping up for years. It had begun in the suite at the Hampshire House while Jule fingered the keys with the *Blondes* score. He had never quite understood that if he earned a hundred dollars at least half of it belonged to the tax collector. He had been running from the crunch for years, ignoring it, frantically mounting projects that shouldn't have been touched, hopefully grabbing at any income, all the while living royally. Then there was the true cause of the crunch—the starting gates at Santa Anita and Hialeah and Belmont Park. Name any track and Jule's money had ridden on the horses.

It was all very embarrassing to Jule now. Yet he would not admit it publicly; he insisted that Margaret not admit it. He delighted in telling friends how she made her own clothes, wallpapered, painted, finished furniture, laid tiles, but the reasons were always—these were her hobbies.

Dorothy Dicker did not cash her pay checks for nine months. They stacked up in her office drawer. She guarded pennies and sweet-talked creditors.

Jule's breaking point came in the office of Comden and Green's attorney, William Fitelson. They were meeting to discuss the upcoming Carol Burnett musical, *Fade In, Fade Out,* new title for *A Girl to Remember,* the show with ABC-Paramount backing. Fitelson was a complete stranger to Jule, but the subject of money arose and Dorothy sat speechless as Jule finally admitted that he was on the verge of complete destruction. His old friends, Comden–Green, were equally taken aback.

A few weeks earlier, a New York music publisher, privy to some aspects of the problem, had said, "The best thing that Jule Styne could do would be to commit suicide." Jule also admitted the depth of his gambling addiction to the lawyer, further shocking Dicker.

Fitelson listened calmly and then said, "There's no reason for a man of your talent to be destroyed. I'm going to get you out of trouble."

Over a period of several weeks, Fitelson met with Louis Dreyfuss, head of Chappell Music Company, and arranged for an interest-free loan of $650,000, most of which went to the IRS. A dim light appeared at the far end of the tunnel. The liens on *Funny Girl* and the ASCAP monies were lifted.

Dorothy Dicker said, "Margaret is by no means the good fairy, but she was more helpful than Jule during the crunch, once she understood the problem. We all made it through, thanks to Bill Fitelson and Louis Dreyfuss." A large portion of gratitude was also owed to Dicker herself.

Fade Out, Fade In, staged by Mr. Abbott, opened at the Mark

Hellinger two months, to the day, after the triumphant entry of *Funny Girl.* Carol Burnett had never really liked the Comden–Green satire about Hollywood, and the reviews, both out-of-town and from the New York critics, weren't too good. However, the show lasted nine months, at which time Burnett took on another nine months' assignment: She was pregnant. The Burnett show had been one of those precrunch straws in the wind, a project that wisdom would have sent to the shelf. A live seal was in the cast, and the animal odor permeated the Styne office long after final curtain.

Okay, Lester Osterman and I dropped $300 thousand of the ABC-Paramount money on Carol and company. Then Buddy Robbins brings me Portofino PTA, *a Gerald Green novel, and soon we had a libretto from Nate Monaster, the film writer. On close examination it was terrible, and once again, I should have stopped. I called in everyone from Paddy Chayefsky to Arthur Laurents to help me. That heavenly voice said, "Quit!" But I didn't listen.*

No one, of any stature, wanted to direct *Something More,* the new title for *Portofino PTA,* music by Sammy Fain, lyrics by Marilyn and Alan Bergman, so Jule decided to stage it himself. "Why not? I thought. I'd written for the theater. I'd produced for it. Why not direct? I'd have to learn to be more patient. I'd have to learn the mechanics of staging. But why not?"

Dorothy Dicker remembers that he was "so excited. For once he was organized. He almost stopped his 'Stynese.' He wasn't frantic. He wanted to show everyone he wouldn't be running up and down the aisle; stopping and playing the piano for everyone. Very dignified, he said, 'Dorothy, my notes.' But in changing his approach to everything he ceased being himself. Creatively, the play lost."

Predictably, *Something More* was always something less. Stars Barbara Cook and Arthur Hill, though they tried hard, weren't suitable for the lead roles. They were Jule's choices, of course. With the show downhill already, Jule voluntarily stepped aside as director in Philadelphia and Joe Leighton took over, making few changes. Not much could be done about the show.

Opening in New York, in November 1964, *Something More* lasted one forlorn week. On closing night, Jule sat on the edge of Margaret's bed and wept bitterly. Finally, he said, "We're going to England."

"Over my dead body," Margaret replied. "You're not going to England with your tail between your legs. If you go, I'm not going with you."

Jule quickly changed his mind and Nicholas Styne, a blond, was born Christmas Day, 1964, in New York, not London. Mother and boy came through the ordeal nicely, mother soon to arise from her bed after seven months of being prone. And the father of Nicky Styne soon became a father in the true and traditional sense. He had not assumed that role very much with Stanley and Norton. With Nicky, there was "kitchy-kooing" and cradle-rocking; knee-bouncing and pushing of the perambulator along Fifth Avenue.

In the early spring of 1965 came news that both *Peter Pan* and *Magoo's Christmas Carol* would be re-aired on television during the winter. The announcement turned Jule toward TV again. He thought that what TV needed was a repertory of children's musical shows. Broadway had always been his only fairy story but now, with Nicky in mind, he was beginning to think about others. *So I started checking the children's classics and found that* Little Red Riding Hood *had been published in twenty-seven languages. Of all things, I read a French version that was studded with sex symbolism and came to think that the story could be something very different from the traditional one we know. Why not tell it from the wolf's point of view?*

Bob Merrill was in town and Jule phoned him. By sundown the next day, they'd completed three songs. Then writer Robert Emmett was brought in to do a quick libretto. Within a week, the trio had a rough book draft and three additional songs. In another two weeks, the final draft of both libretto and score was completed.

Styne and Merrill, within a few days, became the producers of *The Dangerous Christmas of Red Riding Hood,* a film enterprise launched unwittingly by tiny Nicky and now scheduled to air on ABC-TV a few days after Thanksgiving, starring Liza Minelli as Miss Riding Hood and Cyril Ritchard as a most discriminating wolf.

About that time, as Jule and Margaret were sitting down to dinner, he said, "Thank you for having Nicky."

"What do you mean?" she asked.

Jule replied, "I didn't really intend to have any more children. But at your age, you should have them. So I thank you for Nicky."

Margaret stared at her husband, fighting back tears.

Failures and successes, despair or triumph, something was always in the process of birth in the Styne office, either forming slowly or rushing wildly to delivery, TV's *Riding Hood* an excellent example of the latter.

Hallelujah, Baby! began that year of 1965 when Arthur Laurents called Jule to say that he had an idea for a "black" musical. Immediately, Jule thought about the negative reception accorded *Mr. Wonderful.* Yet times had changed somewhat. Just because the Sammy Davis Jr. show had come to a dismal end, there was no reason not to try again, especially with Laurents.

Sultry singer Lena Horne had been a close friend of Arthur Laurents for years, and toward the end of the civil rights turnabout had asked Arthur to write a show for her. He sketched out a tough, hard-hitting black pilgrim's progress through the changing social attitudes of the twentieth century, covering six decades.

Laurents discussed the idea briefly, then Jule read the short synopsis, liked it and agreement to go forward was reached that day. Within the week, Laurents went to work on the libretto and Jule began to seek a top lyricist. Bob Merrill was first choice but decided against the show. He thought that the basic story was "too thin." Comden–Green felt otherwise and signed papers.

David Merrick was then approached, read the synopsis, carefully considered the talents of Laurents and Styne and Comden and Green, and became the producer. Gene Saks was signed as director and as 1965 merged into another year, it appeared that a solid musical was in the making. Everyone who read the rough draft of Laurents's script judged it to be superb.

The foursome went to work.

Of course, Jule was working on other ventures during this period. He wrote songs for a film, *What a Way to Go;* attempted to launch a musical version of *The Apartment,* with Billy Wilder; labored briefly with Bob Merrill on a musical of *Love in the Afternoon,* and put some time in on *Divorce, Italian Style,* with Isobel Lennart. He could not slow the pace of earlier years.

Another cycle of life did not stop, either. Frank Sinatra married actress Mia Farrow in the summer of 1966, and the following week, Mrs. Bennett Cerf, widow of the late publisher, called Jule to say, "Frank would like you to be at the wedding reception I'm giving tomorrow night at '21.' "

Jule was surprised but gladly accepted and attended the party, sitting next to the bride and groom for the first course. Frank said, "Jule, tell them about the old days," so Jule stood up and regaled the guests with humorous stories of those old days.

Then Frank said, "Shtimp, sit down at the piano."

Jule sat down and sang some of the songs that Frank had made famous. It wasn't quite like the old days, but it felt good to be in the same room with Sinatra again.

During the evening, Jule said to Frank that he'd be great playing the part of Nick Arnstein in the upcoming film version of *Funny Girl.* Sinatra replied succinctly, "It's the girl's story."

"We can write four new songs. Stark can add to Nicky's part."

"Come on to Vegas, and we'll talk about it," said Frank. "Have Stark call me."

Jule phoned Stark the following day to carry out the request. "If you ever want a collector's item on records and film, get Sinatra to play Nicky Arnstein." The combination of Streisand and Sinatra was foolproof box office, Jule thought.

Stark answered, "Sinatra's all wrong. We need a big, attractive man. Someone with Cary Grant class."

Disregarding the negative, Jule flew to Las Vegas, where Sinatra was appearing at The Sands Hotel, but didn't tell Frank that Stark wasn't interested. Instead, he talked to the singer about the four new melodies; about Streisand, whom Frank had never really known. They had a "hello" acquaintance. Sinatra seemed pleased and interested.

Jule called Stark again. The flat answer was, "Forget about Sinatra."

The rejection was embarrassing. How could he tell Frank that Stark didn't want him? Where Sinatra was involved, Jule had talked out of turn again. The silence resumed.

Funny Girl opened in London for fourteen weeks that year. The first performance was a charity benefit, and Jule was flanked on the stage after final curtain by Streisand and Stark as the royal family came by to offer congratulations. Princess Margaret asked Jule, "When are you bringing *Gypsy* here?" He knew that the princess had previously inquired about its availability for her charities and replied that he was trying to assemble a London company.

By now, Stark had the movie version in pre-production and Walter Scharf had called Jule to say, "I'd like to do *Funny Girl.*" Scharf was highly qualified to be musical director, and Jule told him to fly over to the British opening; meet Stark and Streisand.

Walter went to London as instructed but had trouble catching up with Jule for two days. On the third morning, Walter visited the Turf Commission, which was near the Hilton Hotel, and heard a very distinctive voice in the back room, talking odds and horses. Where else would he be, thought Walter.

Though I'd promised everyone I'd stop gambling, it was like withdrawal. I couldn't stop overnight. It was all around me, so tempting.

Jule returned to West Fifty-first Street and the Hellinger building just in time to see *Hallelujah, Baby!* begin to crumble. Without hearing one note or reading one word of the script, Lena Horne suddenly decided it wasn't for her. Diahann Carroll was second choice but was definitely too pretty, too sweet, too ladylike, to play the part of Georgina, the cleaning girl who made it in show business.

Reading the pitfalls ahead quite capably, David Merrick departed the project. He was afraid of a "black story" without a Lena Horne in the starring role. Then director Gene Saks quit for much the same reason. The *Mr. Wonderful* haunting had returned. Black wasn't entirely beautiful, as yet, along Broadway. Bert Shevelove was finally set to direct; the new producers were Al Selden and Hal James.

Leslie Uggams was then appearing at a night club in Atlantic City. She could sing; she could act passably well; she had a "name" of sorts. Most important, she was the best candidate available. There was no other black female singer around at the time who came close to what was required of Georgina. Uggams was signed.

But, little by little, the anger and toughness in the script, so perfect for Horne, a tigress by nature, began to slip away. "It all softened. It got softer and softer and softer, and worse and worse," said Laurents. "I relearned the old lesson: Fellows, what we started with is gone. Let's forget it."

Additionally, Selden and James were having money problems, similar to the drought of *Mr. Wonderful.* "It's a story about black people," was the beginning of the spiel to angels. "Oh, well," was often the reaction. Jule and Buster Davis took the score to Philadelphia in hopes of raising money. They returned to New York less traveling and hotel expenses. So Jane Nussbaum and Hal Rigby joined as co-producers and money-raisers. Finally, the budget was collected.

There was an atmosphere of anger in and about *Baby!* from the first day of rehearsals. Frenzy often accompanies rehearsals, but another new and different element was even stronger. The civil rights movement shadowed the play, and each line of "black" dialogue was subjected to careful scrutiny, especially by co-star Robert Hooks. One song, written for the character of Georgina's mother (Lillian Hayman) wasn't racist, in Laurent's opinion, but Hooks refused to remain onstage while it was sung. The song was deleted.

Hooks, Laurents remembers, was deeply involved with the idea that no one was going to take advantage of him. He worked just the hours he was told to work; not a minute more. He advised Uggams to do the same. Under those circumstances, little enthusiasm could be generated; vitality faded early.

Production meetings were constantly called, usually concerning the Comden–Green lyrics and existent or nonexistent racial overtones. At one such shout-down in the mezzanine of the Martin Beck Theatre, Adolph Green faked a heart attack, collapsing on to the carpet. No one paid any attention to him for a few minutes, then Laurents looked over to ask, "Are you all right, Adolph?"

Green sighed and pulled himself up from the floor.

Baby! went to Boston in early spring, 1967, for a trial run and received mixed reviews. The critics seemed a bit puzzled by the show, sensing that they were hearing the framework of something, not the guts. Laurents could have confirmed that for them.

Jule slept very little during the Boston run. He worked daylight hours on *Baby!* and nights on *Funny Girl.* Walter Scharf was on the phone from Hollywood, taking down the melodies for new songs for the movie, Walter at his piano on the coast; Jule at his in the Beantown hotel suite.

"I didn't get all that, Jule."

"I'll play it back for you."

The composition sessions sometimes lasted several hours, often until after midnight.

Baby! played three weeks of previews on Broadway and then officially opened at the Beck on April 26, 1967. Surprising everyone, it ran for ten months. Jule began to think that the general public wasn't against the "black" theme. Entrenched show people and angels appeared to be the racist culprits.

An additional surprise was that *Baby!* won the coveted Antoinette Perry Award as best show of the year. In fact, it won four months after closing curtain. And Jule found it difficult to believe that his score for *Hallelujah, Baby!* won a "Tony." He hadn't won for *Bells Are Ringing;* he hadn't won for *Gypsy;* he hadn't won for *Funny Girl.* In accepting the award, he said plaintively and quite honestly . . . "there comes a time when you say, 'We ought to be fair and give it to him this year.' "

While *Hallelujah, Baby!* was in the middle of its run, Margaret announced to Jule that she'd have her own baby come summer. Jule was very pleased.

23

The saddest ones are the ones that have
the greatest potential and then are screwed up.

—JULE STYNE, 1977

Another show that "might have been" was *Darling of the Day.* Jule so much wanted it to be his Lerner-and-Loewe musical. *The saddest ones are the ones that have the greatest potential and then are screwed up.*

Armina Marshall of the Theatre Guild had called Jule one day shortly after *Baby!* opened to say that she wanted to run an old film, *Holy Matrimony,* for him. Monty Woolley, the impeccable British actor with the flowing beard, unforgettable as the lead in *The Man Who Came to Dinner,* had starred in the picture, based on Arnold Bennett's novel *Buried Alive.* The plot was simple enough: British artist Priam Farll hated the Establishment and abandoned England after being ostracized by Queen Victoria. When King Edward VII came into power, he ordered that the world-famous painter return home to recieve a knighthood. There wasn't a Farll painting anywhere on the British Isles and Edward felt slighted.

The twist in this story was that Farll's butler dies en route to England and Farll assumes his identity, claiming that the famous artist has been buried at sea. Farll then begins a new life. There was great charm to the story.

Marshall, and Joel Schenker, also of the Guild, set *Billy Budd* writers Keith Waterhouse and Willis Hall to do the libretto; Peter Wood to direct, and then asked Jule who should do his lyrics.

He answered, "There's only one man, Yipper Harburg. He's erudite. He knows painters. He can give me sophisticated lyrics."

Armina Marshall was immediately reluctant. Edgar "Yip" Harburg, the *Wizard of Oz* man, lyricist for "April in Paris" and other hits, had an earned reputation for being difficult. He'd also been caught at the art of sneaking social messages into his lyrics. *But Yipper was the right man for it, and Armina finally bought him. I'd been dying to work with him for years.*

At the first meeting of Harburg–Styne–Waterhouse–Hall and Peter Wood, the Yipper immediately objected to the book. Waterhouse and Hall quickly objected to the socially conscious Mr. Harburg. They said he was writing his lyrics for another book, not theirs.

Jule defended the Yipper. "No, if this book was right, Yip would forget his messages."

Wood returned to England after the meeting, but before his departure laid out the whole story, scene by scene. Waterhouse and Hall also went home to London, completed another script and mailed it to Jule, with a note: "We're afraid Harburg won't like this because he is thinking of another story." That was true, more or less. Harburg didn't like the new draft; neither did Styne.

Peter Wood promptly resigned, as did Waterhouse and Hall. Veteran Sam Berman was hired to do another libretto.

Then Armina Marshall screened *Holy Matrimony* for Steven Vinaver, a new, young director who'd scored in an off-Broadway revue, *Diversions.* Vinaver was captivated by the story but said it must have a major British star—Sir Lawrence Olivier or Rex Harrison. "Marvelous," said Jule, a feeling shared by Armina Marshall and Joel Schenker.

Without even seeing the film, Olivier told Vinaver he wasn't interested. But Peter Finch was in town and Jule played the score for him. The late Academy Award winner said he liked the music for *Married Alive,* new title for the production, but concluded the role wasn't for him.

Several months passed and another prime prospect, Rex Harrison, visited New York, expressing an interest in *Married Alive.* He met Jule and Armina Marshall at the St. Regis Hotel about 11:00 P.M., with his wife, Rachel Roberts. He'd been to a champagne party, was slightly drunk, and his first request was for a bottle of the bubbly. Jule sent down for four. A case would have been provided for the asking. Harrison was capable of packing the theater every night.

"Now, let me hear some of the songs," Harrison said.

Jule sat down, playing and singing "The Sunset Tree." On into the early morning, as more champagne was poured, Jule played the entire score. Well past 2:00 A.M., with a cold drizzle falling outside, Jule finished with "I Got a Rainbow Working for Me." Which wasn't true at all.

Harrison was silent for a while, then said, "I can't do this show but my wife would be great for it."

Jule and Armina Marshall eyed Harrison sleepily, realizing that Rachel Roberts was the real reason that Rex had listened to the songs.

Next approached was Robert Shaw. He hated the lyrics. He said, "This isn't British at all. You're using all the euphemisms. We don't speak that way." Shaw was scratched.

Also scratched was Sam Berman. Screenwriter Nunnally Johnson was brought in to rewrite the words of Berman, Waterhouse and Hall. The title of the original Arnold Bennett novel, *Buried Alive,* was now much more appropriate for this sputtering endeavor.

A few weeks later, Steven Vinaver said excitedly to Jule, "You're playing the score on Sunday for Sir John Gielgud."

That was very encouraging news, Jule thought.

So on Sunday, score tucked under his arm, Jule walked over to Gielgud's apartment, not far from his own residence. Even while knocking on the door, he heard a buzz of voices inside; laughter. Gielgud's butler answered and Jule saw that at least thirty-five guests had been gathered. Brunch plates were being carried out. Wine had flowed. The guests were waiting for the afternoon's unpaid entertainment. Jule felt rage.

I saw two fellows sitting at the piano and Gielgud said to me, 'Give them the score. They'll play it and sing it. You just relax. Jule recognized the duo to be Ferrante and Teicher.

Sir John did not know Jule Styne. "They don't play it," said Jule firmly. "I play it, and I sing it, or no one hears it."

Sir John said, "They're quite good."

Styne replied, "I'm quite good, too."

"Oh," said Sir John, and nodded for Ferrante and Teicher to leave the piano bench.

Jule then performed his own work, forgetting his anger, and happily acknowledged the applause. He was also happy to hear Gielgud say, "That's a marvelous score and I love it."

Two days later, Jule was summoned to the Shubert Theatre and onstage was Sir John; also Geraldine Page, the prospective co-star. They acted a scene and then Gielgud sang. *My God, I knew instantly that he was tone deaf. I worked with him a few tortured minutes. Hopeless. Then Geraldine Page sang. She couldn't sing with the piano or without it. Here were these two great stars trying to find a way to exit gracefully.*

Within a few days, Steven Vinaver was released and Albert Marre was the replacement as director. Marre lasted two weeks and then Vinaver was rehired. Meanwhile, Jule flew to London to audition Patricia Routledge, a seasoned performer of the musical stage. Routledge not only looked the part but sang it beautifully, as expected. Jule cabled Vinaver that he'd found Alice Challice.

Then somebody suggested Vincent Price for Priam Farll. Not bad, I thought. He was an art collector. He knew paintings. Some people thought he was British. So I flew to Hollywood, listened to him sing and set him. He had a pleasant if not professional voice, a certain charm and grace.

Pat Routledge took all the honors, and the show, finally titled *Darling of the Day,* lasted one month. It is high on Jule's current list of prospective revivals, with Harburg at work on the libretto for a London company.

Oddly enough, I think it was one of the best scores I'd ever done. Walter Kerr agreed. But it somehow missed. With a Harrison or Olivier, maybe. Maybe. The potential was there.

With comparative ease, Margaret gave birth to Katherine on July 23, 1968. After three sons, Jule was father to a daughter. Margaret said, "He was almost drooling. I knew he was going to spoil her. He fell madly in love with her. One night he walked in, said, 'Hi, Maggi; hi, Nicky, and then began kootchy-kooing over Katherine, who was in my arms. Nicky just sat there. So, at dinner, I said, 'Jule, you have to make a memory. You cannot treat Nicky as an equal. If you want to kootchy-koo over Katherine, you must say "Nicky, I'll play with you after I change my clothes and say hello to Katherine . . .' "

Jule was soon playing catch with four-year-old Nicky in Central Park. It was another new role for a man in his sixties. Earlier, Jule had said to Margaret, "I shouldn't get too close to Nicky in case I die. That way, he won't miss me."

Throughout 1969, Jule prepared two shows—*Prettybelle,* to star Angela Lansbury, and *Look to the Lilies,* reuniting him with Sammy Cahn. Jule had long wanted to do another show with Sammy, firmly believing that his ex-partner could write for Broadway successfully, even though his past attempts had partially failed. Sammy had never really gotten over the attacks on several of his *High Button Shoes* lyrics. Two subsequent efforts with Jimmy Van Heusen, *Skyscraper* and *Walking Tall,* had flopped. Yet, over the twenty years since parting as a team, Sammy had dozens of hit songs to his credit, both individual movie songs and those of a nonmovie variety. Jule also believed that he could use the stage know-how he had gained since *Shoes* to materially aid Sammy in creating dramatic lyrics. The man was enormously talented and deserved better treatment on Broadway.

Sammy agreed to try again, and the reunion vehicle chosen was *Lilies of the Field,* which had starred Sidney Poitier in the film version. Movie writer Leonard Spigelgass constructed the libretto and Jule went to work with Sammy Cahn. *It felt good to be with Sammy once more, but he hadn't slowed down at all. I marveled at his speed but kept feeling that the lyrics, by and large, weren't digging deep enough into character. I'd been spoiled forever by Sondheim in that regard.*

Jule's choice to play the tough Mother Superior was Ethel Merman, an off-beat casting, but director Josh Logan didn't like Merman and selected Shirley Booth. *Shirley's a buttercup and bad picking for that part.*

The Poitier role went to Al Freeman, Jr., after Styne and Cahn flew to London with hopes of signing Sammy Davis Jr. They played the score in a Playboy Club room, and Sammy, within minutes, was singing along.

We could almost count the money. But then Sammy Davis counted money too, and asked for $20 thousand a week. We caught the plane the next morning.

From the start there was friction between Al Freeman and Josh Logan. And Logan quickly discovered that Shirley Booth drew little comfort from being directed. "What are we doing here with these people? Where are we?" Logan asked Jule.

Damned if I knew. It all got so muddy. The character played by Freeman was supposed to be gentle and here we had him singing hip songs. Booth stayed a buttercup. I knew we were dead from the first week of rehearsal.

Prettybelle, which was in rehearsal simultaneously, with libretto and lyrics by Bob Merrill, music by Jule, direction and choreography by Gower Champion, produced by Alexander Cohen, opened first, in Boston, in early March, 1970. The show writhed for two weeks and then collapsed, losing $400,000.

Then at month's end, *Look to the Lilies,* Jule's twenty-second show, opened on Broadway. At intermission of opening night, Alan

Lerner came up to Styne–Cahn to say, "That 'I, Yes, Me' is such a beautiful song. Too bad the show will close."

Lilies did close in three weeks and "I, Yes, Me" went into the trunk, along with "Follow the Lamb," probably one of the best lyrics Sammy Cahn had ever written.

There was one last Styne–Cahn collaboration, *The Night the Animals Talked,* another Christmas special for television. The animals around the Christ Child both talked and sang that evening of December 6, 1970.

24

Gower Champion can drive you right up a wall.

—BOB MERRILL, 1977

Jule had not had a solid hit since *Funny Girl* in 1964, and the year at hand was 1971. The near-misses of *Hallelujah, Baby!* and *Darling of the Day* did little to take away the mortifying stings and losses of *Something More, Prettybelle* and *Lilies.* Jule was no longer shooting a "hot hand" when he was approached by agent Irving Lazar with a deal to compose the music for a stage version of *Some Like It Hot,* the Billy Wilder–I.A.L. Diamond film hit of the late fifties, starring Marilyn Monroe, Jack Lemmon and Tony Curtis.

Producing *Sugar,* new title for the Wilder–Diamond farce, was David Merrick and almost immediately there were negotiating problems. Jule had certain reservations about working with Gower Champion, Merrick's choice of director. Champion tended to be dictatorial, working closely with his cast but practically ignoring the creative staff during rehearsals. There had been many differences between Jule and Champion on *Prettybelle.*

However, Jule's career was at a crucial point, he thought; he was looking for an upswing, and finally told Merrick, "All right, if Champion is the only way you'll go, I'll do it." Then he told Bob Merrill, who would write the lyrics for *Sugar,* "I can smell trouble ahead for me."

Jule flew off to California to begin collaboration in Merrill's Beverly Hills home. A call to Merrill from Margaret preceded Jule's arrival. "He can come out, but promise me you won't let him gamble," said Margaret. Merrill replied that he'd try very hard to keep Jule away from the tracks and out of card games; no guarantees, however.

At the time, Merrill was married to a pretty Eurasian girl, Dolores, and Jule had a wing of the house to himself. His every need was met by Dolores and the Merrill's cook-maid. About the third day of work, Jule said to Merrill, "I'm having a terrible time here. I'm very uncomfortable with all this service."

That was odd, Bob thought. Jule was usually very comfortable with service. He went first class everywhere. As far as Bob knew, Jule preferred luxury. "I don't understand you," said Merrill.

Jule answered, "This is very embarrassing for me. So much fuss being made over me."

Now truly puzzled, Bob said, "Jule, relax. We're treating you like family."

Jule said, "No, you're not, that's the trouble. Let me take you and Dolores to dinner."

"You don't have to do that."

"I insist," said Jule. "We'll go tomorrow night."

Merrill shrugged. If it would make his guest happy, relieve his embarrassment, fine.

Later, Dolores said to her husband, "Jule is taking us to dinner tomorrow night."

"Yes, I know. Where?"

"He said it was a surprise."

Early the next evening, they all got into Merrill's car and Bob asked Jule, "Where are we going?"

"I'll tell you how to get there."

Merrill drove, and drove, and drove, Jule directing each turn. In twenty minutes, La Cienaga's "restaurant row" was far behind and the car finally curved down on the San Diego Freeway. Exasperated, Merrill asked, "Jule, where in hell are we going?"

"You'll see."

Ten minutes later, Bob did see. Jule directed the car off the freeway and soon the unmistakable grandstand of Hollywood Park loomed up. The trotting races were in season. Jule said, "We'll have dinner in the clubhouse and watch the horses run."

Remembering what Margaret had said, Merrill warned, "No betting."

"Just a little, but don't tell Margaret." The "little" was six or seven hundred dollars a race, an improvement, certainly, over some of the past visits to tracks.

Jule's gambling habits had not materially changed since *Funny Girl,* nor had some aspects of the Styne–Merrill collaboration. "It was still like walking with Mr. Magoo through a holocaust," Merrill maintained, citing a typical exchange:

Merrill: "Jule, please let's try this chord."

Styne: "It doesn't work."

Merrill: "Try it once."

Styne: "I don't have to try it once. I can hear it without playing it. It doesn't work, I tell you."

Five minutes later, Jule would play the identical requested chord and then turn toward Merrill.

Styne: "How do you like it, Bob?"

Merrill: "I like it very much. That's the chord I was trying to get you to play."

Styne: "Well, I'll tell you why I'm doing it now."

Merrill: "Why, Jule?"

Styne (grinning): "Because it's better."

The trouble with Gower Champion that Jule had "smelled" long before rehearsal soon became reality. Champion locked the creators—librettist Peter Stone, Styne and Merrill—out of the rehearsal hall. Whenever the red light over the rehearsal studio door was aglow, Champion was snug inside with his cast and conductor. Until the red light was turned off, Messrs. Stone, Styne and Merrill were not welcome. They fumed.

Merrill said, "Gower is the type of man who will take a show away from you. He'll battle producers, actors; anyone. He'll disappear for two days to get his way. He's perfectly capable of taking David Merrick for a fall. Example—'All right, fellows, if you have something to say, let's have breakfast at eight o'clock.' The trouble is that Gower doesn't show. He doesn't intend to show."

Champion "took" *Sugar* away from the creators, in their opinion. It soon became "the Creators *vs.* Gower Champion" and the creators stumbled around between confusion and frustration and anger, hardly the ingredients to mix a good musical.

Washington's Kennedy Center had been selected as the first tryout site, cast and technicians and creators moving into the Watergate

Hotel, a fitting place for the *Sugar* intrigues. Across the street was a Howard Johnson's and Stone–Styne–Merrill met there regularly, eating their way through problems. The more irritating the day, the more they ate. Pancakes with ice cream; pie à la mode; root-beer floats; sundaes; whipped cream desserts.

Feeling separated from the show, unable to make changes, the trio hung on stubbornly. In Jule's opinion, Champion had already dropped the best songs, without consultation.

One night they were at Howard Johnson's devouring pancakes and root-beer floats when Merrick dispatched his production supervisor, Biff Liff, to say, "David told me to find you and tell you you're off per diem. I'm not about to tell you that. I didn't see you." Biff Liff trudged off.

The big question in their minds now was: "Who will be my replacement?"

Every night the threesome diligently checked to see who was sitting in the producer's house seats. Who would replace Peter Stone? Who would replace Jule Styne? Bob Merrill? In a state of siege with both producer Merrick and director Champion, Peter Stone was the logical first man out. Neil Simon, the playwright, came down from New York to occupy one of Merrick's seats and a rumor swept the company before final curtain that Simon was the new librettist; Stone had been fired. The rumor was unfounded, but insecurity spread to the cast and soon Bobby Morse was visiting Jule's suite for verbal hand-holdings.

The show went on to Toronto, opening to mixed reviews, and there was even greater replacement pressure now. It was said that Champion wanted *Hello, Dolly!* writer Michael Stewart to rework Stone's script; was seeking composer Jerry Herman to replace Styne. For the first time in a theatrical career that had spanned almost a quarter of a century, Jule was in danger of being fired.

Tipped that Herman was in town, Jule located the composer at a hotel far away from the theater. Jule made a call, then talked some twenty minutes with Herman about the show and Champion, having made up his mind to fight the dismissal.

A meeting between Champion and Jule had already been arranged for that night, to take place in Jule's suite. Champion was late for the meeting because of a prior conference across town with Jerry Herman. The director finally walked in, seething. "Now, you've done it," he yelled.

"Done what?"

Gower put his hands on his hips, Jule remembers. "You talked to Jerry Herman."

Jule quietly confessed that he had, as well as to his lawyer in New York. He remained the composer.

Sugar opened on Broadway April 9, 1972, and the reviews were not any better than those in Washington and Toronto. Douglas Watt, of the New York *Daily News,* said, "*Sugar* is a musical of such unswerving mediocrity that it sometimes is hard to keep one's mind on it."

The musical, which ran an unexpected eighteen months at the Majestic, did little to pull Jule out of the longest slump of his career, nor did it particularly help his bank account. He was on half-royalty while the investors were paid off.

25

One of the best performances of the Gypsy *revival was in Jule's hotel room. He demonstrated a strip-tease number in his jockey shorts.*

—BARRY BROWN, 1976

There was one tried-and-true work of art sitting on the shelf—*Gypsy.* There were also two young producers, Barry Brown and Fritz Holt, who very much wanted to revive *Gypsy;* present it in London, then bring it on to New York. They'd first approached Jule in 1971, and his quick answer had been, "My God, yes. See if Ethel will do it."

Ethel Merman wouldn't repeat her performance. Her aged parents were both ill. She even rejected the Brown–Holt offer to fly them to London and place them under medical care there. Merman had toured only briefly in the original production and had previously rejected a London company run in 1961, an opening locked up for Princess Margaret.

Holt and Brown had, of course, talked to David Merrick, Stephen Sondheim and Arthur Laurents. Each of the show's partners, in addition to Jule, thought the *Gypsy* revival was a fine idea. And Laurents did not see the loss of Merman as a major obstacle. He'd always wanted to direct his own version of *Gypsy* with Angela Lansbury as Mama Rose, believing that Lansbury would bring a new dimension to the role.

Sondheim and Styne seconded the Lansbury choice. She was also ideal, in the thinking of Brown and Holt, as well as Bobby Tucker, a choreographer who had assisted Jerry Robbins in the original show. Lansbury not only had the depth of talent necessary to handle the difficult role, she was "box office" in both London and New York. But in late 1971 Angela was living on a farm in Ireland, temporarily retired from the stage, solving family problems. She rejected the bid from Brown and Holt.

The producers then sought Elaine Stritch, who was eager to play Rose. However, she was not "box office" insofar as potential backers were concerned, and the revival plans were halted. More than a year passed and then Lansbury suddenly notified Brown that she wanted to work again; that she'd do *Gypsy* for them.

Arthur Laurents was quickly signed to direct Angela and by the end of 1972, the *Gypsy* revival was well and alive in London. The young producers, who had no personal money to invest, had raised all but $90,000 of the needed $275,000 budget. Lansbury herself solved the problem. She said to Brown, "Why don't you talk to my brother?"

Edgar Lansbury, with partner Joseph Beruh, had produced *The Subject Was Roses* and *Godspell,* as well as individual successes, and they wrote a check a day later for the $90,000. Brown and Holt then contracted for the Piccadilly Theatre, not ideal for a musical because of its small size, and *Gypsy* was scheduled for a May opening.

Angela had insisted that Jule come to London for four weeks of work, with rehearsals scheduled to begin six weeks later. She wanted to go into rehearsal knowing every note of the score. *So I started work with her and within an hour knew I'd have a surprise for everyone. No one was sure she could sing the* Gypsy *songs. She was primarily an actress. She'd sung* Mame, *and a Sondheim show,* Anyone Can Whistle, *but the* Gypsy *songs were more demanding than either of those shows. By the end of the day, I knew she'd be superb. I let her have her own way. She began to act the pants off the part. Not as forceful as Merman, vocally not as blatant, but doing it a different way, her way. I called Brown and Holt, Sondheim and Laurents. She started with "Some People" and then did "Everything's Coming Up Roses." They all flipped. Arthur couldn't get over it.*

Laurents went into rehearsal with two major changes in mind. "The striptease had never been successful. I'd always wanted the girl to talk, because that's what Gypsy did, chatter, and by the time we got to Philly in the original, Jerry Robbins didn't have much faith in Sandra Church, and wasn't interested in trying it. So I made that change and it became successful with Zan Charisse. She chattered away as Gypsy

Rose Lee had done, never taking her clothes off. The other major change that I made was solely because Angela was a brilliant dancer. Sondheim had never been happy with 'Together' because Robbins had cut a lot of the lyrics. So I put them back and Angela danced, and brought the house down. Otherwise, I just made some line cuts here and there. There was a difference in the directorial approach, and of course, Angela played it differently than Merman. A more personal performance."

There was a third major change in the revival, basically a technical change. In the original production, Laurents had wanted to send the whole stage forward during the strip number, letting Gypsy go upstage, through the curtains, and then return to the laps of the audience on an extended stage.

Merrick and Hayward had advised that it couldn't be done because the audience in the balcony would lose sight of the actress.

"They were wrong," said Laurents. "It became a thrilling theatrical effect."

Jule flew back to London with Sondheim just before the opening to do additional scoring and also supervise the orchestra during rehearsal. Dismayed at the postage-stamp size of the Piccadilly orchestra pit, which accommodated only nineteen musicians, Jule pleaded for one additional instrument, a viola. In a calculated, tear-welling performance, Jule got his viola. The vulnerable young producers pushed and crowded another chair into the pit.

Eventually, the young producers also pushed and crowded Jule out of the theater to stop a British musicians' rebellion. Not once did the London musicians play the way Jule wanted them to. The same old shouts and curses, so familiar to Milt Rosenstock, rang in the theater. "That eighth note is off!" Groans came out of the pit. "That should be A flat, not A natural!" Finally, the union threatened to pull the orchestra unless the composer was banned from rehearsals. Holt and Brown exiled him.

Gypsy, with Angela Lansbury, opened to rave reviews in London. Katharine Hepburn attended the first preview and climbed up on the runway, crossing the orchestra pit like a tomboy, to congratulate Lansbury. They'd never met.

Eleven curtain calls were counted for Miss Lansbury on opening night, and on the eleventh call she stepped out of character to say, "The night doesn't belong to me. It belongs to the authors, and you should meet them."

Laurents, Sondheim and Styne had never heard a star make that kind of speech on opening-night curtain call. They mounted the stage and joined her.

Throughout the comparatively easy rebirth of *Gypsy,* another remake was under way. *Lorelei* was a strange animal that got its start in San Francisco when producer Dick York wanted to revive *Gentlemen Prefer Blondes,* starring Bernadette Peters.

Carol Channing heard of the plans, but considered *Blondes* her private domain and informed producer Lee Guber that she wanted to star in any revivals. She also wanted the story updated, believing she was too old to play the original part. Carol also thought it might be best to road-show for a year prior to a New York opening.

Guber and co-producer Shelly Gross saw wisdom in that. The sets should be designed for easy travel. The cast would be committed to a long-term stay on the road. Five musicians would form the nucleus for an orchestra to be filled in with local people.

Gail Parent and Kenny Solms, who were Carol Burnett's TV writers, young and inexperienced, were signed to rewrite the book. Comden and Green were again associated with Jule for additional lyrics to his new music. The hit songs from the original production, "Diamonds Are a Girl's Best Friend" and "A Little Girl from Little Rock," with Leo Robin's lyrics intact, were too good to discard, and were integrated into the new score, along with "Keeping Cool with Coolidge."

Lorelei opened in Oklahoma City, first stop on the nine-month road schedule, and Channing drew $190,000 the first week. The Oklahoma critics were bedazzled by *Lorelei,* especially by Channing, but the reviews in such places as Chicago and Los Angeles indicated the new show was not likely to turn Broadway upside down.

Jule spent a week or so during each opening attempting to polish the score, and when *Lorelei* was in Los Angeles he chatted with Buddy Robbins whose late father had, of course, been responsible for Jule's involvement in *Blondes.*

"Do you know what I did today?" Jule asked Robbins. "Well, I couldn't get an orchestrator. So I sat down on the curb in front of the Shubert, in Century City, and worked on the orchestration. Can you imagine? The greatest composer in America today, writing music on the curb of the Avenue of the Stars?"

Lorelei began its New York run the night of January 27, 1974, at the Palace Theatre, and Douglas Watt of the *Daily News* termed it "creaky." As other tallies came in, it was evident that only Carol

Channing saved the show. It ran for a year on the strength of her performance.

The theater was also used for a one-performance SRO turnout on the night of May 19, when the man who wrote music on the curbside of the Avenue of the Stars was saluted by his associates and fellow artists in "Jule's Friends at the Palace," a black tie, fund-raising affair for the American Musical and Dramatic Foundation and other charities.

The four-hour journey through Jule Styne's music, performed by Liza Minelli, Tony Bennett, Carol Channing, Betty Comden, Adolph Green, Chita Rivera, Dolores Gray, Robert Morse and others, visited Jule's life in Chicago and Hollywood and then went on to Broadway. Jerome Robbins, Arthur Laurents, Sammy Cahn and Marvin Hamlisch were among those who reminisced, telling Jule anecdotes.

At evening's end, the composer did his own turn at the keyboard, happily weeping at the standing ovation as he arose from the piano bench.

Another happy evening occurred on September 23, 1974, when the New York production of *Gypsy* opened at the Winter Garden. The Broadway critics discovered that *Gypsy* had miraculously gathered strength while on the shelf. The reviews were equal to, or better, than the assays given to the Merman cast and staging. Laurents and Lansbury and Sondheim and Styne had somehow added to a show already claimed to be a landmark of American musicals.

26

We all have these hidden things. Yes, I wanted to star in my own show; perform my own work before a live, paid audience; hear the applause . . .

—JULE STYNE, 1977

In the spring of 1976, Jule was out in California. He was approaching his seventy-first birthday, a good time to tell the story of any man's life, and was thinking about what had gone by, talking a lot about the past and some about the future.

You know, I seldom think about it, but I've led an exciting and hopefully a productive life. I've worked with some marvelous people, even a few creative giants, in both films and on the stage. A few have been the best talents of our time. Any composer who could write for both a Sinatra and a Streisand in one lifetime is lucky. And if I think about Gypsy, *I think what a privilege it was to work with Jerry Robbins, Arthur Laurents, Steve Sondheim, Ethel Merman. That's a lot of talent for one show. Listen, I'm very proud of* Gypsy *and some of the others, but I don't operate in the past. It's more fun to think about what's happening right now and what's coming up. . . .*

Imminent for Broadway was *One Night Stand*, an original by Herb Gardner. In the late sixties, Jule had approached Gardner with the idea of converting his *A Thousand Clowns* to the musical stage. Gardner had said, "No, if I do something with you, I want it to be an original." Ten years later, script and score were completed.

Scheduled to open in London was another Jule Styne musical, *Bar Mitzvah Boy,* based on the prizewinning BBC television production. Then there was an unscheduled project, a movie musical of *Treasure Island.* The score for Long John Silver and company was also complete.

Yet, to some degree the frantic years of simultaneous shows and juggling three scores at once were over. Or, on close analysis, were they? *What it is, really, is more care and selection. I'll still have my losses but I don't think they'll be back-to-back anymore. I'll start projects and abandon them when I think they won't work. Some will work, and they'll be brought to the stage. I haven't slowed down all that much but I don't feel the urgency now. I'm not compelled to put things into production just to make a quick buck . . .*

The days of the bookies are definitely over. *Now, I walk two blocks to OTB—Off-Track Betting—and place my six dollars on a race . . .* This pleases Dorothy Dicker and Margaret Styne and assorted collaborators; almost anyone who knows Jule.

The little portable radio near his desk in the office on Fifty-first Street is still tuned in each afternoon to catch the race results. *I'll always have my hobby, but it's under control now . . .*

Songwriter and pop singer Neil Sedaka lived in an apartment two floors below the Stynes, and both Nicky and Katherine were smitten with him. Sedaka was often on the road, appearing in night clubs or concerts, but when he was at home the Styne children were regular visitors. Sedaka sometimes talked to Nicky and Katherine about his shows in Las Vegas or Lake Tahoe, or wherever.

One day, Katherine returned upstairs to say to her mother, "My Daddy writes songs but he never goes to those places to sing." Margaret told Jule of Katherine's remark. He thought about it.

Jule had played and sung in many living rooms in New York, Florida, California, or wherever, but it wasn't the same. These were parties. And, yes, he did want to perform sometime, somewhere, for his children, and before a paying audience. Oddly enough, in the late fall of 1976, he'd had an offer to do just that—give a series of concerts at a dozen universities. But he'd hesitated, uncertain about doing an "act."

Then it was suggested that he get himself acclimated by playing two weeks at the Rainbow Grill, high above Rockefeller Center in New York. *Lo and behold, it was financially attractive. If people liked the "act," then I'd do it for the colleges. I suppose it was an idea whose time had come. Other composers had done it. Sammy Cahn had done it, on Broadway no less. And I really did want Katherine and Nicky to see their old man work an audience. Entertain. Get some applause. Ego, I guess, persuaded me to do the gig.*

So, on the frigid night of January 17, 1977, Jule opened high up in the snow clouds, in the Rainbow Grill, wearing a black satin shirt beneath his dinner jacket; displaying a beatific smile on a face that still belied time on earth. The room was packed, and scattered in the audience were notables from show business past and present, as well as the beaming Styne family.

Musically backed by the Bernie Layton Quartet and a trio of singers, Jule performed at the grand piano, attacking it as always, mixing jokes and patter and some fifty songs, including, "The Guy with the Polka-Dot Tie," late-late of Chicago's Tuley High School. Introduced by protégé Marvin Hamlisch, he went about it as if he'd been doing this same act for fifty years, and in a way he had. The voice was husky, and still very much Tin Pan Alley. The evening was fast and fun, Jule enjoying himself immensely, reveling in murmurs of, "I didn't know he wrote that."

The act paraded through *High Button Shoes* and *Gentlemen Prefer Blondes* and *Bells Are Ringing* and *Gypsy* and *Funny Girl* and some shows not as well known, a song from here and a song from there: "Let It Snow" and "It's Magic" and "Just in Time" and "Three Coins in the Fountain" and just for Isadore and Anna, a touch of Haydn.

At the end of almost an hour and a half of a singing love-in, Hoagy Carmichael was among the first to leap to his feet, acknowledging a rather rare moment in show business. Jule was grinning and bowing, as if he'd finally made it on *the street* and didn't quite believe it.

Weekly Variety said, in part:

> Jule Styne, who has written about 1,400 songs, including the scores for such hits as *Funny Girl* and *Gypsy,* is playing the first sustained café date of his career. It's an event for which he has practiced much of his adult life, being one of the most avid volunteer entertainers at parties and other functions. He has now put this developed skill to use in an act that practice has made almost perfect.
>
> Styne is an ingratiating personality. His chatter is informal and spontaneous. However, performance is not the key in this case. There is a pervasive spirit engendered by the music that makes this event. There is a tremendous listenability in Styne's comps. The audience sings along almost involuntarily. There is laughter, camaraderie, and an enor-

mous rapport between the performers and the audience. All have rarely enjoyed themselves as much.

Eight other reviewers said much the same.

Jule was invited back to the Rainbow Grill in May 1977, this time for a six-week run. A reporter from the *Daily News* said, "You're over seventy. How can you keep up this pace at your age?"

"What age?" Jule replied. An answer that wasn't an answer. Pure "Stynese."

On closing night, June 18th, Jule didn't seem weary, though he'd been doing two shows nightly for more than a month. He seemed exhilarated, as if he might like this to go on forever, a sharing feast of his best music.

Broadway star Bobby Van, one of the back-up singers for this finale, asked, in the closing moments, "Jule, what's your favorite song? After six weeks here, you've got to tell me."

"I love them all."

"That's not an answer," protested Van.

The moment was unrehearsed and Jule broke into "The Party's Over" as the audience rose to give him a standing ovation; then smiling, almost to himself, contradicted: "No, the party isn't over . . ."

Then he segued to the last part of "Time After Time" and rasped:

I only know what I know
I always bet win, place and show
It's kept me young and feeling fine
So time after time
I tell myself that I'm so lucky, so lucky
To be Jule Styne . . .

Margaret Styne's obviously biased description of her husband was rather accurate, after all: ". . . impossible, infuriating, inconsistent, irresponsible and illogical. Exhilarating, exciting, irrepressible, irreplaceable and never ever boring. He calls himself Peter Pan—he must be right because he's never grown up enough to forget where dreams are born. I'm glad."

So are many others.

Index

ABOUT THE AUTHOR

Theodore Taylor is a former newspaper reporter. He adds Jule, *his twentieth book, to works on a wide variety of subjects, ranging from the assassination of Senator Robert Kennedy to an award-winning study of the quiet life of a Basque shepherd. Twelve years of film work at major studios provided insight for Jule Styne's "Hollywood period." He lives in California.*